T0256190

Graphing Data with R

John Jay Hilfiger

Beijing · Boston · Farnham · Sebastopol · Tokyo

Graphing Data with R

by John Jay Hilfiger

Copyright © 2016 John Jay Hilfiger. All rights reserved.

Printed in the United States of America.

Published by O'Reilly Media, Inc., 1005 Gravenstein Highway North, Sebastopol, CA 95472.

O'Reilly books may be purchased for educational, business, or sales promotional use. Online editions are also available for most titles (*http://safaribooksonline.com*). For more information, contact our corporate/institutional sales department: 800-998-9938 or *corporate@oreilly.com*.

Editors: Laurel Ruma and Shannon Cutt
Production Editor: Shiny Kalapurakkel
Copyeditor: Bob Russell, Octal Publishing, Inc.
Proofreader: Rachel Head

Indexer: Ellen Troutman
Interior Designer: David Futato
Cover Designer: Karen Montgomery
Illustrator: Rebecca Demarest

November 2015:   First Edition

Revision History for the First Edition

2015-10-16:   First Release
2016-03-25:   Second Release

See *http://oreilly.com/catalog/errata.csp?isbn=9781491922613* for release details.

While the publisher and the author have used good faith efforts to ensure that the information and instructions contained in this work are accurate, the publisher and the author disclaim all responsibility for errors or omissions, including without limitation responsibility for damages resulting from the use of or reliance on this work. Use of the information and instructions contained in this work is at your own risk. If any code samples or other technology this work contains or describes is subject to open source licenses or the intellectual property rights of others, it is your responsibility to ensure that your use thereof complies with such licenses and/or rights.

978-1-491-92261-3

[LSI]

Table of Contents

Part I.   Getting Started with R

Part II.   Single-Variable Graphs

Part III. Two-Variable Graphs

Preface

"A picture is worth a thousand words," says the proverb. Sometimes, a picture is worth a lot of numbers, too! Complex relationships are often more easily grasped by looking at a picture or a graph than they might be if one tried to absorb the nuances in a verbal description or discern the relationships in columns of numbers. This book is about using graphical methods to understand complex data by highlighting important relationships and trends, reducing the data to simpler forms, and making it possible to take in a lot of numbers at a glance.

Who Is This Book For?

Just about anyone who needs to visualize and analyze data will find something useful here. My primary aim, however, is to make graphical data analysis accessible to a wide range of people—especially those who do not have much (or any) previous experience with R but who need or want to create various types of graphs to help them understand data important to them. This will likely include people working in business, media, graphic arts, social sciences, and health sciences who have real needs for data analysis but might not have backgrounds in advanced mathematics and computer programming. Although this book is designed for self-study, it might also find a place as a supplemental text for courses in elementary and intermediate statistics or research methods.

The vehicle for this book is R, but this is not a comprehensive course on R. Many computer classes and computer books attempt to show you every possible thing one can do with a language or tool. For many of us who have attempted to learn this way, it gets to be quite confusing and boring. This book will focus on understanding the elements of graphics for data analysis and how to use R to produce the kinds of graphs discussed here; it will show you how to use some of R's built-in resources for finding help, and leave a lot of the other stuff for you to pursue elsewhere. You should have access to a computer and feel comfortable using it for some task(s), such as sending email, browsing the Internet, or perhaps using applications such as word processor or spreadsheet. Familiarity with basic statistics will be helpful for some of the topics covered here, but it is not necessary for most of them.

Why R?

It is possible to make useful graphs of small datasets by hand. It is much more efficient, however, to take advantage of computer technology to produce accurate and appealing visual data analyses. For large datasets, hand work is effectively impossible. Computer software, conversely, makes producing complex graphs of even very large datasets practical.

This technology is now readily available through open source software to virtually anyone who has access to a computer. "Open source" refers to programs for which the source code is made available to all—to examine, to use, or to make one's own modifications or additions.

Open source software products are offered as free downloads to anyone who wants them. Perhaps you suspect that stuff given away for free cannot be of high quality. Let me assure you that some of this free software conforms to the highest professional standards.

The particular software chosen for this book, R, is a programming language and collection of statistical, mathematical, and graphing programs used by literally millions of people around the world, including many leading professionals in science, business, and media. You have likely seen graphics produced by R on websites, in major newspapers, and in other publications. You will be able to produce this kind of professional data visualization, too, because R works on computers running Windows, Macintosh, or Linux operating systems. This covers just about all the desktop and laptop computers out there today!

How to Use This Book

The way to get the most out of this book is to make a lot of graphs yourself. To this end, read the book while seated in front of your computer and reproduce all of the commands given here. Further, many sections have exercises that challenge you to go a step beyond the illustrations in the text, either by refining the example commands or by making another graph of a different dataset. It would be best to do this before going on to the next topic.

Conventions Used in This Book

The following typographical conventions are used in this book:

Italic
> Indicates new terms, URLs, email addresses, filenames, and file extensions.

`Constant width`
> Used for program listings, as well as within paragraphs to refer to program elements such as variable or function names, databases, data types, environment variables, statements, and keywords.

`Constant width bold`
> Shows commands or other text that should be typed literally by the user.

`Constant width italic`
> Shows text that should be replaced with user-supplied values or by values determined by context.

 This element signifies a general note.

Using Code Examples

This book is here to help you get your job done. In general, if example code is offered with this book, you may use it in your programs and documentation. You do not need to contact us for permission unless you're reproducing a significant portion of the code. For example, writing a program that uses several chunks of code from this book does not require permission. Selling or distributing a CD-ROM of examples from O'Reilly books does require permission. Answering a question by citing this book and quoting example code does not require permission. Incorporating a significant amount of example code from this book into your product's documentation does require permission.

We appreciate, but do not require, attribution. An attribution usually includes the title, author, publisher, and ISBN. For example: *Graphing Data with R* by John Jay Hilfiger (O'Reilly). Copyright 2016 John Jay Hilfiger, 978-1-491-92261-3."

If you feel your use of code examples falls outside fair use or the permission given above, feel free to contact us at *permissions@oreilly.com*.

Safari® Books Online

 *Safari Books Online* is an on-demand digital library that delivers expert content in both book and video form from the world's leading authors in technology and business.

Technology professionals, software developers, web designers, and business and creative professionals use Safari Books Online as their primary resource for research, problem solving, learning, and certification training.

Safari Books Online offers a range of plans and pricing for enterprise, government, education, and individuals.

Members have access to thousands of books, training videos, and prepublication manuscripts in one fully searchable database from publishers like O'Reilly Media, Prentice Hall Professional, Addison-Wesley Professional, Microsoft Press, Sams, Que, Peachpit Press, Focal Press, Cisco Press, John Wiley & Sons, Syngress, Morgan Kaufmann, IBM Redbooks, Packt, Adobe Press, FT Press, Apress, Manning, New Riders, McGraw-Hill, Jones & Bartlett, Course Technology, and hundreds more. For more information about Safari Books Online, please visit us online.

How to Contact Us

Please address comments and questions concerning this book to the publisher:

O'Reilly Media, Inc.
1005 Gravenstein Highway North
Sebastopol, CA 95472
800-998-9938 (in the United States or Canada)
707-829-0515 (international or local)
707-829-0104 (fax)

We have a web page for this book, where we list errata, examples, and any additional information. You can access this page at *http://www.oreilly.com/catalog/0636920038382.do*.

To comment or ask technical questions about this book, send email to *bookquestions@oreilly.com*.

For more information about our books, courses, conferences, and news, see our website at *http://www.oreilly.com*.

Find us on Facebook: *http://facebook.com/oreilly*

Follow us on Twitter: *http://twitter.com/oreillymedia*

Watch us on YouTube: *http://www.youtube.com/oreillymedia*

Acknowledgments

A number of people helped to make this book come into being. First, my wife, Karen, whose patience, understanding, and encouragement throughout the process were essential to my completing the task. Our son Eric and daughter Kristen read the first chapter and offered brutally frank assessments, which was humbling but very helpful. The technical reviewers, Drs. Raymond Bajorski, Sarah Boslaugh, and Philipp K. Janert, were invaluable for their insights, corrections, and suggestions. My editor, Shannon Cutt, was extraordinarily capable and positive. She helped me navigate not only the writing but all the technical and practical details of preparing a manuscript for publication. I had no idea there was so much to do! Finally, the O'Reilly Media team, who do all the things you don't see and do see that are absolutely essential to producing the quality library of books for which they are so respected. Thank you, all.

## PART I

Getting Started with R

In this section, we will learn some of the basic commands in the R language. We will also learn about data types and how to prepare data for use in R, as well as how to import data created by other software into a form in which you can use R to analyze it. This will be followed by a discussion of some special properties of R graphs, such as how to save them for use in other programs and the differences between graphs used for data analysis and graphic presentation. Finally, we will look briefly at several graphics systems available to R users.

# CHAPTER 1

R Basics

Downloading the Software

The first thing you will need to do is download the free R software and install it on your computer. Start your computer, open your web browser, and navigate to the R Project for Statistical Computing at *http://www.r-project.org*. Click "download R" and then choose one of the mirror sites close to you. (The R software is stored on many computers around the world, not just one. Because they all contain the same files, and they all look the same, they are called "mirror" sites. You can choose any one of those computers.) Click the site address and a page will open from which you can select the version of R that will run on your computer's operating system. If your computer can run the latest version of R—3.0 or higher—that is best. However, if your computer is several years old and cannot run the most up-to-date version, get the latest one that your computer can run. There might be a few small differences from the examples in this book, but most things should work.

Follow the instructions and you should have R installed in a short time. This is *base R*, but there are thousands (this is not an exaggeration) of add-on "packages" that you can download for free to expand the functionality of your R installation. Depending on your particular needs, you might not add any of these, but you might be delightfully surprised to discover that there are capabilities you could not have imagined and now absolutely must have.

Try Some Simple Tasks

If you are using Windows or OS X, you can click the "R" icon on your desktop to start R, or, on Linux or OS X, you can start by typing **R** as a command in a terminal window. This will open the *console*. This is a window in which you type commands and see the results of many of those commands, although commands to create graphs will, in most cases, open a new window for the resulting graph. R displays a prompt, the greater-than symbol (>), when it is ready to accept a command from you. The simplest use of R is as a calculator. So, after the prompt, type a mathematical expression to which you want an answer:

```
> 12/4
[1] 3
>
```

Here, we asked for "12 divided by 4." R responded with "3," and then displayed another prompt, showing that it is ready for the next problem. The [1] before the answer is an *index*. In this case, it just shows that the answer begins with the first number in a *vector*. There is only one number in this example, but sometimes there will be multiple numbers, so it is helpful to know where the set of numbers begins. If you do not understand the index, do not worry about it for now; it will become clearer after seeing more examples. The division sign (/) is called an *operator*. Table 1-1 presents the symbols for standard arithmetic operators.

Table 1-1. R arithmetic operators

Operator	Operation	Example
+	Addition	$3 + 4 = 7$ or 3+4 (i.e., with no spaces)
–	Subtraction	$5 - 2 = 3$
*	Multiplication	$100*2.5 = 250$
/	Division	$20/5 = 4$
^ or **	Exponent	$3^2 = 9$ or $3**2 = 9$
%%	Remainder of division	5 %% 2 = 1 (5/2 = 2 with remainder of 1)
%/%	Divide and round down	5 %/%2 = 2 (5/2 = 2.5, round down, = 2)

You can use parentheses as in ordinary arithmetic, to show the order in which operations are performed:

```
> (4/2)+1
[1] 3
> 4/(2+1)
[1] 1.333333
```

Try another problem:

```
> sqrt(57)
[1] 7.549834
```

This time, arithmetic was done with a *function*; in this case, sqrt().
Table 1-2 lists somecommonly used arithmetic functions.

Table 1-2. Some commonly used R mathematical functions

Function	Operation
cos()	Cosine
sin()	Sine
tan()	Tangent
sqrt()	Square root
log()	Natural logarithm
exp()	Exponential, inverse of natural logarithm
sum()	Sum (i.e., total)
mean()	Mean (i.e., average)
median()	Median (i.e., the middle value)
min()	Minimum
max()	Maximum
var()	Variance
sd()	Standard deviation

The functions take *arguments*. An argument is a sort of modifier
that you use with a function to make more specific requests of R. So,
rather than simply requesting a sum, you might request the sum of
particular numbers; or rather than simply drawing a line on a graph,
you might use an argument to specify the color of the line or the
width. The argument, or arguments, must be in parentheses after
the function name. If you need help in using a function—or any R
command—you can ask for assistance:

```
> help(sum)
```

R will open a new window with information about the specified function and its arguments. Here is a shortcut to get exactly the same response:

```
> ?sum
```

Be aware that R is case sensitive, so "help" and "Help" are not equivalent! Spaces, however, are not relevant, so the preceding command could just as well be the following:

```
> ? sum
```

Sometimes, as in the sqrt() example, there is only one argument. Other times, a function operates on a group of numbers, called a *vector*, as shown here:

```
> sum(3,2,1,4)
[1] 10
```

In this case, the sum() function found the total of the numbers 3, 2, 1, and 4. You cannot always type all of the vectors into a function statement like in the preceding example. Usually you will need to create the vector first. Try this:

```
> x1 <- c(1,2,3,4)
```

After you enter this command, nothing happens! Actually, nothing happens *that you can see.* Any time the special operator made of the two symbols, < and - appears, the name to the left of this operator is given the value of the expression to the right of the operator. (Newer versions of R allow the use of one symbol, =, to accomplish the same thing. After Chapter 1, we will use the simpler form as well.) In this case, a new vector was created, which the user called x1. R is an *object-oriented language,* and the vector x1 is an *object* in your workspace.

What Is an "Object?"

Think of an object as a box filled with items that are related to one another. These items could be simple numbers, or names, or the results of a statistical analysis, or some combination of these or other items. Objects help you to keep things organized, putting things related to one another in the same box and unrelated things in a different box; they also inform R what kinds of things are in them so that R can take appropriate actions on items in a particular object. A vector is one kind of object that contains a bunch of

things all of the same type—perhaps all numbers or all alphanu-
meric values. An object can even contain other objects. After all,
you could put a box inside a bigger one. So, you could put a vector,
or several vectors, into a *data frame*, which is another kind of
object. You can see what objects are in your current workspace by
typing the command `ls()`.

Creating a new vector requires typing the letter "c" in front of the
parenthesis preceding the numbers in the vector. See what happens
when you type the following:

```
> x1
```

The set of numbers 1, 2, 3, 4 has been saved with a name of x1. Typing the name of the vector instructs R to print the values of x1. You
can ask R to do various kinds of operations on that vector at any
time. For example, the command:

```
> mean(x1)
```

returns, as evidenced by printing to the screen, the mean, or average,
of the numbers in the vector x1. Try using some of the other operators in Table 1-2 to see some other things R can do.

Create another object, this time a single number:

```
> pi <- 3.14
```

At any time, you can get a list of all the objects presently in your
workspace by using the following command:

```
> ls()
```

And, you can use any or all of the objects in a new computation:

```
> newvar <- pi*x1
```

This creates yet another object named newvar.

User Interface

The examples you have seen so far are all *command-line instructions*.
In other words, you directed R what to do by typing command
words. This is not the only way to interface with R. The basic installation of R has some *graphical user interface* (GUI, pronounced
"GOO-ee") capabilities, too. The GUI refers to the point-and-click
interface that you have probably come to appreciate with other

applications you use. The problem is that each of the types of installation—Windows, OS X, and Linux—has somewhat different GUI capabilities. OS X is a little "GUI-er" than the others, and you may quickly decide that you prefer to issue a lot of commands this way. Whichever operating system you are using has a menu at the top of the console window. Before you enter important data, experiment a little to see what point-and-click commands you can use.

This book uses the *command-line interface* because it is the same for all three versions of R—Windows, OS X, and Linux—so only one explanation is necessary, and you can easily move from one computer to another. Listing *code*—that is, a set of command lines—is far easier and terser than trying to explain every menu choice and mouse click. Further, learning R this way helps you to understand the logic of the software a little better. Finally, the command language is more precise than point-and-click direction and affords the user greater control and power.

Installing a Package: A GUI Interface

No matter which operating system you are using, you can download a free "frontend" program that will provide a GUI for you. There are several available. After you have learned a little more about R, and appreciate its considerable usefulness, you might be ready to try one of these GUI interfaces. For example, earlier I mentioned that a large number of packages are available that you can add to R; one of them is a well-designed GUI called "R Commander." If you are connected to the Internet, try the following command:

```
> install.packages("Rcmdr", dependencies=TRUE)
```

R will download this package and any other packages that are necessary to make R Commander work. The packages will be permanently saved on your computer, so you will not need to install them again. Every time you open R, if you want to use R Commander, you will need to *load* the package this way:

```
> library(Rcmdr)
```

We are all different. For some of us, the command language is great. Others, who dislike R's command-line interface, might find R Commander just the thing to make R their favorite computer tool. You can produce many of the graphs in this book by using R

Commander, but you can't produce all of them. If you want to try R Commander, you can find additional information in Appendix C.

To retrieve a complete list of the packages available, use this command:

```
> available.packages()
```

You can learn a lot more about these packages, by topic, from CRAN Task Views at *http://cran.r-project.org/web/views/*.

You can see a list of all packages, by name, by going to *http://cran.r-project.org/web/packages/available_packages_by_name.html*.

To get help on the package you just downloaded, type the following:

```
> library(help=Rcmdr)
```

Error Messages

If you make a mistake when typing a command, instead of the expected result you will see an *error message*, which might or might not help! Appendix G has some guidance on dealing with the most likely types of errors.

Data Structures

You can put data into objects that are organized or "structured" in various ways. We have already worked with one type of structure, the vector. You can think of a vector as one-dimensional—a row of elements or a column of elements. A vector can contain any number of elements, from one to as high a number as your computer's memory can hold. The elements in a vector can be of type *numeric*; *character*, with alphabetic, numeric, and special characters; or *logical*, containing TRUE or FALSE values. All of the elements of a vector must be of the same type. Here are some examples of vector creation:

```
> x <- c(14,6.7,5.1,-8)                    #numeric
> name <- c("Lou","Mary","Rhoda","Ted") #character/quotes
                                         #needed
> test <- c(TRUE,TRUE,TRUE,FALSE,TRUE) #logical/caps needed
```

Anything that appears after the *octothorpe* (#) character is a comment. This is information or notes intended for us to read, but it will be ignored by R. (Being a musician, I prefer *sharp* for this symbol.) It is a good idea to get in the habit of putting comments into code to remind you of why you did a particular thing and help you to fix problems or expand upon a good idea when you come back to your program later. It is also a good idea to read the comments in the R code examples throughout the book.

The *data frame* is the main kind of structure with which we will work. It is a two-dimensional object, with rows and columns. You can think of it as a box with column vectors in it, or as a *rectangular dataset* of rows and columns. For better understanding, see the next section on sample datasets and the exercise on reading CO_2 emissions data into R. A data frame can include column vectors of all the same type or any combination of types.

R has other structures, such as matrices, arrays, and lists, which will not be discussed here.

You can use the str() function to find out what *structure* any given object has:

```
> str(x)
 num [1:4] 14 6.7 5.1 -8

> str(name)
 chr [1:4] "Lou" "Mary" "Rhoda" "Ted"

> str(test)
 logi [1:5] TRUE TRUE TRUE FALSE TRUE
```

Sample Datasets

The base R package includes some sample datasets that will be helpful to illustrate the graphical tools we will learn about. To see what datasets are available on your computer, type this command:

```
> data()
```

Ensure that the empty parentheses follow the command; otherwise, you will not get the expected result. Many more datasets are available. Nearly all additional packages contain sample datasets. To see a description of a particular dataset that has come with base R or that you have downloaded, just use the help command. For instance, to get some information about the `airquality` dataset, such as brief description, its source, references, and so on, type:

```
> ?airquality
```

Look at the first six observations in the dataset by using the following:

```
> head(airquality)
```

```
  Ozone Solar.R Wind Temp Month Day
1    41     190  7.4   67     5   1
2    36     118  8.0   72     5   2
3    12     149 12.6   74     5   3
4    18     313 11.5   62     5   4
5    NA      NA 14.3   56     5   5
6    28      NA 14.9   66     5   6
```

This dataset is a data frame. There are 153 rows of data, each row representing air quality measurements (e.g., Ozone, Solar.R, and Wind) taken on one day. The `head()` command by default prints out the names of the variables followed by the first six rows of data, so that we can see what the data looks like. Had we wanted to see a different number of rows—for example, 25—we could have typed the following:

```
>head(airquality,25)
```

Had we wanted to see the last four rows of the dataset, we could have typed this command:

```
> tail(airquality,4)
```

Each row has a row number and the values of six *variables*; that is, six measurements taken on that day. The first row, or first day, has the values 1, 41, 190, 7.4, 67, 5, 1. The values of the first variable, Ozone, for the first six days are 41, 36, 12, 18, NA, 28. This is an example of a *rectangular dataset* or *flat file*. Most statistical analysis programs require data to be in this format.

Notice that among the numbers in the dataset, you can see the "NA" entries. This is the standard R notation for "not available" or "missing." You can handle these values in various ways. One way is to delete the rows with one or more missing values and do the calculation with all the other rows. Another way is to refuse to do the calculation and return an error message. Some procedures offer the user a means to specify which method to use. It is also possible to *impute*, or estimate, a value for a missing value and use the estimate in a computation. Treatment of missing values is a complex and controversial subject and not to be taken lightly. Kabacoff (2011) has a good introductory chapter on handling missing values in R.

There are two ways to access the data. The first method is to use the `attach()` command, issue some commands with variable names, and then issue the `detach()` command, as in the following example:

```
> attach(airquality)
> table (Temp)          # get counts of Temp values
> mean (Temp)           # find the average Temp
> plot(Wind,Temp)       # make a scatter plot of Wind and Temp
> detach(airquality)
```

The advantage of this method is that, if you are going to do several steps, it is not necessary to type the dataset name over and over again. The second method is to specify whatever analysis you want by using a combination of the dataset name and variable name, separated by a dollar sign ($). For example, if we wanted to do just this:

```
> attach(airquality)
> plot(Wind,Temp)
> detach(airquality)
```

We could use the equivalent code:

```
> plot(airquality$Wind,airquality$Temp)
```

The advantage of this method is that if you are calling upon several datasets in quick succession, it is not necessary to use many `attach` and `detach` statements.

The Working Directory

When using R, you will often want to read data from a file into R, or write data from R to a file. For instance, you might have some data that you created using a spreadsheet, a statistical package such as SAS or SPSS, or a text editor, and you want to analyze that data using R. Alternatively, you will often create an R dataset that you want to save and use again. Those files must be stored somewhere in your computer's file structure. With each read or write operation, it is possible to specify a (frequently long) path to the precise file containing the data you want to read or the place where you will write the data. This can be cumbersome, so R has a *working directory*, or default location for files. In other words, if you do not instruct R where to find a particular file, it will just assume that you mean it is in the working directory. Likewise, if you do not specify where to save something, R will automatically write it in the working directory. You can find your current working directory with this command:

```
> getwd()
```

Suppose that you got the response that follows (your actual result will be quite different, of course!):

```
[1] "/Users/yourname/Desktop/"
```

The last folder in the chain (i.e., the last name on the righthand side) is the place where R looks for files and writes files unless you direct it to look elsewhere. You can change the working directory by using the setwd() command. You might want to create a new folder specifically for the use of R, or even specifically for your exercises with this book. Call it something that clearly suggests its purpose, such as "R folder" or "R graphical data." Assuming you have created a folder called "R things" within the folder "Desktop," you can then issue the following command:

```
> setwd("/Users/yourname/Desktop/R things")
```

From this point on, R will consider the folder "R things" to be your working directory, until the next time you give a setwd() command or shut down R by typing q(), for "quit." If you do not want to have to set the working directory every time you start R, see the section "Sourcing a Script" on page 22 to learn how to do this.

Putting Data into R

You now know how to use the sample datasets that come with various R packages. This is a tremendous resource for learning to use R, but you are learning R because you want to do graphical analysis of your own data. The method you choose to put your data into R will depend on several factors:

- How large your dataset is
- Whether the data already exists as a data file in any one of various forms

- How comfortable you are with using tools outside of R to create a file
- How much time you have to devote to data entry
- Your threshold for pain ;)

Beginner Alert!

The next three sections show various ways to enter data. If you are a beginner and find these sections too demanding, you might want to read the section "Typing into a Command Line" (coming up next) and then try an easy data entry problem, such as Exercise 1-4, at the end of the chapter. You can return to the sections "Using the Data Editor" on page 14 and "Reading from an External File" on page 16 later. In fact, after doing Exercise 1-4, you could actually go directly to Chapter 3 and then read from the section "Using the Data Editor" through Chapter 2 later, when you need the information there.

If you are not especially interested in data entry because you expect to use datasets that have already been created as spreadsheets, statistical package datasets, ASCII files, or other types of data files, you should skim the remainder of this section and consult Appendix E for the data file type of interest.

Typing into a Command Line

The most direct way to enter data into R is to type, from a command line, a statement creating a vector, as you have already done. If your need is to analyze one or a few fairly short vectors, that is probably the easiest thing to do.

Exercise 1-1.

Backblaze, a data backup company, runs about 25,000 disk drives and reports on survival rates (in percent) of hard drives. It showed the following annual survival rates for its drives (read from a graph; source: *http://bit.ly/1KVU57t*):

```
year rate
1    94    # (i.e., after one year, 94% of drives still work)
2    92
3    90
4    80
```

Create two vectors by using the following commands:

```
> year <- c(1,2,3,4)
> rate <- c(94,92,90,80)
```

Be sure that you enter the numbers in the proper order; for example, if 1 is first in the year vector, 94 must be first in the rate vector, and so on. You can examine the relationship of these two vectors by using this command:

```
> plot(year,rate)
```

Most graphic commands open a new window. If you have several open applications, you might miss it and be forced to look for it.

The plot statement in the previous code snippet called the plot() function and instructed it to do an analysis on the two arguments, year and rate. The graph we just made is a simple one, but it is possible to make very elaborate graphs with R. The plot on the right side of Figure 1-1 shows a few ways in which you could customize the basic plot. We will examine many such options throughout this book. You can enter the **?plot** command to see a long list of available options.

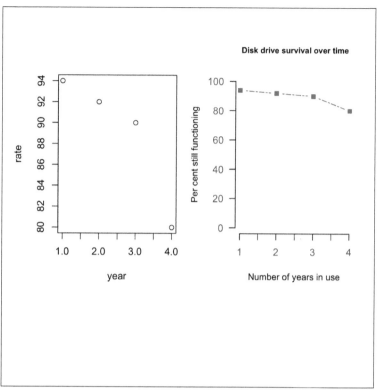

Figure 1-1. The plot on the left side, disk drive survival rate versus years in use, was created by the simple command plot(year,rate). The plot on the right is customized and required many choices. How many differences do you see?

You could combine the two vectors, year and rate, into a new data frame, mydata, as shown here:

```
> mydata <- data.frame(year, rate)
```

Using the Data Editor

If your data is just a little more complex or larger, you could use the simple data editor from the R console. Even if you do not enter your data this way, it is a good thing to know about the editor because someday (or maybe lots of days) you might need to fix an occasional problem data point in an object in your R workspace. I suspect that for most people it will be an unnecessary effort to try to use the editor for data entry. Read this section to learn some terms and to see how to save a file. You will probably prefer to use your favorite spreadsheet program for data entry, but you might need to use the editor if you do not have a spreadsheet program. See the section "Reading from an External File" on page 16 to learn how to read your spreadsheet data into R.

Exercise 1-2

The data presented in Table 1-3 (from the US Energy Information Administration) concerns worldwide carbon dioxide emissions over a recent eight-year period. You will enter it into R by using the built-in data editor, but let us see what is in this dataset first.

Table 1-3. Per capita carbon dioxide emissions from energy use (metric tons of carbon dioxide per person), by region of the world

Year	North America	Central/South America	Europe	Eurasia	Middle East	Africa	Asia/Oceania
2004	16.2	2.4	7.9	8.5	7.1	1.1	2.7
2005	16.2	2.5	7.9	8.5	7.6	1.2	2.9
2006	15.9	2.5	7.9	8.7	7.7	1.1	3.1
2007	15.9	2.6	7.8	8.6	7.6	1.1	3.2
2008	15.4	2.6	7.7	8.9	7.9	1.2	3.3
2009	14.2	2.6	7.1	8	8.3	1.1	3.5
2010	14.5	2.7	7.2	8.4	8.4	1.1	3.6
(source: http://1.usa.gov/1R6sj99)							

The top row in Table 1-3 is *header* information, naming each of the variables recorded. Each row contains all the information gathered during one year. Each row is said to be a *statistical unit*. Social scientists usually call the row a *case*, whereas natural scientists most often refer to the row as an *observation*. Computer professionals usually call the row a *record*. Each of the columns is called a *variable*, or in the case of computer science, a *field*. The emissions dataset has seven rows (observations) and eight variables: the year, and the amount of emissions from each of seven regions in the study.

The editor looks like a spreadsheet and has some of the features of a good spreadsheet, but is not as convenient to use as Excel or Numbers. It is also easy to lose your changes if you are not careful. To begin, choose an object name and assign this name to a new data frame. There are several ways to do this. I find the safest way is to name each variable, identify its type, and specify how many rows:

```
> emissions <- data.frame(Year=numeric(7),N_Amer = numeric(7),
CS_Amer=numeric(7), Europe=numeric(7),Eurasia=numeric(7),
Mid_East=numeric(7),Africa=numeric(7), Asia_Oceania=numeric(7))
```

This creates an empty data frame, called emissions. To open up the editor, call the edit() function by assigning an object to hold the empty data frame:

```
> emissions <- edit(emissions)
```

Remember, emissions is empty. By calling the object "emissions" in the preceding command, you are telling R to overwrite the empty data frame with whatever edited data you enter. Enter the data by double-clicking the cell that you want to write/edit. When you are done, click the upper-left corner of the spreadsheet in OS X or the "X" in the upper-right corner in Windows. *Do not* click Stop, which is on the edit window in OS X or at the top of the screen in Windows. If you click Stop, you will lose any changes. After the data is entered, check carefully to ensure that there are no errors. If you see an error, just double-click the cell that you want to fix and type the corrected number. If necessary, you can use the previous command again to go back to the editor and fix any problems. Save this data frame so that you can use it again later without the need to retype it:

```
> save (emissions,file="emiss.rda")
```

The preceding command writes the emissions data frame into a file called *emiss.rda* in the working directory. You can retrieve the data by using the following command, assuming that you still have the same working directory:

```
> load("emiss.rda")
```

Reading from an External File

You might already have a favorite tool that you use for data entry; for many people this is a spreadsheet program, but it also could be a text editor. I like Numbers on my Mac, but Excel or another spreadsheet will work just as well. The general approach is to create the file in the spreadsheet program and save it to your working directory. After it's there, you can read it into R for analysis.

Exercise 1-3

Prolific English composer Edward Elgar (1857–1934) is, perhaps, most famous for two celebrated works: "Pomp and Circumstance," the processional march for innumerable graduation ceremonies; and the "Enigma Variations," for symphony orchestra. Although the entire latter work is a popular part of symphony programs, the extraordinarily beautiful "Nimrod" variation is often performed by itself, not only by orchestras, but also by other ensembles (musical groups) or soloists.

One of the most fundamental questions one must ask before performing a musical work is, "What should the tempo be?" In other words, "How fast should it be played?" Although the composer usually gives an indication, some works have received a wide range of interpretations, even among the most highly regarded musicians. Learning how other musicians perform the work can be quite instructive to someone planning her own performance. The "Nimrod" tempo data presented in Table 1-4 comes from a number of recorded performances that were available on YouTube on November 9, 2013.

Table 1-4. Performance times of "Nimrod" by various ensembles

Performer	Medium	Time	Level
Barenboim–Chicago SO	so	240	p
Solti–London Phil	so	204	p
Davis	so	270	p
Remembrance2009	cb	236	p
Belcher	org	254	p
Bish	org	232	p
ColdstrGuards	cb	239	p
Pallhuber–3 Lions BB	bb	257	a
Bernstein–BBC	so	315	p
Dudamel–SBolivarSym	so	239	p
John	org	252	p
Sunshine Brass	bb	186	a
Mahidol Sym Band	cb	173	a
Hills	org	240	p
Grimethorpe CollB	bb	200	p
Barbirolli_Halle O	so	200	p

Performer	Medium	Time	Level
Stokowski	so	244	p
Boult–London SO	so	211	p
Kindl–Marktoberdorfer BB	bb	238	a
Carter–Charlotte CB	cb	196	a
Cord–IndianaU	bb	188	a
Mack–SUNYFredonia CB	cb	160	a
U Akron CB	cb	193	a
Akron Youth Sym	so	188	a
BP–Ostwestfalen	cb	198	a
Santarsola–MoldovaPO	so	320	p
Klumpp_NWD PO	so	187	p
Burke–MancunianWinds	cb	257	a
US Army Field Band	cb	235	p
EE–Phonograph	so	186	p
Niemczyk–NWC O	so	169	a
Allentoff–Brockport SO	so	200	a

The Nimrod dataset has 32 rows (cases/observations) and 4 columns (variables). This data will become a data frame in R.

Nimrod codebook

All but the simplest datasets need a "codebook," which offers an explanation of the meaning of each of the values of the variables. The codebook for the Nimrod dataset is as follows:

performer

>   Name of both conductor and ensemble, if available. At least one must be available for inclusion in the study.

medium

>   bb   brass band
>   cb   concert band
>   org organ solo
>   so   symphony orchestra

time

>   Performance time, in seconds, from first note to last note, leaving out announcements, tuning, applause, etc. Proxy measure for tempo; i.e., assumes same tempo throughout.

```
level (proficiency level of the performers)
```
a amateur (or student)

p professional

The variable time is a *quantitative variable*; that is, it's a measurement of an amount. You can use quantitative variables in arithmetic, so one could calculate the sum or the average of the variable time. These are R numeric vectors, as discussed in the section "Data Structures" on page 7. All the other variables in this particular dataset are *categorical variables*; i.e., the observations are assigned to categories. Some people refer to categorical variables as *qualitative* or *nominal variables*. These are R character vectors. We cannot calculate the average of medium, because the values bb, cb, and so on are not numbers; calculation does not even make sense. There are some things we can do with categorical variables, though, such as finding the *frequency* of bb or of cb. We might also use the values of categorical variables to form groups. So, for instance, we might break the dataset into parts, according to the values of level, so we could compare the average time in the amateur group to average time in the professional group.

You can enter the data in one of the following ways:

- Type the data into your favorite spreadsheet program and save (export) the spreadsheet to your working directory as a *.csv* file, with the name *Nimrod.Tempo.csv*. R can read other file types, but *.csv* seems to be the easiest and the least prone to error. Then open R and type the following command:

  ```
  > Nimrod <- read.csv("Nimrod.Tempo.csv",header=TRUE)
  ```

  If you want to read a file that does not have a header, use header=FALSE.

- If you want to read Excel files without converting them to *.csv* files, there is a package called XLConnect that is meant for exactly this purpose. XLConnect can do many other tasks, such as editing a spreadsheet and writing R data to an Excel file. You will not be able to use this package if you have an old version of R (before version 3.0). The code that follows shows how to read the Nimrod data when it has been saved as an Excel file with the name *Nimrod.xls*:

```
> install.packages ("XLConnect")
> library (XLConnect)
> Nimrod2 <-readWorksheetFromFile("Nimrod.xls",
    sheet = 1, header = TRUE)
```

What if a command is too long for one line?

If you need to issue a command (like the preceding one) that is
too long to fit on one line in the console, just keep on typing,
and R will place the remaining text on the next line. Do not
press "return" or "enter" until you reach the end of the command. If you press the "return" key before the command is
complete, R will not understand your request and will probably
return a cryptic error message.

---

*You do not actually need to have Excel installed on your computer
to use this package.* There are many datasets, freely available
from government agencies and sundry other sources, that you
can download in Excel format. See Appendix E for more information on this topic. You can copy them and read them into R
for your own analysis with XLConnect. This package can read or
write *.xls* or the newer *.xlsx* formats. You can find complete documentation at *http://cran.r-project.org/web/packages/XLConnect/
XLConnect.pdf*.

- Use a text editor or word processor to create a text file called
  Nimrod.Tempo.txt that uses spaces as separators between values.
  The file can be read as follows:

```
> Nimrod <-read.table("Nimrod.Tempo.txt", sep = "",
    header=TRUE)
```

If you find yourself in a situation that the preceding discussion of
methods for putting data into R did not cover, consult the R help
file, "R Data Import/Export." This file is included in the "R Help"
that is part of the base R installation. After you have read the data
into R using any one of the aforementioned methods, check to see if
it worked by using one of the following:

```
> Nimrod # types out complete dataset

> head(Nimrod) # types out first 6 rows

> fix(Nimrod)  # opens Nimrod data in editor
```

The final option will open the editor (see Figure 1-2) so that you can check the data or change data values, if necessary.

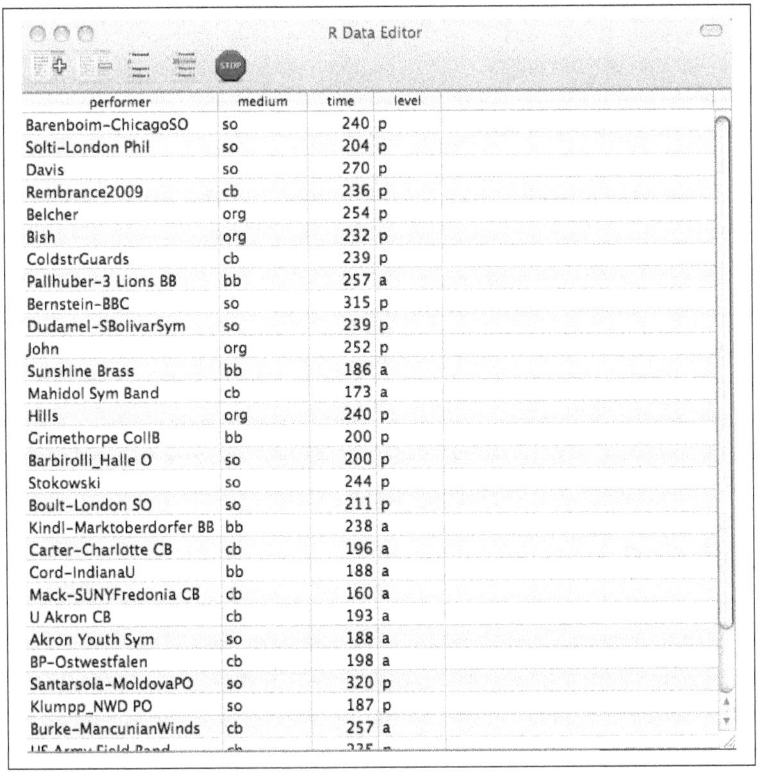

performer	medium	time	level
Barenboim-ChicagoSO	so	240	p
Solti-London Phil	so	204	p
Davis	so	270	p
Rembrance2009	cb	236	p
Belcher	org	254	p
Bish	org	232	p
ColdstrGuards	cb	239	p
Pallhuber-3 Lions BB	bb	257	a
Bernstein-BBC	so	315	p
Dudamel-SBolivarSym	so	239	p
John	org	252	p
Sunshine Brass	bb	186	a
Mahidol Sym Band	cb	173	a
Hills	org	240	p
Grimethorpe CollB	bb	200	p
Barbirolli_Halle O	so	200	p
Stokowski	so	244	p
Boult-London SO	so	211	p
Kindl-Marktoberdorfer BB	bb	238	a
Carter-Charlotte CB	cb	196	a
Cord-IndianaU	bb	188	a
Mack-SUNYFredonia CB	cb	160	a
U Akron CB	cb	193	a
Akron Youth Sym	so	188	a
BP-Ostwestfalen	cb	198	a
Santarsola-MoldovaPO	so	320	p
Klumpp_NWD PO	so	187	p
Burke-MancunianWinds	cb	257	a
US Army Field Band	cb	235	p

Figure 1-2. The R data editor, with the Nimrod data. You can use the editor to view the data and/or change specific values.

You can also give R commands to analyze the data in various ways, such as shown here:

```
> mean(Nimrod$time)
[1] 222.0938
> table(Nimrod$medium)      # get counts within each medium
 bb  cb org  so
  5   9   4  14
```

And you can create some cool graphs, which we will get to in due course.

You can also ask R for some general information about the dataset Nimrod:

```
> summary(Nimrod)
                     performer   medium           time        level
 Akron Youth Sym         : 1    bb : 5    Min.    :160.0    a:13
 Allentoff-Brockport SO: 1    cb : 9    1st Qu. :191.8    p:19
 Barbirolli_Halle O      : 1    org: 4    Median :221.5
 Barenboim-ChicagoSO     : 1    so :14    Mean    :222.1
 Belcher                 : 1              3rd Qu. :241.0
 Bernstein-BBC           : 1              Max.    :320.0
 (Other)                 :26
```

Save the Nimrod data frame the same way you did the emissions dataset (but with a different filename, of course), because you will need to retrieve it for a later exercise:

```
> save (Nimrod,file="Nimrod.rda")
```

You can retrieve it later by using the load() command:

```
> load("Nimrod.rda")
```

You can find more information about reading and importing external files in Appendix E.

Sourcing a Script

Up to this point, we have typed single-line commands. Most of the time, this will work just fine. There might be instances, however, when you want to perform a sequence of commands and repeat the entire sequence. This can get to be quite tedious if the sequence is very long or you want to repeat it many times. Fortunately, R can work with *scripts*. A script is a list of commands, set up in the order in which you want them to be performed. You can create a script by using a text editor and save it in a file. Then, you can *source the script*, which means to retrieve the script and execute the saved commands.

To see how this works, imagine that you are updating the Nimrod data on an ongoing basis. You add a few new observations from time to time in an Excel spreadsheet and would like to do some analysis in R to see where things stand with the latest data included. The list of commands for this analysis that follows requires that you have previously installed a couple of packages. If you are not sure of what packages you have installed on your computer, you can find out by using the command:

```
> installed.packages()
```

If you do not have gmodels and XLConnect, install them now:

```
> install.packages("gmodels")
> install.packages("XLConnect")
```

Now, here is a list of commands that you might use to carry out this analysis. Note that when we use a block of commands, we will usually not precede each one with the R prompt, >:[1]

```
# The following group of commands is a script
library(gmodels)  # required to use the CrossTable command
library (XLConnect) # must have installed XLConnect
Nimrod2 <- readWorksheetFromFile("Nimrod.xls",sheet=1,
  header=TRUE)
attach(Nimrod2)
CrossTable(medium,level,
  prop.r=FALSE,
  prop.c=FALSE,
  prop.t=FALSE,
  prop.chisq=FALSE)
# above command prints table with counts in each cell,
# but no percents
perf_time <- summary(time)     # save summary output
title  = "Summary of performance times:"
cat(title,"\n", "\n")          # print title and 2 linefeeds
print(perf_time)               # print results of summary(time)
detach(Nimrod2)
```

It would be a bit of a bother to key in these exact same commands every time you wanted to see results. So, I recommend that you use an editor to create a file that contains the preceding commands. A text editor is provided in R. In most versions of R, you can access it from the File menu at the upper-left corner of the R console. Choose New Document or New Script to open a text window, and enter the commands. Save the edited script in the working directory, using the name *NimTotals.R* for this example. Then, use the following command to execute all of the commands in the file:

---

1 Many of the remaining examples of code will be written as scripts, without the > prompt at the beginning of each line. Furthermore, long commands, such as the CrossT able() command in the example, are often broken up over several lines; this makes reading them a little easier.

```
> source("NimTotals.R")
```

```
   Cell Contents
|-------------------------|
|                       N |
|-------------------------|
```

```
Total Observations in Table:  32
```

```
             | level
    medium   |        a |        p | Row Total |
-------------|----------|----------|-----------|
          bb |        4 |        1 |         5 |
-------------|----------|----------|-----------|
          cb |        6 |        3 |         9 |
-------------|----------|----------|-----------|
         org |        0 |        4 |         4 |
-------------|----------|----------|-----------|
          so |        3 |       11 |        14 |
-------------|----------|----------|-----------|
Column Total |       13 |       19 |        32 |
-------------|----------|----------|-----------|
```

```
Summary of performance times:

   Min. 1st Qu.  Median    Mean 3rd Qu.    Max.
  160.0   191.8   221.5   222.1   241.0   320.0
```

The CrossTable() command in your script created a *contingency table* or *cross tabulation*. At the top of the table is a header row, which includes values for the variable level. The column on the left gives the names of the values for the variable medium. The first row below the header shows information for "bb"—brass bands. There are four brass bands that are "a," or amateur groups, and one that is "p," or professional. The column on the right and the row on the bottom give totals for the respective rows or columns. For example, the Row Total column shows that there are five brass bands of all kinds. Statisticians call the totals *marginal values* or just *marginals*.

Below the table, you will find summary information for the variable time—the performance time. We see a *minimum* time of 160 seconds and a *maximum* time of 320 seconds. There are two measures of the center of the distribution of time: the *mean*, or ordinary average, where all the numbers are added and then the sum is divided by the total number of numbers; and the *median*, which is the number that is higher than 50 percent of the numbers and lower than 50 percent. Finally, we have the *first quartile*, 191.8 (the point at which one quarter of the numbers are lower), and the *third quartile*, 241 (the point at which three-quarters of the numbers are lower).

You might also find it convenient to write a script containing library() and setwd() commands so that you can, with one command, execute many such commands that you would otherwise need to enter separately. If you have downloaded several packages that you use frequently, it might be a good idea to load them all in one step rather than trying to remember when you need a particular package. Even though it is not a great inconvenience to issue a source() command each time you start R, some people prefer having R source such a script automatically. This is possible, but the method is a little different for each platform. In OS X, at the top of the screen, open the R menu and choose Preferences. You will be able to specify a working directory that will apply every time you start R. Configure it so that R starts by dragging and dropping a file containing a script that will be sourced at startup. In Windows, you will need to find the *.Rprofile* or *Rprofile.site* file and edit it to include the commands that you want to execute at startup. To see examples, try this:

```
> ?Startup
```

User-Written Functions

Sourcing a script is a great tool when you need to repeat a sequence of commands exactly. However, there may be times when you want to do some procedure repeatedly, but not always on the same variables or same arguments. If you wanted to use the script we created in the previous section, but not always on the same file, you could write your own function that would let you choose which file to retrieve and analyze.

The general format for a *user-written function* is as follows:

```
name <- function (argument1, argument2,...){
    commands
}
```

Suppose that you want to name your function "update" and have it retrieve an Excel file that you will name each time you use the function. The code that follows, which is almost the same as the script in the previous section, would do this. The argument fn appears in the function statement and in the Nimrod2 statement, indicating whatever argument is supplied by the user in the function call will be substituted in the Nimrod2 command when R executes the commands:

```
# a user-written function, called "update"
update <- function (fn){
library(gmodels)
library (XLConnect)
Nimrod2<-readWorksheetFromFile(fn,sheet=1,header=TRUE)
attach(Nimrod2)
CrossTable(medium,level,
  prop.r=FALSE,
  prop.c=FALSE,
  prop.t=FALSE,
  prop.chisq=FALSE)
 # print table with counts in each cell, but no percents
perf_time = summary(time)  # save summary output
title  = "Summary of performance times:"
cat(title,"\n", "\n")   # print title and 2 linefeeds
print(perf_time)
detach(Nimrod2)
}
```

To use this function, you must first save it, as you would save any R script, and then load it or source it. You can then issue any number of commands until you are ready to call the function, which you would do the following way, where myfile.xls is the name of the Excel file that you wish to analyze:

```
> update("myfile.xls")  # filename in quotes because myfile.xls
                        # is the value of a character variable
```

Of course, you might want to analyze a different file the next time. Just substitute the name of the new file. You can also create simple mathematical functions or quite complex programs, such as one that produces a special type of graph, as we will see later.

A Taste of Things to Come

Figure 1-3 displays several graphs based on the Nimrod data. All of these types of graphs will be discussed in the following chapters, and you should be able to produce any of them, and many more, by the time you finish this book.

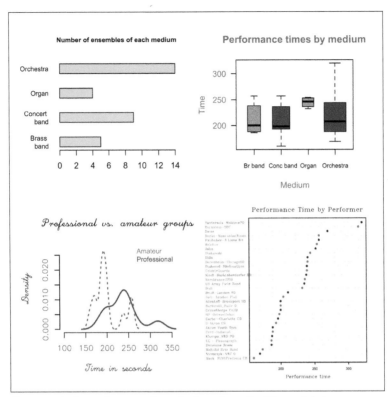

Figure 1-3. Several types of graphs based on the Nimrod data.

Exercise 1-4

If you had trouble entering data in "Exercise 1-2" on page 15 or "Exercise 1-3" on page 17, try entering the simple dataset from "Exercise 1-1." on page 12 by one of the following methods. First, here is the data again:

Year	Rate
1	94
2	92
3	90
4	80

Method 1: spreadsheet
Open your spreadsheet program. Enter the data into five rows (including the header) and two columns, just as the data is laid out

here. Export the file into your working directory (see the section "The Working Directory" on page 10) as a *.csv* file with the name *simple1.csv* Then, create the new data frame mydata:

```
> mydata = read.csv("simple1.csv",header=TRUE)
> mydata

  year rate
1   1   94
2   2   92
3   3   90
4   4   80
5  NA   NA
```

In this case, there was a blank row in the spreadsheet, so the last row of the R data frame has missing values. You can fix this by using the nrows argument to read in only the specified number of rows:

```
> mydata= read.csv("simple1.csv",header=TRUE,nrows=4)
> mydata

  year rate
1   1   94
2   2   92
3   3   90
4   4   80
```

If you had an extra (blank) row before the header, here would be the result:

```
> mydata

    X  X.1  X.2 X.3
1 NA year rate  NA
2 NA    1   94  NA
3 NA    2   92  NA
4 NA    3   90  NA
5 NA    4   80  NA
```

You could use the skip argument to ignore the first row:

```
> mydata= read.csv("simple1a.csv",header=TRUE,skip=1, nrows=4)
> mydata

    X year rate X.1
1 NA    1   94  NA
2 NA    2   92  NA
3 NA    3   90  NA
4 NA    4   80  NA
```

In this last example, we have extra columns. This is not a big problem, because we could simply ignore them. The important thing is that the two vectors of interest, year and rate, have the right number of rows. If you want to delete one of the useless columns, you can do it this way:

```
> mydata$X = NULL
> mydata

  year rate X.1
1    1   94  NA
2    2   92  NA
3    3   90  NA
4    4   80  NA
```

Method 2: text

Open your word processor or text editor. Type in the data with a space between each entry and the next on a line, and a carriage return at the end of each line, like so:

```
year rate
1 94
2 92
3 90
4 80
```

Extra spaces should not matter, but the data should be saved as plain text, not rich text. If your word processor allows you to save a .txt file, use the Save As command to save your file into your working directory, with the name *simple2.txt*. Otherwise, you will probably need to use the Export command, again using the name *simple2.txt*. Read the data into R and create the data frame newdata by using the following command:

```
> newdata = read.table("simple2.txt",sep="",header=TRUE)
> newdata

  year rate
1    1   94
2    2   92
3    3   90
4    4   80
```

# CHAPTER 2

An Overview of R Graphics

This chapter discusses how to export a graph and the differences between exploratory and presentation graphs. There is also a brief overview of several graphics systems in R. If you have some past programming experience or substantial experience with graphics, you will probably appreciate having this information before going on to the specifics of R graph types. If you're not coming from that background, you might find this material a little too technical and unnecessary at this point. If so, go directly to Chapter 3 and come back to this one when you are ready for it.

Exporting a Graph

After you have made a graph, you will probably want to save it or put it in a document. How you do this will depend on what other software you are using. With some word processors, for instance, you can simply copy the graph by opening the graph window in R and clicking Copy in the Edit menu or a context menu connected to the graph. You can then paste it into the word processor.

Other software will require a little more effort on your part. If you have tried the copy-and-paste method and it does not work, you will need to choose a file type and instruct R to save your graph in this format, to a specific file. You can save the graph in any one of several formats, including *.bmp*, *.pdf*, *.jpeg*, *.png*, *.tiff*, *.ps* (PostScript), and others. The code example that follows shows how to save the graph we made in "Exercise 1-1." on page 12 to a *.jpeg* file, named *test.jpeg* (you could, of course, give it any other name you choose, as long as the extension is ".jpeg"; for example, you might name it *mywork.jpeg*):

```
jpeg("test.jpeg") # opens a device
plot(year,rate)
dev.off()   # closes the graphic device - you must do this
```

After the graph has been saved in this manner, you can insert it into the word processor document. For example, in OpenOffice, you open the Insert window, click Picture, click From File, and then select the file *test.jpeg* from the working directory. Of course, after your graph is saved in a file, it is ready to load into all kinds of applications, such as drawing or illustration programs—for example, you can "brush up" your R graphs in Adobe Illustrator or Inkscape, if so desired. The graphs in this book were saved as *.png* files and uploaded, with no brushing up, to my editor's Google Drive account. For a higher resolution graph, I used this code:

```
dpi=600
png("filename.png", width = 6*dpi, height = 6*dpi,
  res = dpi)
graphic commands
dev.off()
```

For more information on saving files this way, type **?png**.

What Is a "Device"?

Specifying a *device* is a way to instruct R where to draw a graph and define what form it will take. If no device is specified, graphs appear in a graphic window on the computer screen. If you want to save a graph to a file (on a hard drive, flash memory, or whatever), you must instruct R what file (device) to write to, by "opening a device." You do that by using a command that also informs R what format the file will be, such as *.jpeg*, *.pdf*, *.png*, and so on. Then, you can draw a graph on the device by using whatever graphic commands you need to make the kind of graph you want. Finally, "close the device"; that is, stop writing to that file. After you've closed the device (by using dev.off()), any further results go to the screen, or to another device if you open a new one. For more information about devices, type **?device**.

Exploratory Graphs and Presentation Graphs

Graphs are useful both for *exploration* and for *presentation*. Exploration is the process of analyzing the data and finding relationships and patterns. Presentation of your findings is making your case to others who have not studied the data as intensively as you have. While you are exploring the data, your graphs can be stark, lean, and somewhat unattractive. In the role of data analyst—the person who knows the data, and is getting to know it better with each graph made—you do not need all the titles, labels, reference details, and colors that someone sitting through a presentation might expect, and indeed might find necessary. Furthermore, adding all this extraneous detail just slows down the exploration phase. Also, some graphs will prove to be dead ends or just not very interesting. Consequently, many graphs might be discarded during the discovery journey.

As the process of exploration continues, adding some details can make relationships a little clearer. As you get closer to presentation and/or publication, the graphs become more detailed and prettier. You will probably create many plain graphs in the process of analysis and relatively few beautiful graphs to appear in the final report.

Following are two graphs of the mtcars dataset included with the base installation of R, which shows the relationship between mpg (miles per gallon) and wt (weight of the car). The first graph (see Figure 2-1) is an early attempt to discern the relationship between the two variables by using a *scatter plot*. It clearly shows that as the weight of a car increases, the mileage per gallon decreases. If you are not familiar with scatter plots, you might want to come back to this example after you have read Chapter 12. The second graph, shown in Figure 2-2, shows quite a bit of refinement over the first effort. It includes a title, labels on the axes, and a breakdown of cars by the number of cylinders, and, of course, color is applied. This might be something that appears in a PowerPoint presentation. Between these two examples, there might have been several other relatively plain exploratory graphs. Because this book is about the process of graphic analysis, many of the examples included will be plain and skeletal, but they lead toward an attractive finished product.

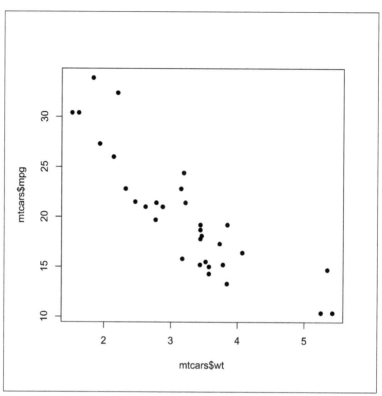

Figure 2-1. An exploratory graph of wt versus mpg.

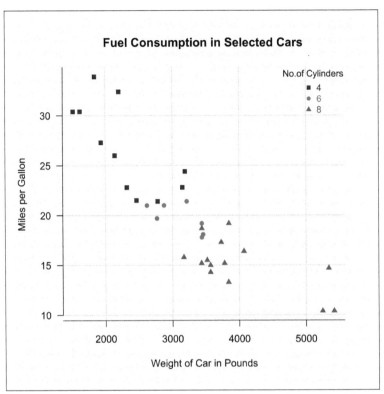

Figure 2-2. Presentation graph of wt versus mpg; a refinement of the graph in Figure 2-1.

One line of code produced the graph in Figure 2-1:

```
plot(mtcars$wt, mtcars$mpg, pch=16)
```

The more colorful and elaborate graph in Figure 2-2 required several more lines of code. It took more work, but its usefulness as a presentation object makes this worth the effort. The various types of commands that went into this graph are not explained here; we will examine them in several chapters later in the book. The point is that simple and effective graphs are easy to make with R, but if you want very fancy graphs, you can get them with a bit of extra labor. The script to produce Figure 2-2 looks like this:

```
# Script producing Figure 2-2
library(car)
attach(mtcars)
par(bg="snow",fg="snow",col.axis="black",bty="l")
mtcars$wt2 = 1000*wt
attach(mtcars)
scatter plot(mpg~wt2|cyl,
  smoother=FALSE,
  reg.line=FALSE,
  col=c("indianred4","blue","purple"),
  pch=c(15,16,17),
  main="Fuel Consumption in Selected Cars",
  ylab="Miles per Gallon",
  xlab="Weight of Car in Pounds",las=1,
  legend.plot=FALSE,bty="l")
axis(2,col="black",at=c(10,15,20,25,30,35),las=2)
axis(1,col="black",at=c(1000,2000,3000,4000,5000,6000))
legend("topright",
  title="No. of Cylinders",
  c("4","6","8"),
  inset=-.005,
  text.col=c("indianred4",
  "blue","purple"),
  title.col="black",
  cex =.65,
  pch=c(15,16,17),
  col=c("indianred4","blue","purple"),
  bty="n")
detach(mtcars)
```

Graphics Systems in R

There are several graphics systems available in R. Base R includes many useful graphic functions, but different R users have extended the graphics capabilities by contributing new graphics packages. The following discussion characterizes the strengths and styles of various graphics packages.

Base Graphics and grid

Base R includes a graphics package that is automatically installed when you first install R, and is also automatically loaded each time you start R. It is quite powerful in that it is able to produce many kinds of graphics that you can customize extensively. Many R users will never need more power or flexibility than what is provided in base R, so this is a good place to begin. Most of the graphics in this book were produced by the base R graphics package.

Even though base R graphics are quite impressive, there are sometimes applications that call for more control over the details of graphic output. For this reason, a package called grid was developed for low-level graphics. "Low-level" means that grid provides a number of tools or materials that are used by developers of still other packages that will be used, in turn, to make finished graphs.

In this respect, grid is somewhat like a lumber mill that makes boards (low-level material) that will be used by builders or homeowners for projects in a house (high-level), such as floors or bookshelves. One can be a fine builder without being concerned about how the lumber mill sections trees, rough-cuts planks, and planes them smooth. The builder starts with the board, not the tree. The grid package provides processed materials used to make the other graphics systems discussed in this chapter, as well as some graphic procedures included in various other R packages. It does not provide any functions that we will use directly to make finished graphs. However, some of the graphic functions we will use have been built from grid functions. For detailed information about grid, see Murrell (2011). Because users generally do not write grid code directly, there is no grid example given here.

lattice

The lattice package was developed to provide improved graphics for *multivariate data*—i.e., for graphing more than two variables at a time. lattice is modeled on the *trellis graphics* described by Cleveland (1985, 1993). The idea here is that sometimes the most effective way to visualize relationships of several variables is not to attempt to put all of them in one graph, but to look at several related graphs, organized in a purposeful way. For example, Figure 2-3 shows a trellis plot of four windows, or *panels*, from the BP dataset in the epiDisplay package. In each panel, there is a plot of systolic blood pressure by diastolic blood pressure. Each panel shows the plot for a combination of sex and saltadd (whether salt was added to the diet).

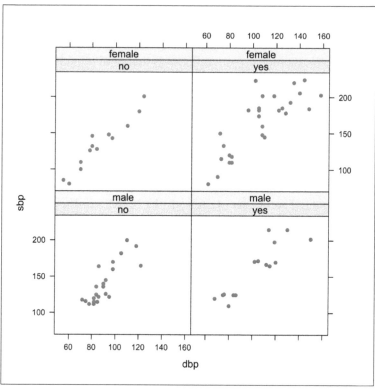

Figure 2-3. A trellis plot produced by using the lattice package.

Figure 2-3 demonstrates a way of examining the relationship of four variables at once by scanning four related graphs on one page. Here is the code to do it:

```
# Figure 2-3
library(lattice)
library(epiDisplay)
attach(BP)
xyplot(sbp~dbp|saltadd*sex,pch=16)
detach(BP)
```

lattice comes with the base R installation, but you must load it during each session for which you need it. In addition to trellis graphics, it includes functions for many other graphic types as well. Although this book uses only a few examples of lattice, it is an excellent graphics package that extends the capabilities of R. You might find it worth the time to learn, after you become more familiar with R and base graphics.

ggplot2

The ggplot2 package is designed to have a syntax that is consistent across all graphic types; that is to say, the command language is surprisingly similar from one type of graph to another. This is in marked contrast to base R, for which there are many arguments that can be used for several different kinds of graphs, but there are also a number of inconsistencies. The ggplot2 package is also quite versatile, enabling you to customize graphical displays relatively easily. Because the syntax of this package differs so much from that of base R graphics, very few examples of its use appear in this book. I should mention, however, that there are a few commands that are designed to look similar to base R, so you can try some of the capabilities of ggplot2 without much effort. If you have need for some of the special features of this package, it might be something for you to learn after you have acquired a greater understanding of R. The aesthetic style of ggplot2 is rather different from base R graphics, and you might or might not like it. An example appears in Figure 2-4, and the code that follows is what created it:

```
# Figure 2-4
library(ggplot2)
ggplot(mtcars, aes(x=wt, y=mpg)) + geom_point()
```

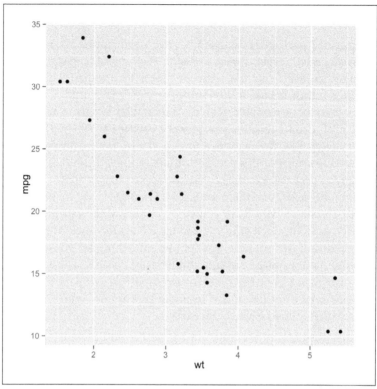

Figure 2-4. A simple graph produced by ggplot2, based on the same data as the base R graphs in Figure 2-1 and Figure 2-2.

ggplot2 does not come with base R, so if you want it, you must install it first and then load it during every session for which you want to use it.

Special Applications/Graphs Incorporated into Packages

Many packages, even those that are not primarily graphics packages, include some graphic capabilities. You can get a sense of the diverse and plentiful graphic offerings at the CRAN Task Views web page (*http://cran.r-project.org/web/views/*). Click Graphics to see a one-page overview of the types of graphics included in many packages, but keep in mind that this does not include all graphics. Also, some packages might have only a few graphic functions mixed in with many other features, and these kinds of packages will not usually appear in Task Views. Use your favorite search engine to scour the Internet for references to a particular graphic in R. Among the thousands of R packages, it can be a daunting quest to find exactly what you need!

User-Written Graphic Functions

If you just cannot find the right graphic for your data, it is possible to write your own graphic function. This is simply an extension of the method covered in Chapter 1, but later I will introduce a number of graphics tools that you can include in such functions. An example of a user-written graphic function to produce a Bland-Altman plot is presented in Chapter 14.

## PART II

Single-Variable Graphs

Exploratory analysis of a dataset usually begins with an examination of a single variable at a time. In this section, we will consider several graphical methods for discovery of patterns in a single characteristic. For instance, if people are the statistical units of interest, how much variability is there in a characteristic such as height, weight, or IQ? If automobiles are the units, we might be curious about how they vary in maximum speed, fuel consumption, or horsepower. As we gain insight about each variable alone, it usually makes sense to examine the relationships between variables, but that will be the topic of the next section.

The single-variable methods in the next several chapters are designed for quantitative variables, except for the bar chart and pie chart, which are appropriate for categorical variables. You also can expand most of the graphs in this section to study the effect of a second variable on the variable of primary interest. These expansions are equivalent to two (or more) single-variable graphs, arranged by value of the second variable. For this reason, they are included in this section with their corresponding single-variable graphs.

# CHAPTER 3

Strip Charts

A Simple Graph

One of the simplest yet still quite useful graphs is the *strip chart* (called a "dot plot" by some analysts). This graph provides a way to view how a set of numbers is *distributed*. That is to say, what is the shape of the data? Can we identify what the maximum and minimum numbers are, how spread out they are, and whether some of the numbers cluster together?

Let's examine the `trees` dataset provided with base R. To see a description of this data, type the following:

```
> ?trees
```

A new window opens, describing the data. Following is the information provided in the window:

Description
This is a brief narrative about the data.

Usage
This displays the dataset name.

Format
This explains that the structure is a data frame and that it has 31 observations with 3 variables, and gives the variable names and the units of measurement.

Source
This indicates where the data came from.

References

This gives examples of books or articles in which an analysis of the data appears. I sometimes copy and paste a reference into a search engine to see such an analysis. This does not always work, but when it does, it is usually very helpful.

Examples

This gives some R code using the dataset. It is sometimes very interesting to copy and paste one or more of the examples into the R console and see what kinds of statistical analyses and/or graphs are produced. In this particular case, the kinds of plots produced will be discussed later in the book, but there is also some statistical analysis that is not covered here.

Most help files for datasets give information for most of the previous categories.

When You Need a Little Help...

R provides several kinds of readily accessible help. For example:

- ?numbers gives help for a dataset named numbers.
- ?mighty gives help for a function named mighty.
- example(x) gives example output for the function x. Try example(stripchart).
- vignette() lists all vignettes for packages installed on your computer. Try it!
- vignette(x) shows the vignette for x. Vignettes can be almost anything, from a user manual to R code and sample output.

All the variables in the trees dataset measure, in different ways, the size of the 31 trees in the sample. Consider first the variable, Volume. Try the commands that follow. Be sure to use an uppercase "V" in Volume; otherwise, R will indicate that there was an error, because it does not recognize the variable volume:

```
> attach(trees)
> Volume
```

You will see the following:

```
[1] 10.3 10.3 10.2 16.4 18.8 19.7 15.6 18.2 22.6 19.9 24.2 ...
[19] 25.7 24.9 34.5 31.7 36.3 38.3 42.6 55.4 55.7 58.3 51.5 ...
```

R printed out the volume of each of the 31 trees. Index numbers are included in the output, showing that the first line begins with [1], the first element of the vector. The second line begins with the 19th element. It might take a while to process this information. You need a strategy. Perhaps you should look first for the smallest and largest numbers. You might also try to guess at the average, or see if several trees have the same volume. Even with a relatively small dataset like this one, the process can seem difficult. Now try a simple graph:

```
> stripchart(Volume)
```

The strip chart appears in Figure 3-1.

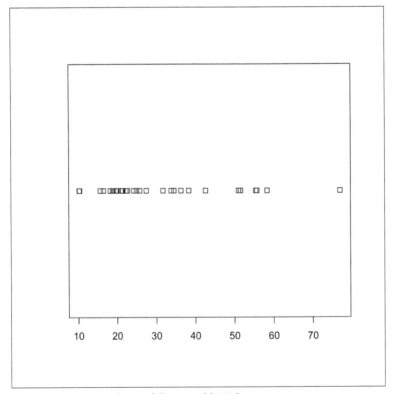

Figure 3-1. A strip chart of the variable Volume

The axis on the bottom shows the numerical values of the volumes of the 31 trees. The graph shows that many of the values are clustered around 20–30 cubic feet, with a smaller cluster between 50 and

60. There is one extremely large value, well over 70. This one large value may raise some important questions. Was there some overlooked factor that could explain the unusual size? Was there a mistake in measuring or recording the measurement of this tree? Is there some way to verify or correct this number? If there will be further analysis of this data, should this extraordinary value be included or excluded? All these questions might have been neglected had the analysis begun with consideration of numbers alone—in other words, asking simply about the average volume.

There are not 31 distinct squares on the plot, because some of the trees have the same, or nearly the same, volume. You can separate those trees competing for the same location on the graph by adding an argument in the stripchart() command:

```
> stripchart(Volume, method = "jitter")
```

Figure 3-2 is a marked improvement over the previous graph.

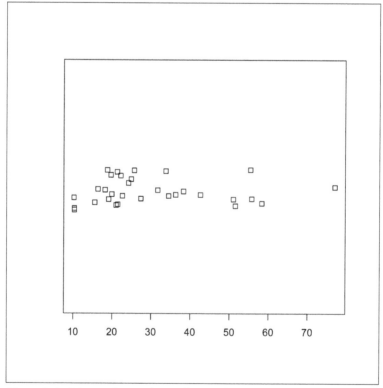

Figure 3-2. A jittered strip chart of tree volume.

There is still some overprinting in Figure 3-2, but careful counting shows that there are now 31 points. Some of the points that had been sharing the same space are "jittered" above or below each other, making the graph much easier to read. One way to improve this display further would be to increase the amount of jittering in this graph. You can use a help command to see what options are available:

```
> ?stripchart
```

The help file for stripchart() has a lot of useful information, including a great deal that is not described in this book but might be of use to you later. It contains the following sections:

Description
> This indicates what the function does and what circumstances are appropriate for its use.

Usage
> This shows the basic syntax and default options. In other words, if you do not specify a particular argument, what will happen?

Arguments
> This describes the choices that you can make to alter the results to your own liking. (Arguments were defined in the section "Try Some Simple Tasks" on page 2.)

Details
> This provides various details such as where to find more information, who developed the function, and so on.

Examples
> This presents code that you can copy and paste into the console to get a feel for what the function really does.

The help file shows that the default value of jitter is 0.1. Experiment with the jitter argument and the stack argument to see how they work. Another way to improve the graph is to change the character representing each point with the pch (think "plot character") parameter. This time, add a label to the x-axis by using the xlab argument:

```
> stripchart(Volume, method = "jitter", pch = 20,
    xlab = "Volume in cubic feet")
```

You can see the results of this change in Figure 3-3.

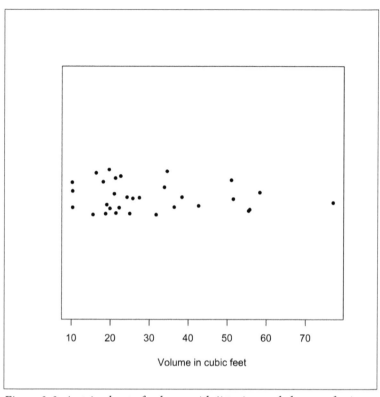

Figure 3-3. A strip chart of volume with jittering and change of print character.

The separation of tree volumes is much clearer in Figure 3-3 because the print characters are smaller and do not overlap as in the previous graph. If you look at Figure 3-2 and Figure 3-3 very closely, you will see that the placement of the points seems a little different. Actually, they are both right! When you use method = "jitter", the points are placed *at random* above or below the horizon. Therefore, each time you issue the stripchart() command with jittering the result will be slightly different, even with exactly the same data. That is, the *vertical placement* will vary slightly, but the horizontal placement will be exactly the same, and the horizontal position is what we are concerned about. (Actually, there is a way to fix this, but it brings up a technical issue that I would prefer not to introduce at this point. If you want to see the points in the same place on every chart, just type the command set.seed(1) before the stripchart() command, each time you use it.)

The command:

```
> ?points
```

opens a help window that includes, among a lot of other information, the options for the pch parameter. In Figure 3-4, pch options are extracted and displayed in a much more convenient form.

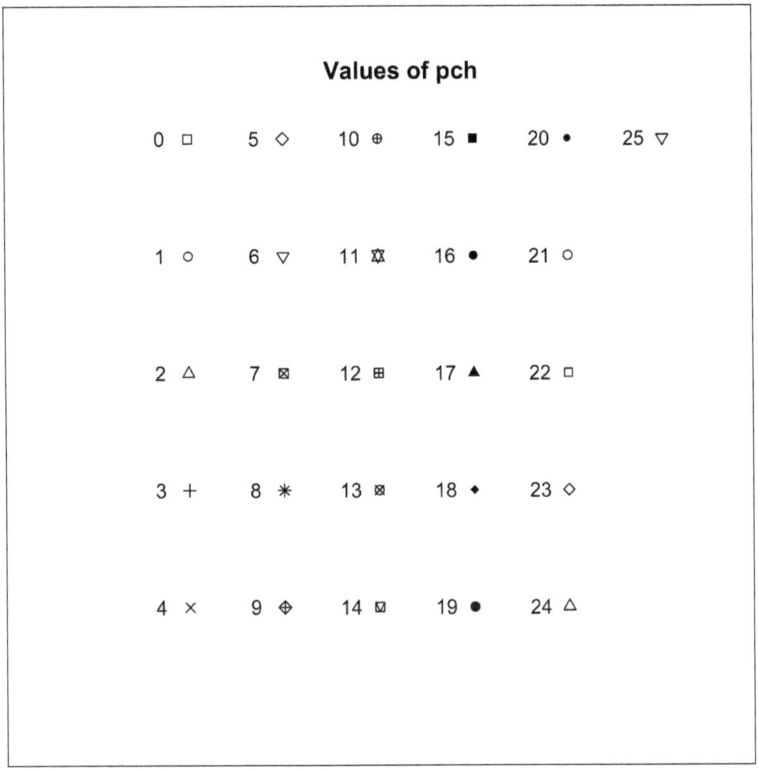

Values of pch

0 □	5 ◇	10 ⊕	15 ■	20 •	25 ▽
1 ○	6 ▽	11 ✡	16 ●	21 ○	
2 △	7 ⊠	12 ⊞	17 ▲	22 □	
3 +	8 ✳	13 ⊠	18 ◆	23 ◇	
4 ×	9 ⊕	14 ⊠	19 ●	24 △	

Figure 3-4. Options for the graphical parameter pch.

The best symbols for this kind of plot—the ones that overlap the least—tend to be open circles (pch=1) or very small symbols (pch=20 or pch=18). You can also use other characters, so if you wanted a really small plot symbol, you could use the period:

```
pch = "."
```

Data Can Be Beautiful

Figure 3-3 is a perfectly fine display for our understanding of the data. For the purpose of presentation, however, we might like something a little more eye-catching. There are several things that can be done to make this graph a little more interesting. The options examined here will be useful for later graphs, as well.

Most R graphs are created with a box around them. These boxes are often unnecessary, look unappealing, and can be distracting. (Some people like the box, but play along with me here; there probably will come a time when you would like to know how to get rid of it.) Fortunately, you can remove them quite easily. There are many arguments available to control graphic output. To see a list of graphic parameters, type the following:

```
> ?par
```

You can use many of these parameters in various graphic commands. A few of them must be used only with a par() command, usually given before calling another graphic function. The argument controlling the box around a graph is bty (i.e., box type). To suppress the box entirely, issue the par(bty="n") command before typing the graphic command. The following two commands produce Figure 3-5, with no box around the plot:

```
> par(bty = "n")  # Figure 3-5
> stripchart(Volume, method = "jitter", pch = 20,
  xlab = "Volume in cubic feet")
```

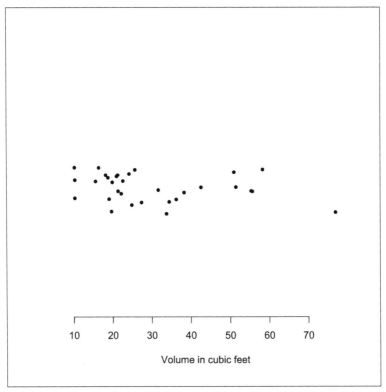

Figure 3-5. A strip chart of Volume, without a box around the plot.

A Box Around Your Graph?

You can have a box, a partial box, or no box around a graph. The options available with the bty argument of the par() function are "o" (the default), "l", "7", "c", "u", or "]". Each one creates a partial box around the plot, in the shape suggested by the parameter. bty = "n" removes the box entirely. The best way to understand this is to try one or more of them yourself. For more information, type **?par**.

Notice that with no box around the plot in Figure 3-5, the single extreme value of Volume looks out of place, beyond the graph. You can fix that by using the xlim argument to extend the x-axis, as shown in Figure 3-6.

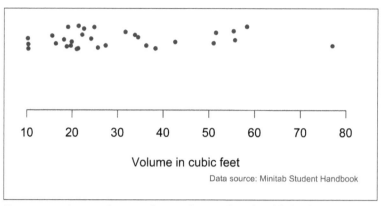

Figure 3-6. A strip chart without a box and with added color, an extended x-axis, and added margin text.

Probably the next thing that comes to mind is color. It is easy to change the color of the points by adding one more argument to the `stripchart()` command:

```
# Figure 3-6
par(bty = "n")
stripchart(Volume,
  method = "jitter", jitter = .3,
  pch = 20,
  xlab = "Volume in cubic feet",
  col = "dodgerblue4",
  ylim = c(0,8),
  xlim = c(10,80)) # xlim forces x between 10 & 80
  # and ylim closer to x-axis
```

Notice that the `col` argument gives a color name. R has 657 named colors for you to use. You can see them listed in Appendix B. You can also see the R colors on your computer screen by issuing the following command:

```
> demo(colors)
```

After looking at the plot produced by the preceding command, which changes the color of the points only, you might also like to change the color of the axis. You can do this by using the `axis()` command, as shown in the code that follows. This operates on an existing graph. The `axis()` command changes the color of the axis in the graph produced by the previous command (again, refer to Figure 3-6 to see the result):

```
> axis(1, col = "dodgerblue4", at = c(10,20,30,40,50,60,70,80))
```

Take Control of the Axis

The axis() function adds an axis to the current plot. The parameters in the axis() command used here are:

- Which axis to operate upon: 1. This parameter is required and you do not need to include the parameter name (side). Possible values are 1 = bottom, 2 = left, 3 = top, and 4 = right.
- The color of the axis: col = "dodgerblue4".
- Where to put tick marks and labels: at = c(10,20,30,40,50,60,70,80).

There are several other arguments that allow you to specify features such as fonts, labels, line width, and so on. You can add this function to most graphs, not just strip charts. axis() is not required for any plot, but it gives you a great deal of control over the final result. For more information, type **?axis**.

The mtext() command adds a note outside of the plotting area of the graph.

```
> mtext("Data source: Minitab Student Handbook",
side = 1, line = 4, adj = 1, col = "dodgerblue4", cex = .7)
```

Add Text to Your Plots

You can use the text() and mtext() functions to add text within the plotting area or in the margins, respectively, of an existing graph. The mtext() command in the strip chart example specifies the following:

- Text to be displayed: in our example, "Data source: Minitab Student Handbook".
- Where it should be: side = 1 specifies the bottom. Other possible values are 2 (left), 3 (top), and 4 (right).
- How many lines below (or above, left of, or right of) the graph: line = 4.
- Justification: adj = 1 specifies far right, adj = 0 means far left, and a number between 0 and 1 can be provided to indicate how far to the left/right.
- Color: col = "dodgerblue4".
- Type size: cex = .7.

For more information, type **?mtext** or **?text**.

Being finished with the trees dataset, type:

```
> detach(trees)
```

Exercise 3-1

Try your hand at strip charts with another dataset, mtcars. Do a simple strip chart of the variable mpg. What do you learn? Try a more sophisticated chart by looking at the mpg strip chart broken down by the number of cylinders a car has; that is, a subplot of mpg for each value of cyl (i.e., cylinder). The following command does that by using a grouping variable, cyl, after the symbol ~ (tilde). Usually, a grouping variable is a categorical variable. In this case, it is actually a quantitative variable that has a small number of possible values—the car can have 4, 6, or 8 cylinders:

```
> attach(mtcars)
> stripchart(mpg~cyl)
> detach(mtcars)
```

Is this an improvement? What additional information did you glean from this plot? Try jittering the plot. Does this help?

Exercise 3-2

Many of the packages that you can add to R offer alternatives to the functions provided in base R. Try out an alternative to strip chart() by installing the plotrix package and testing the function dotplot.mtb() on the variable Volume from the trees dataset. How is this function like stripchart(), and how is it different? Do you like one better?

# CHAPTER 4

Dot Charts

Basic Dot Chart

The *dot chart* (sometimes called "dot plot") is quite similar to the strip chart in that it shows how spread out or clumped together points are. But the dot chart goes beyond this and gives us the opportunity to glean even more information from our data. You might consider the next dataset a bit gruesome, but consider that some readers of this book might indeed deal with this kind of data on a regular basis. Because the methods introduced in this book can be applied to a wide range of subjects, for readers with varying needs, diverse types of data have been chosen to illustrate the use of graphs. So, let's look at the USArrests dataset, which gives arrest rates per 100,000 population for serious crimes in each of the US states in 1973:

```
> attach(USArrests)
> head(USArrests) #shows first 6 rows, can get all with:
    USArrests

           Murder Assault UrbanPop Rape
Alabama      13.2     236       58 21.2
Alaska       10.0     263       48 44.5
Arizona       8.1     294       80 31.0
Arkansas      8.8     190       50 19.5
California    9.0     276       91 40.6
Colorado      7.9     204       78 38.7
```

This dataset includes values for four named variables. There is also one column without a variable name in the top row. The values in the lefthand column are row.names—in this particular case, the names of states. Many times, the row name is simply a number.

Let's explore this dataset. First, see what a strip chart can tell you about murder arrests. Try it and ponder what you have learned about murder arrests from the strip chart. Are the arrest rates nearly the same or very different? Are they clustered together or spread out? What would you have expected? Although you might have arrived at some interesting insights, consider the further capabilities of the dot chart:

```
> dotchart(Murder)
```

The graph in Figure 4-1 is similar to the strip chart in that it shows the location (along the x-axis) of each state. It is different, however, in that each state has its own "row," or horizontal line. Therefore, there is no overprinting and no need for jittering.

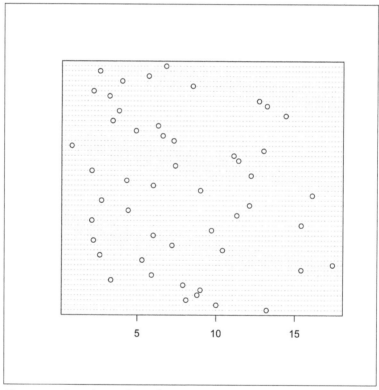

Figure 4-1. Dot chart of murder arrest rates in each of the states.

Another useful refinement is possible. All data frames include a character vector containing a row identifier that is recognized by the name row.names. Notice that each row in the data frame has a state name. You can label each row in the dot chart with its state name by adding the argument labels = row.names(USArrests). The labels could also be the values of any other variable, if we wanted that:

```
# Figure 4-2
dotchart(Murder, labels = row.names(USArrests), cex = .5)
```

Figure 4-2 demonstrates that it is easy to identify exactly which states had the lowest and highest murder arrest rates and to find some that are typical or nearly average rates. The labels argument placed the state names on the plot; the cex argument changed the character size. The default value of cex is 1, so any smaller value makes the characters smaller.

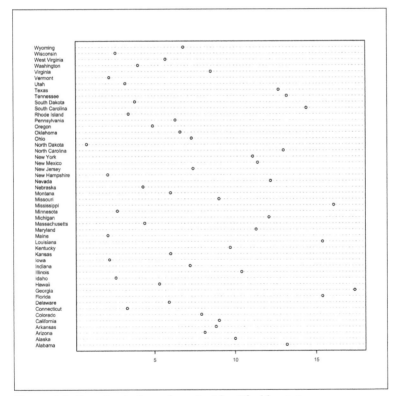

Figure 4-2. Dot chart of murder rate, identified by state.

A more interesting view of this data might be to see the murder arrest rates arranged by size. To do that, the data must first be sorted by Murder. This means that the dataset's rows will be rearranged in order of their murder arrest rates. You can create a new dataset sorted this way by using the order() function. The name of the sorted dataset could be just about anything. This one is arbitrarily called data2 (no awards for originality here):

```
> data2 = USArrests[order(USArrests$Murder),]
```

Next, redraw the graph (see Figure 4-3) using this newly sorted data and add a title and label:

```
> dotchart(data2$Murder, labels = row.names(data2),
    cex = .5, main = "Murder arrests by state, 1973",
    xlab = "Murder arrests per 100,000 population")
```

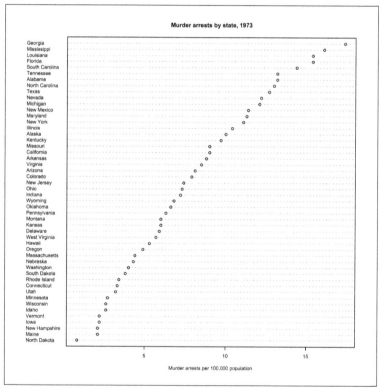

Figure 4-3. Dot chart of states sorted by murder rate.

Now, it is easy to see which states are the leaders and the laggards in murder arrest rates. Of course, you could see that information in a table of numbers, but with this chart you can see at a glance the relative differences among the states. Are the results what you would have expected? Remember that the rates in our data are rates of arrests, not rates of murders.

The plot could be made a little more attractive with a few small adjustments. The plot character would stand out more if it were solid, so add `pch = 19`. Color would catch the viewer's attention, so make the points and labels a different color by using the `col` argument. The lines are quite close together, too, so try using color to facilitate reading by alternating colors, line by line. To do this, use the argument `col = c("darkblue","dodgerblue")`. Make the horizontal reference lines a different color by using `lcolor = "gray90"`.

Recycling Arguments

Many R functions *recycle* arguments. This means that if there are not enough items in a vector, for instance, R will reuse items. So, to make Figure 4-4, the argument `col = c("darkblue","dodgerblue")` applies to the 50 states. Because there are only two colors specified, when R needs to apply a color to the third state, it goes back to the first color, and so on until all the states have colors. The `col` argument could have included any number of colors. If there were 50 or more, R would have used the first 50 colors. If there were any number less than 50, R would recycle as necessary until each state had a color.

You can see what colors are available by using the following command:

```
> demo(colors)
```

Here's how you can get a list of the color names:

```
> colors()
```

Appendix B contains a color chart. The R code that created the chart is also there, so you can print one out if you want. A couple of nice R color charts are also available on the Internet at *http://www.stat.columbia.edu/~tzheng/files/Rcolor.pdf* and *http://research.stowers-institute.org/efg/R/Color/Chart/*.

The title of the graph would stand out more if it were larger, so add cex.main = 2; that is, make the main title twice its size. The complete command looks like this:

```
> dotchart(data2$Murder, labels = row.names(data2),
    cex = .6, main = "Murder arrests by state, 1973",
    xlab = "Murder arrests per 100,000 population",
    pch = 19, col = c("darkblue","dodgerblue"),
    lcolor = "gray90",
    cex.main = 2, cex.lab = 1.5)
```

Figure 4-4 presents the results.

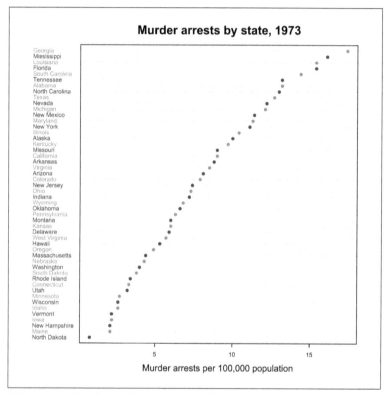

Figure 4-4. Dot chart of states by murder arrest rates with added color.

Exercise 4-1

To understand why cex was added to the plot in Figure 4-2, try the dotchart() command without this parameter and see what happens.

Exercise 4-2

Make a dot chart of the variable `time` from the `Nimrod` dataset. Remember that you will first need to use the `load()` command to retrieve the data.

# CHAPTER 5

Box Plots

The Box Plot

Sometimes, it can be helpful to look at summary information about a group of numbers instead of the numbers themselves. One type of graph that does this by breaking the data into well-defined ranges of numbers is the *box plot*. We will try this graph on a relatively large dataset, one with which our previous types of graphs do not work very well.

There are some interesting datasets in the `nlme` package. Get this package and load it by using these commands:

```
> install.packages("nlme")
> library(nlme)
```

Next, take a look at the `MathAchieve` dataset. With more than 7,000 rows, this is much larger than the datasets we have dealt with previously. What problems will this create for us if we want to examine the distribution of `MathAch` scores? Let's see what happens with a strip chart of this data.

In the code that produces Figure 5-1, as in many following examples, the `mfrow` argument is used in `par()` to make multiple graphs appear on one page. The format is `mfrow = c(i,j)`, where i is the number of rows of graphs and j is the number of columns:

```
# Figure 5-1
library(nlme)
par(mfrow=c(2,1)) # set up one graph above another: 2 rows/1 col

stripchart(MathAchieve$MathAch, method = "jitter",
  main = "a. Math Ach Scores,
  pch = '19'", xlab = "Scores", pch = "19")

stripchart(MathAchieve$MathAch, method = "jitter",
  main = "b. Math Ach Scores,
  pch = '.'", xlab = "Scores", pch = ".")
```

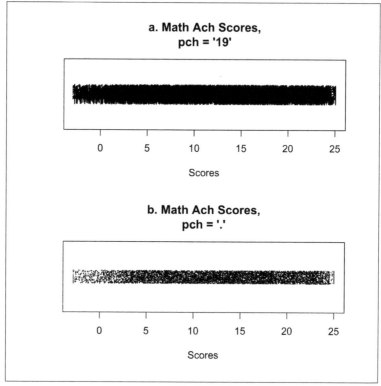

Figure 5-1. Strip charts of math achievement scores

These strip charts show the results of using the plot character from Figure 3-4 (in Figure 5-1a), and using a different, smaller character (in Figure 5-1b). Even then, the plot is very dense. There are too many points, so it is difficult to judge the shape of the distribution. Where is the center? Maybe at about 10, or a little higher? Is the distribution a little *skewed*, or less dense, to the left? How many points are extreme values? Unfortunately, the help file gives no reference to the study. It would be interesting to know something about the scoring of the math test, because there are many scores below zero.

Perhaps a different kind of chart would be more revealing. The box plot graphically displays several key measurements that are not obvious in the strip chart. First, let's make some box plots with the code that follows. Note that this time the mfrow argument creates a different layout of graphs on the page, with one row and two columns:

```
# Figure 5-2
library(nlme)
par(mfrow = c(1,2)) # two graphs side-by-side: 1 row, 2 cols

boxplot(MathAchieve$MathAch,
  main = "Math Achievement Scores", ylab = "Scores")

boxplot(MathAchieve$SES,
  main = "Socioeconomic Status", ylab = "SES score")
```

The graph, shown in Figure 5-2 (also known as a *box-and-whiskers plot*) shows a dark line in the center representing the *median*, the point at which half of the scores are lower and half are higher. Reading off the chart, it appears that the median is about 13. Other ways to describe the median are as the *50th percentile*, the point at which 50 percent of the scores are lower, or as the *second quartile*, the point at which two quarters of the scores are lower. The lower edge of the box is the *first quartile*, the point at which one quarter, or 25 percent, of the scores are lower. The upper edge of the box is the *third quartile*, the point at which three-quarters, or 75 percent, of the scores are lower. The vertical lines coming out of the box are the "whiskers," which go to the highest and lowest points if they are no more than 1.5 times the *interquartile range* (the distance between the first and third quartiles). If the points are beyond the whiskers, they appear as small circles.

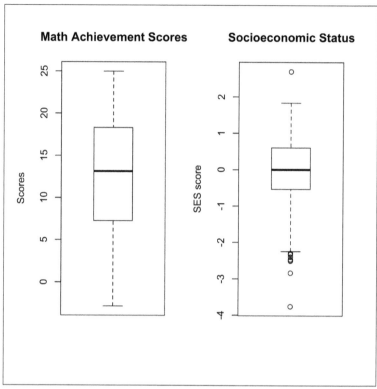

Figure 5-2. Box-and-whiskers plots of math achievement scores and SES

Figure 5-2 shows the distribution of math achievement scores to be nearly symmetrical but slightly skewed to the lower scores; that is, the lower whisker is a little longer.

One of the other variables in the dataset, SES (socioeconomic status), is interesting to examine. Compare its box plot (the right side of Figure 5-2) to that of the math scores. There are several points beyond the whiskers in the SES plot. Extreme values always raise some questions about the variable under scrutiny as well as the accuracy of the data. You might want to check the extreme values to ensure that the data has been entered correctly. If so, it might be appropriate to consult the literature on the SES measure to look for explanations of the extremes and to think about the nature of the sample selected for the study.

Let's return to the math scores. It might be illuminating to break the sample into smaller groups so that we can compare test scores. Figure 5-3 shows the results of generating box plots of MathAch with several group breakdowns. The par() function sets the page for four graphs by passing to the mfrow argument a vector indicating two rows and two columns. Each graph has a label—on the x-axis—of the command that creates that graph. This is accomplished by including the argument sub = 'text to appear'.

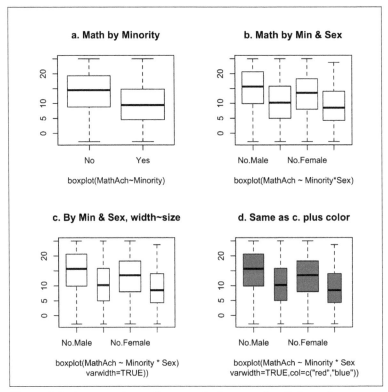

Figure 5-3. A comparison of progressively more detailed graphs.

Here are the commands for creating Figure 5-3:

```
# Figure 5-3, i.e. 4 graphs
par(mfrow=c(2,2))    #set up page for 2 rows of 2 graphs each
attach(MathAchieve)

boxplot(MathAch ~ Minority, xlab = "boxplot(MathAch~Minority)",
  main = "a. Math by Minority", cex = .4)

boxplot(MathAch~Minority*Sex,
  xlab = "boxplot(MathAch ~ Minority*Sex)",
  main = "b. Math by Min & Sex", cex = .4)

boxplot(MathAch ~ Minority * Sex,
  xlab = "boxplot(MathAch ~ Minority * Sex)",
  sub = 'varwidth=TRUE))', varwidth = TRUE,
  main = "c. By Min & Sex, width~size", cex = .4)

boxplot(MathAch ~ Minority*Sex,
  xlab = 'boxplot(MathAch ~ Minority * Sex',
  varwidth = TRUE, col = c("red","blue"),
  main = "d. Same as c. plus color",
  cex = .4, sub = 'varwidth = TRUE,
  col = c("red","blue"))')
```

Let's examine the four graphs. Figure 5-3a shows a box plot for non-minority students and another box plot for minority students. We see that although the median and quartile scores of nonminority students are higher, the maximum and minimum scores are similar. In Figure 5-3b, each of the minority groups has been further broken down by sex. We see not only lower math scores for minorities in both genders, but also lower math scores for females among both minorities and nonminorities. Figure 5-3c and Figure 5-3d are both improvements on Figure 5-3b. In these graphs, the width of each box is related to the size of the group it represents. We can see that fewer of the students are minorities, and there are fewer males than females in each of the minority and nonminority groups. Figure 5-3d uses color to make the groups more easily distinguishable. The color vector specifies only two colors, which are given to the first two boxes and then *recycled* to give the same two colors to the last two boxes. The effect of this recycling is to give nonminority males and females red, and minority males and females blue. (As we saw in the previous chapter, R recycles any vector that is not long enough to accomplish the task given to it.)

Nimrod Again

Now is a good time to revisit the Nimrod dataset. We can use box plots to look at the distribution of performance times in the various performance media and in amateur versus professional ensembles. Furthermore, we can look at one important piece of information that I neglected to mention earlier. Let's begin with box plots of time broken down by level and medium:

```
# Figure 5-4a, first must have loaded Nimrod
#  load("Nimrod.rda")  /  see Chapter 1
attach(Nimrod)
par(mfrow=c(2,1)) #graphs laid out in 1 display w/ 2 rows, 1 col
boxplot(time ~ level * medium,
  main = "a. Performance time by level and medium")
```

The result of this command is depicted in Figure 5-4a. We see considerable variation by group. Except for the brass bands, professional groups tend to play the piece slower than amateur groups. In the next version of this graph, it might be clearer to highlight amateur versus professional status with color. Because professional groups consistently play the piece slower, does this difference indicate that the "correct" tempo is rather slow? It is certainly something to think about.

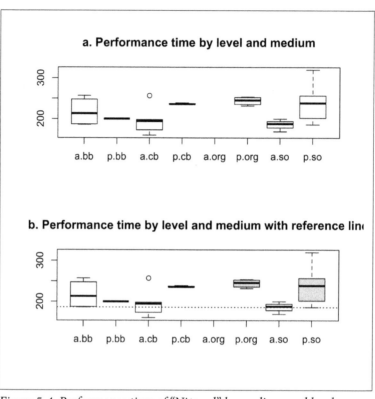

Figure 5-4. Performance time of "Nimrod" by medium and level

Now it's time to reveal the identity of a secretly coded performer in the dataset. "EE" is none other than Edward Elgar, the composer himself! Despite the learned execution of the highly trained professional musicians in the sample, we can reasonably argue that the composer should be taken as a more authoritative source of information about the proper tempo of this work. Of course, we have only one performance by the composer and do not know if he conducted at this tempo, or near this tempo, every time. Nonetheless, it might be revealing to show Elgar's tempo, in comparison to all the others, on the graph. We can do this by adding a *reference line*. Upon consulting the spreadsheet we started with (Table 1-4), we find that Elgar's performance time was 186. A horizontal line, across all the boxes, at the level of 186 would make it easy to compare each performance time to the composer's. We can do this with the abline() command, which will place a line on the graph produced immediately before this command:

```
# Figure 5-4b
boxplot(time ~ level * medium,
  main = "b. Performance time by level and medium with reference
  line", col = c("white", "light blue"))
abline(h = 186, lty = "dotted")
detach(Nimrod)
```

Adding Lines on the Graph

You can use the abline() function to put one or more *reference
lines* on a graph (you can use the function as many times as necessary to put multiple lines on a single graph). This function draws
only straight lines; different methods are used for curves. The line
can be specified by its intercept and slope (if you do not remember
the meanings of *intercept* and *slope* from high school math, see the
brief review of lines in Chapter 12), or, as in the Nimrod example,
you can draw a horizontal line by giving only the y-intercept (h =
186; i.e., time = 186). Where appropriate, a vertical line could be
requested by using v = instead of h. Various line types can be called
for, as in the present example, which uses lty="dotted". For more
information, type **?abline** or **?par**.

The graph in Figure 5-4b shows that amateur musicians were in
much closer agreement with the composer's idea of tempo than professional musicians. This is a surprising result and will make for a
provocative graph. Of course, we have only a small sample of performances. Were it our purpose to make generalizations to professional and amateur performances, our present sample would not be
sufficient. However, we are just exploring possible relationships and
formulating a hypothesis that we might wish to investigate further,
and we have enough data for this.

Making the Data Beautiful

Figure 5-4b does the basic job of showing the relationship of time
with level and medium. If this is all you want at this point, you can
skip to the exercises at the end of the chapter. You might want to
come back to this section later, as you begin to feel more comfortable writing R code and find yourself wanting a more attractive
graph.

We can make the Nimrod graph much more eye-catching and appealing as well as easier to interpret. One of the most unsatisfying features of Figure 5-4b is the names of the instrumental groups, "a.bb" and so on. Longer names, such as "amateur brass band," simply will not fit in the limited space. One way to fix this problem is to make the bars go horizontally, dedicating a line for each group name in the margin. We will also give meaningful names to instrumental groups and put some text on the graph. This new graph appears in Figure 5-5.

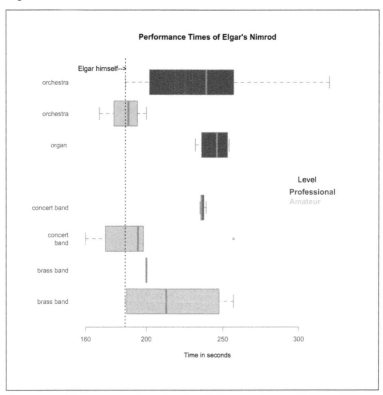

Figure 5-5. The improved graph of performance time of "Nimrod" by medium and level. Compare this to Figure 5-4.

Do you agree that Figure 5-5 is an improvement over Figure 5-4b? If so, let's see how to make these improvements.

The following script will produce the new graph. There are several commands that are set apart by blank lines between them to make reading them a little easier. The comments above each command explain the arguments' meaning:

```
# Script for Figure 5-5
attach(Nimrod)

# par() sets bkgrnd color, foreground color, axis color,
# text size (cex), horiz.
# text on y-axis (las=1), margins (mar). Graph too big for
# default margins. ?par for more info on above arguments.

par(bg = "white", fg = "white",
  col.axis = "gray47", mar = c(7,8,5,4),
  cex = .65, las = 1)

# boxplot() determines formula (time ~ level * medium),
# makes plot horizontal,
# sets color for box border and box colors (col),
# creates titles (main, xlab), creates names
# for the combinations of level*medium (names), names size
# (cex.names). One of the names is "" because there is no
# category "amateur organ."

boxplot(time ~ level * medium, horizontal = TRUE,
  border = "cadetblue",
  main="Performance Times of Elgar's Nimrod",
  col = c("deepskyblue","peachpuff4"),
  xlab = "Time in seconds",
  names = c("brass band","brass band","concert
  band", "concert band","", "organ ", "orchestra","orchestra"),
  cex.names = .4)

# abline() puts vert. line at time = 186 sec. to show the
# performance conducted by Elgar. Line type (lty) dotted & color
# (col) black.

abline(v = 186, lty = "dotted", col = "black")

# legend() chooses legend text & color & location on the graph.
# Legend shows that pros are peachpuff4 & amateurs are
# deepskyblue.

legend("right", title = "Level", title.col = "black",
  c("Professional","Amateur"),
  text.col = c("peachpuff4","deepskyblue"),
  text.font = 2, cex = 1.2)

# mtext() puts text at a place specified by the user
mtext(" Elgar himself - - >", side = 3,
  line = -2, adj = 0,
  cex = .7, col = "black")
```

```
# axis() modifies x-axis (1)  & sets the color & length and
# tickmarks
axis(1, col = "cadetblue", at = c(160,200,250,300))

detach(Nimrod)
```

What Do the Symbols Mean? The legend() Function

A *legend* is a notation on a graph that indicates the meaning of particular symbols or colors. In Figure 5-5, for instance, the legend on the right side stipulates that brown (R's "peachpuff4") boxes represent professional ensembles, whereas the blue boxes represent the times of amateur groups. The legend() function allows specification of the location on the graph, specific text, colors, fonts, and so on. For more information, type **?legend**.

The lesson learned from study of Figure 5-4 and Figure 5-5, again, is that with R, you can produce basic plots for exploring data quickly and easily (often with one line of code)—and if really pretty graphs are needed for presentation purposes, R can make that possible, too (but it might take considerably more effort!).

Exercise 5-1

As I have said before, correlation does not prove causation. The apparent relation between math scores and minority status in Figure 5-3 may actually be a function of other factors. Perform a box plot analysis of the SES variable, grouped by Minority and Sex. Save your graphs (see Chapter 2 for information on how to save graphs) to use in further analysis later. Using a word-processing program, write a paragraph or two about what you discovered, and insert the graphs that illustrate your points. In a later exercise, we will examine the relationship between the math scores and SES directly.

Exercise 5-2

An alternative to box plots comparing two or more groups is the *Engelmann-Hecker-Plot* (EH-Plot). Compare the box plot of mpg in the mtcars dataset with cyl as a grouping variable (see "Exercise 3-1" on page 56) to an EH-Plot that you can create by using the

---

ehplot() function in the plotrix package. In what ways is the EH-Plot better? How is the box plot better?

# CHAPTER 6

Stem-and-Leaf Plots

Basic Stem-and-Leaf Plot

This short chapter might be considered "nostalgia" by some because it describes a type of graph that was important in the paper-and-pencil days of data analysis. You probably will not see many examples of this type of graph in modern presentations, but it is included here because it will help you to understand the histogram a little better, which is the topic of Chapter 7. You might also find it useful in the exploratory phase of your data examination. If you are already knowledgeable about histograms, you can skip this chapter without fear of missing necessary material.

The sbp dataset in the multcomp package includes the variables sbp —the systolic blood pressure of 69 patients—and the gender of each of those people as well as the age of each. We can look at the distribution of the blood pressures with a *stem-and-leaf plot*. This type of graph reveals not only the general shape of the data distribution, but the (rounded) value of each data point as well.

The stem-and-leaf plot works by putting all of the values in order, from lowest to highest. Then, it reserves a line for all of the values in a common range and writes the last significant digit of each number on the appropriate line. You can use the stem() command in base R to create a stem-and-leaf plot of the sbp variable in the sbp dataset. This type of display, sometimes called a *textual display*, appears in the R console, not in a graphic window. We can produce the display shown in Figure 6-1 as follows:

```
> library(multcomp)
> stem(sbp$sbp)
```

```
The decimal point is 1 digit(s) to the right of the |

11 | 046
12 | 00444588
13 | 000244568889
14 | 002224444589
15 | 00234466788889
16 | 00224589
17 | 002244566
18 | 045
```

Figure 6-1. A stem-and-leaf plot of the sbp variable

The display in Figure 6-1 shows all the blood pressures in the dataset. The column on the left side of the display, including the numbers 11, 12, 13, and so on, contains the "stems." The blood pressures
are all three-digit numbers, so the stem contains the first two digits,
and the "leaf" contains the last digit of each number. Reading from
the top of the display, the numbers represented in the first stem are
numbers beginning with "11" and the leaves are 0, 4, and 6. Thus,
the numbers represented on the first line are 110, 114, and 116. The
next stem includes the numbers 120, 120, 124, 124, 124, 125, 128,
and 128. We can see that there are exactly two systolic blood pressures of 170 and four of 158, but only one of 185.

Figure 6-1 shows the distribution of the data to be approximately
symmetrical. There are about the same number of low blood pressures as there are high blood pressures, and a relatively large number of blood pressures near the center of the distribution (i.e., blood
pressures of about 130 to 160). In this figure, the width of a stem is
about 10 (e.g., 110–119, 120–129). If the width of the stem is
changed, the shape of the graph may well change, too. You can make
such a change to the stem width by adding another argument to the
stem() command. The argument scale = x, where x is a positive
number, controls how wide each stem will be. For example, try this
command:

```
> stem(sbp$sbp, scale = 2)
```

In Figure 6-2, the graph is twice as long as before. Each stem is half
as wide (i.e., width 5 instead of 10), but there are twice as many
stems. The general shape of the distribution has not changed very
much, although there is a dip in the center, around 145, that we did
not see earlier. In some distributions, a change of scale will dramati-

cally change the shape. The width of leaves corresponds to the size of what we will call *bins* in the histogram. Perhaps the stem-and-leaf plot does not look as appealing as some other types of graph, with nicely formed rectangles and colors. However, this type of plot shows the precise value of each number in the vector studied. This can aid in understanding the data and suggest modifications to make in a graph.

```
The decimal point is 1 digit(s) to the right of the |

11 | 04
11 | 6
12 | 00444
12 | 588
13 | 000244
13 | 568889
14 | 002224444
14 | 589
15 | 002344
15 | 66788889
16 | 00224
16 | 589
17 | 002244
17 | 566
18 | 04
18 | 5
```

Figure 6-2. Stem-and-leaf plot of sbp, with twice as many stems.

The stem-and-leaf plot works best for small to medium-sized datasets. If there are too many numbers in one stem, they will run off the page! When this happens, we lose all sense of the real shape of the distribution. One way to deal with this is to make the `scale` bigger. This makes more leaves with fewer numbers in each one of them. Sometimes, even this strategy will not help enough. Again, you might not use this type of plot in a final presentation, but perhaps you will find this elegant tool helpful to understand the histogram and revealing during the exploratory phase of your project.

Exercise 6-1

Try your hand at picking a suitable `scale` for the blood pressure data. The numbers you choose do not need to be integers. They can also be smaller than 1. Try the same thing with some of the datasets we have examined in earlier chapters.

Exercise 6-2

Sometimes, it is useful to compare the distributions of two variables on the same plot. It is possible to do two stem-and-leaf plots back-to-back with the stem.leaf() function in the aplpack package (you will need to install and load the package). Do this for Height and Volume in the trees dataset. Do you see what you expected? Why or why not? (Hint: what units is each variable measured in?) Try the same kind of plot for pretest.1 and post.test.1 in the Baumann dataset in the car package. Is the posttest higher or lower than the pretest? Is this a useful tool?

# CHAPTER 7

Histograms

Simple Histograms

Let's revisit the sbp dataset from the multcomp package. A useful tool for examination of the blood pressure data is the familiar *histogram*. In this type of graph, the range of values of a numeric variable of interest (e.g., sbp) is usually laid out on the horizontal scale (x-axis). This scale is divided into sections, called *bins*. The vertical scale (y-axis) shows how many observations fall into each bin.

Figure 7-1 was produced by calling the hist() function four times, once for each graph in the figure. Of course, you could have accomplished the same thing by typing several command lines at the console. The basic command is simply hist(sbp).

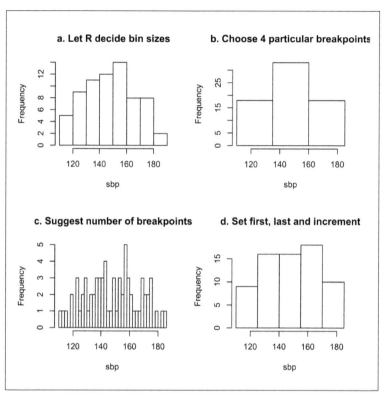

Figure 7-1. Histograms of the sbp variable from the sbp dataset, displaying the effect of differing numbers of bins.

Here is the script to produce Figure 7-1:

```
# Script for Figure 7-1
library(multcomp)
attach(sbp)
par(mfrow = c(2,2))
hist(sbp, main = "a. Let R decide bin sizes")
hist(sbp, main = "b. Choose 4 particular breakpoints",
  breaks = c(110,135,160,185))
hist(sbp, main = "c. Suggest number of breakpoints",
  breaks = 30)
hist(sbp, main = "d. Set first, last and increment",
  breaks = seq(110,190,15))
detach(sbp)
```

This code leaves the choice of number of bins to R, which is often a pretty good decision. In addition, each command line adds the argument main = to produce a title for that particular histogram. Finally, except for the first graph, the breaks = argument suggests the number of bins to use and/or how wide the bins should be. Note that in all of the graphs created here, the bins in any one graph are all the same size; in other words, the bars are all the same width. This is the usual practice for histograms. Anything else would be very difficult to interpret.

You can use the breaks argument to do the following:

- Provide a number of breaks between bars; for example, breaks = 30.
- Define specified breakpoints; for example, breaks = c(110,135,160,185).
- Give first, last, and increment values; for example, breaks = seq(110,190,15).
- Provide any other valid specification of a series of numbers; for example, breaks = c(110:190).

When using breaks, be careful to begin with the lowest number in the vector; otherwise, you will get an error message. In the previous example, the lowest value in sbp is 110.

Figure 7-1 shows several examples of histograms of the sbp data. All of them are histograms of the same variable, but they look quite different. This is because they all have different numbers of bins. You might draw different conclusions about the distribution of the sbp scores from the various histograms.

Figure 7-1a gives the impression that many patients have an sbp score of about 150–160, but fewer patients have higher and lower scores. Further, the distribution is not symmetrical. Figure 7-1b, however, which was created by using the argument breaks = c(110,135,160,185), gives the impression that the distribution is perfectly symmetrical. Figure 7-1c, which was created by using the argument breaks = 30, is more like 7-1a than 7-1b, but shows more detail than either; it is also more volatile than any of the other histograms, with more sudden ups and downs. Figure 7-1d, created by using the argument breaks = seq(110,190,15), seems to be similar to 7-1a, but does not show the big drop in blood pressure at the high end (near 180).

Figure 7-1a uses the default number of bins; this is the number that R chooses if you do not specify one. Figure 7-1a gives higher resolution than Figure 7-1b—there are more bars and a clearer understanding of just where the data falls—but lower resolution than Figure 7-1c. Looking at all of the histograms, it seems that a lack of symmetry and falling off at the high end are two important features of the data that we would want to show. In this particular example, the default option (Figure 7-1a) gives a very good result. This is often but not always true. See "Exercise 7-1" on page 94 for an example of a contrary case.

You can control the number of bins in a histogram, but not as easily as you might hope. If you specify the number of breaks, as in Figure 7-1c, this is treated as a suggestion only. R will select a number that is probably close, but satisfies a "pretty" criterion. To find more information about this rule, type **?pretty**.

You can add many other arguments to the hist() command. A few of them are demonstrated in the next example and shown in Figure 7-2. For example, las = 1 flips the numbers on the y-axis so that they are upright instead of on their sides, label = T adds the frequency number at the top of each bar, col="maroon" determines the color of the bars, and the xlab = argument provides a more descriptive label on the x-axis:

```
# Figure 7-2
hist(sbp, main = "sbp dataset", las = 1, label = T,
    col = "maroon", xlab = "Systolic blood pressure")
```

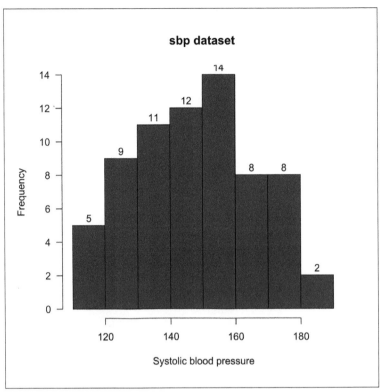

Figure 7-2. A histogram with added features.

Histograms with a Second Variable

Sometimes, it is important to delve deeper into the data than we're able to do with the simple histogram. For instance, it would be interesting to know if the distribution of blood pressures is similar or different for each gender. One way to assess this possibility is by using a *stacked histogram*. The sbp dataset includes the variable gender, which we can use with a stacked histogram to divide each of the bars in Figure 7-1a to show how many observations are males and how many are females. Although the hist() function does not allow us to do this, histStack(), a function provided in the plotrix package, makes this easy to do:

```
# Figure 7-3
library(plotrix)
library(multcomp)
histStack(sbp$sbp, z = sbp$gender,
  col=c("navy","skyblue"),
  main = "Systolic blood pressure by gender",
  xlab = "Systolic blood pressure", legend.pos = "topright")
```

The result appears in Figure 7-3.

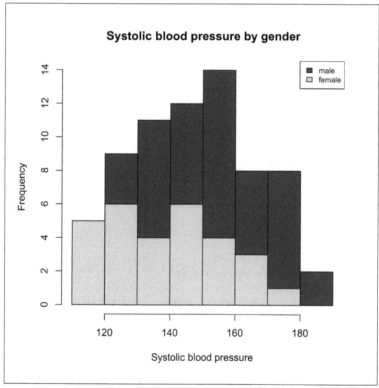

Figure 7-3. A stacked histogram of systolic blood pressure by gender.

The stacked histogram readily provides a lot of useful information. First, it is easy to see the distribution of female blood pressures, in light blue. However, the male distribution is not so easy to interpret: because the bottoms of the bars are all at different levels, it is hard to compare their heights. Nonetheless, we can tell that males have some higher scores than females, and vice versa. There is another way to present this data that most people find easier to read. Rather than putting all the information on one graph, it is possible to break the information up into two graphs that can appear side-by-side or one atop the other. There are several ways to do this in R. One of the easiest is by using the Hist() function in the RCmdrMisc package:

```
# Figure 7-4
library(RcmdrMisc)
library(multcomp)
Hist(sbp$sbp, groups = sbp$gender,
  main = "Systolic blood pressure by gender",
  col = "navy ", xlab = "Systolic blood pressure")
```

Figure 7-4 presents the results.

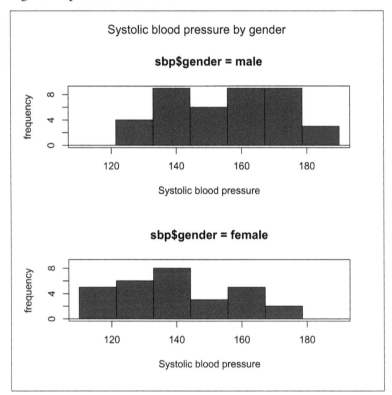

Figure 7-4. Separate histograms of systolic blood pressure for males and females.

The graphs in Figure 7-4 more clearly display not only that males have the highest blood pressures, but that they cluster toward the high end. The Hist() function is fine for a small number of groups, but it is not so convenient when the number of groups is large. For that, we can turn to the lattice package.

The lattice package has a very nice layout for *trellis graphics*—the graphics are broken down by groups of observations, appearing as separate graphs for each group. The Salaries dataset from the car package includes nine-month salary data for faculty at a college in the United States for the years 2008–2009. It was collected for the purpose of studying differences between male and female compensation. Let's produce a set of histograms for each combination of rank (three ranks) and gender (two genders), or six groups in all. Install and load the necessary packages first. Then, look at the information provided in the dataset. Notice the slightly different syntax for the histogram() command. The variable Salaries$salary is preceded by a tilde (~). The combination of variables that will form the groups follows the vertical bar symbol (|), and we use an asterisk (*) to indicate crossing the two variables. We get a very readable display in Figure 7-5, in which it is easy to compare male and female faculty salaries at a glance. The order of the grouping variables is important, however. If we had reversed the order, it would have resulted in a display that is not so easy to read. Try it for yourself:

```
# Figure 7-5
install.packages("lattice") # you probably already have it
install.packages("car")
library(lattice)
library(car)
head(Salaries)

        rank discipline yrs.since.phd yrs.service  sex salary
1       Prof          B            19          18 Male 139750
2       Prof          B            20          16 Male 173200
3   AsstProf          B             4           3 Male  79750
4       Prof          B            45          39 Male 115000
5       Prof          B            40          41 Male 141500
6  AssocProf          B             6           6 Male  97000


histogram(~ Salaries$salary | Salaries$rank * Salaries$sex,
    type = "count", main = "Faculty Salaries by Rank & Gender")
```

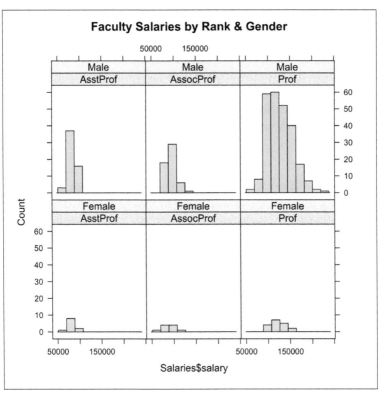

Figure 7-5. Histograms by groups, produced by using the histogram() function in the lattice package.

We can make several observations about the data presented in Figure 7-5. First, comparing the top row of histograms, which show data for males, to the bottom row, we can see that there are many more males than females in this study. Next, looking at the histograms from left to right, it is quite clear that there are many more professors (the highest rank) than associate professors or assistant professors. Finally, the salary distributions of males and females have about the same median for each rank, but there are more males at the high end of salary in both the professor and associate professor ranks.

Exercise 7-1

Consider the case0302 dataset from the Sleuth2 package. Make a histogram of the Dioxin variable, without specifying the number of breaks. Next, try several different ways of creating bins of various sizes. Does the distributional shape seem to change? Look at a strip chart of Dioxin. What does this tell you about the histograms?

Exercise 7-2

Sometimes, you might want to compare two variables. There are many ways to do this, one way being to look at their histograms. If two variables are measured on the same scale, it may be enlightening to look at the histograms back-to-back. The package Hmisc includes the histbackback() function for just this purpose. You can use this function to study the relation between the IQ measurements of brothers in the Burt dataset from the car package. Also, you can compare male and female salaries from the Salaries dataset.

# CHAPTER 8

Kernel Density Plots

Density Estimation

A common problem in science is to estimate, from a data sample, a mathematical function that describes the relative likelihood that a variable (such as the systolic blood pressure in the sbp example in the previous two chapters) takes a particular value. We tried to make a rough estimate of such a graph with histograms in Chapter 7. So, for instance, if you take a glance at the histogram in Figure 7-2, you can see that systolic blood pressures close to 150 are very likely to occur, but scores of about 110 are relatively unlikely. The rule, or formula, that gives the likelihood of a given value of, for example, blood pressure is called the *density function*.

Histograms are a good tool for many problems, being easy to understand and relatively easy to compute. There is, however, a shortcoming of which you should be aware. Many functions of interest are *continuous*; that is, they can take any value within a certain range. A blood pressure value could be 120 or 123 or 129.2, yet the histogram might force all of those values to be in the same bin and thereby all to take the value of 120. (Remember that the bin width in the histogram in Figure 7-2 was 10, so all scores equal to or greater than 120 and less than 130 fall within the same bin.) That is to say, we used a *discrete* function—one that can only take selected values of blood pressure—to estimate the density function, which is continuous. The graph in Figure 8-1a, a *kernel density plot*, is a smooth line approximation of the density function.

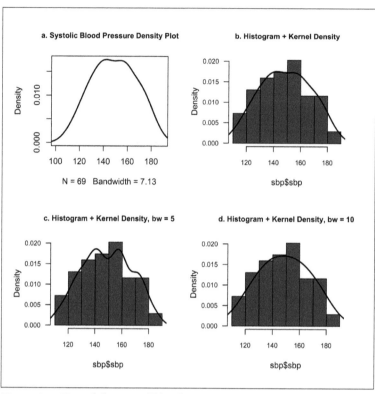

Figure 8-1. Kernel density of blood pressures and kernel density imposed on a histogram of blood pressures.

Look at the graph in Figure 8-1b to see the density estimate produced by R's `density()` function superimposed on the histogram. You can see that the density curve sometimes goes above the histogram and sometimes below. Imagine that you took several weighted averages of numeric values of groups of adjacent bins and replaced the histogram values with smooth lines connecting those averages. This is a type of *smoothing*. Several examples appear in Figure 8-1, the script for which is presented here:

```
# Script for Figure 8-1; there are 4 graphs
library(multcomp)
par(mfrow = c(2,2), cex.main =.9)

# Figure 8-1a
eq = density(sbp$sbp) # estimate density curve of sbp
plot(eq, xlim = c(100,190),
   main = "a. Systolic Blood Pressure Density Plot",
   lwd = 2) # plot estimate
```

```
# Figure 8-1b
# use histogram to estimate density
hist (sbp$sbp,
  main = "b. Histogram + Kernel Density", col = "maroon",
  las = 1, cex.axis = .8, freq = F) # freq=F: prob. densities
lines(eq,lwd = 2) # plot density curve on existing histogram

# Figure 8-1c
eq2 = density(sbp$sbp, bw = 5)
hist (sbp$sbp,
  main = "c. Histogram + Kernel Density, bw = 5",
  col = "maroon", las = 1, cex.axis = .8,
  freq = F) # freq=F: prob. densities
lines(eq2,lwd = 2) # plot density curve on existing histogram

# Figure 8-1d
eq3 = density(sbp$sbp, bw = 10)
hist (sbp$sbp,
  main = "d. Histogram + Kernel Density, bw = 10",
  col = "maroon", las = 1,
  cex.axis = .8, freq = F) # freq=F: prob. densities
lines(eq3, lwd = 2) # plot density curve on existing histogram
```

Figure 8-1a is a kernel density plot. The term *kernel* refers to the method used to estimate the points that make up the plot. In Figure 8-1b, a new plot is superimposed on top of the existing histogram by using the `lines()` command. Combining two graphs this way is very useful, and we will use variations of this trick often. In this case, we view two different methods of summarizing a single distribution.

Putting Curved Lines on a Graph

The `lines()` function is one more tool (remember `abline()`, `text()`, `axis()`, etc.?) that you can use to put new information on the current graph. Unlike `abline()`, which only draws straight lines, `lines()` can draw lines of almost any shape. `lines()` takes an argument of either a vector containing points that define a line, such as the eq vector in the script for Figure 8-1, or a pair of variables, x and y, that are used to draw the line. Further arguments can be most of the parameters in `par()`. For more information, type **?** **lines**.

The plot in Figure 8-1a shows the default label on the x-axis, which gives the sample size, N, and the *bandwidth*. The bandwidth indicates how spread out the plot is. Figures 8-1b, 8-1c, and 8-1d show the effects of changing the bandwidth. Figure 8-1b shows the default bandwidth, the same as Figure 8-1a. Note that it conforms to the general shape of the histogram. It changes direction three times—that is, there are three (very small) bends in the line—and we may well conclude that it is a reasonably good fit to the histogram. Figure 8-1c shows a smaller bandwidth, which fits more tightly to the histogram and changes direction five times. Figure 8-1d shows a larger bandwidth, which results in a flatter line that bends only once.

Choosing a Bandwidth

Which bandwidth should we use? That is not always easy to determine, and a precise answer is beyond the scope of this book. It might seem that making the bandwidth very small—creating a line that fits very closely to the histogram—would be best. Remember, however, that the histogram is based on a *sample* of data. If we took another sample, even a sample from the 69 blood pressures in the sbp dataset, the peaks and valleys in the histogram would be somewhat different. Maybe a lot different! The more precise we try to make the density curve, the less likely it is that it will be a good fit to the histogram from a new sample. Making estimates that are more detailed than the data warrants is called *overfitting* and can lead to embarrassing failures to be replicated on new data. On the other hand, if we make the bandwidth large, it will probably be a reasonably good fit to most samples but will not capture much detail. In many cases, you might find that trial and error with different bandwidths gives you some additional insight. In general, very dense data (i.e., a lot of data) probably warrants a smaller bandwidth, and very sparse data suggests a larger bandwidth. Many R packages offer density estimation and methods for finding an appropriate bandwidth. For example, ASH and KernSmooth are especially fast for large datasets, whereas np offers bandwidth calculation based on the data but is comparatively slow.

Comparing Two or More Density Plots

It is sometimes desirable to compare two or more density plots. For example, you might want to compare the means of two distributions and see if they have similar shape and variance. Consider the emis sions data from Chapter 1, in the section "Using the Data Editor" on page 14:

```
> load("emiss.rda") # load emissions data from Chapter 1
> emissions  # look at emissions data

  Year  N_Amer CS_Amer Europe Eurasia Mid_East Africa
1 2004   16.2    2.4    7.9    8.5      7.1    1.1
2 2005   16.2    2.5    7.9    8.5      7.6    1.2
3 2006   15.9    2.5    7.9    8.7      7.7    1.1
4 2007   15.9    2.6    7.8    8.6      7.6    1.1
5 2008   15.4    2.6    7.7    8.9      7.9    1.2
6 2009   14.2    2.6    7.1    8.0      8.3    1.1
7 2010   14.5    2.7    7.2    8.4      8.4    1.1
  Asia_Oceania
1     2.7
2     2.9
3     3.1
4     3.2
5     3.3
6     3.5
7     3.6
```

Suppose that we wanted to compare the emission profiles of Europe and Eurasia. We could first make a density plot of the European emissions data and then use the lines() function to plot the Eurasian data on top of it. Notice that the following code for Figure 8-2 makes use of the xlim and ylim arguments. This is a way of forcing the plot of the European density to be big enough that the plot of the Eurasian density does not run off the graph. Do not be overly impressed by my seemingly awesome foresight here—I tried it first without extending the limits of the graph and made a mess! Sometimes trial and error is the only path to enlightenment. The script to produce the figure follows:

```
# Script for Figure 8-2
# following par() sets white characters on black background
load("emiss.rda")
par(bg = "black", col.lab = "white",
  col.axis = "white", bty="l",
  fg = "white", col.main = "white")
euro = density(emissions$Europe) # points on density(Euro)
ea = density(emissions$Eurasia)  # points on density(Eurasia)

# use xlim & ylim so 2nd plot does not go out of range
plot(euro, xlim = c(6.9,9), ylim = c(0,2),
  main = "CO2 Emissions in Europe and Eurasia",
  col = "goldenrod1", lwd = 2)
lines(ea, xlim = c(6.9,9), ylim = c(0,2),
  lty = 2, lwd = 2, col = "cyan")
# lty=2 is dotted line
```

```
# lwd = 2 is a wider line than default line

legend("topleft",c("Europe","Eurasia"),
    text.col = c("goldenrod3","cyan"), bty = "n")
```

Figure 8-2 illustrates what the preceding code produces.

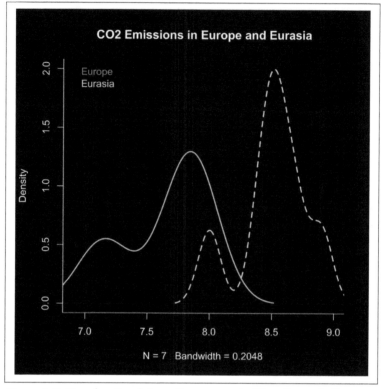

Figure 8-2. Two density plots on the same axis. The xlim and ylim arguments were used in the first plot to make the plotting area big enough to include the second plot, which otherwise would have gone out of range.

A Background That Is Not White

Most of the graphs in this book are on white backgrounds, which looks clean and clear. Notice that Figure 8-2 is on a black background; this was done just to show what you can do, if you're so inclined. If you run the script for Figure 8-2 without the par() command, the usual white background will be used. Run the script again, this time with the par() command included, and a black background will appear. If the black background is produced first, though, reverting to the white background is not as simple as just leaving par() out. Running it once will have changed some parameters, and those changes will still be in effect. Each parameter will need to be reset as an argument in another par() command, changing "black" to "white," and vice versa. By the way, if you ever need to know, you can see just what parameters are in effect by typing the par() command, with no arguments.

The Cumulative Distribution Function

As enlightening as density plots can be, they do not always give us the information we really need. Even though the density plot gives a sense of the relative likelihood of a value on the horizontal axis, oftentimes we would like to know the likelihood of, for example, a systolic blood pressure of 120 or less, or 135 or greater, or between 120 and 140. A plot of the *cumulative distribution function* (CDF) displays on the y-axis the probability of a score equal to or less than the value on the x-axis.

Consider a data distribution that follows the *normal distribution*— the so-called "bell curve." Our example comes from a *simulation*, or a computer imitation of selecting a large sample of numbers from a population of numbers with specified characteristics. The following code for Figure 8-3 shows how to do this with the rnorm() function:

```
# code for Figure 8-3
library(multcomp)
library(Hmisc)
par(mfrow = c(2,2), cex.main = .9, bg = "white")

# get 100,000 numbers sampled from a normal dist
# with mean = 0 and sd = 1
sam <- (rnorm(100000))  #mean = 0 and sd = 1 are default values
plot(density(sam),
   main = "a. Density (sampling from Normal distribution)",
   col = "coral4")  # Figure 8-3a
polygon(density(sam), col = "coral4") # color area under curve

plot(ecdf(sam),
   main = "b. Cumulative distribution function of sample in
   Figure 8-3a", col = "turquoise")

plot(ecdf(sbp$sbp), main = "c. ecdf(sbp$sbp) - base R")
```

```
Ecdf(sbp$sbp,
    main="d. Ecdf(sbp$sbp) - Hmisc pack. + grid()",
    xlab = "sys blood pressure", col = "deepskyblue3")
grid(col = "gray70") # adds gray grid to current plot
```

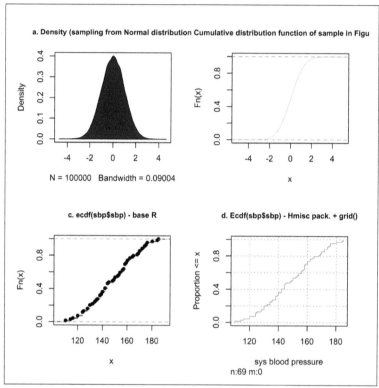

Figure 8-3. The empirical cumulative distribution function.

The graph in Figure 8-3a is the density plot of the sample of 100,000 numbers generated by the computer. Figure 8-3b shows the CDF of the dataset. You can see from this plot that about half of all the numbers on the y-axis are less than or equal to the x value of 0. You can also easily see that nearly (but not quite) all of the numbers are less than 2. The CDF plot in Figure 8-3b was produced by using R's ecdf() function, which plots the *empirical cumulative density function*. It is a smooth curve because there are so many numbers and the distribution is continuous. Figure 8-3c shows what happens when the ecdf() function is applied to the small sbp dataset. The "curve" is interpreted in the same way as it was in Figure 8-3b, but the data is so sparse that there are breaks in the plot, making it less attractive and more difficult to read. Practice reading Figure 8-3c.

What blood pressure is greater than about half of all the blood pressures? Find the place on the y-axis equal to proportion = 0.5. The *x* coordinate is about 150, or slightly less, so about 50 percent of the blood pressures are equal to or less than 150.

An alternative method to find the CDF is to use the Ecdf() function in the Hmisc package. You can see the plot produced by this function in Figure 8-3d. It is a step function rather than a smooth curve, but it is more appealing than the graph in Figure 8-3c, and easier to read. There are many advanced features available with this function, such as the ability to produce graphs for multiple groups and some labeling options. Although there are still other options for producing CDFs, one that is especially interesting is the stat_ecdf() function in the ggplot2 package. Figure 8-4 shows a graph produced by this function. It is both attractive and easy to read, largely because of the grid lines. Following is the code to produce it:

```
# code for Figure 8-4
library(ggplot2)
ggplot(sbp, aes(x=sbp)) + stat_ecdf()
```

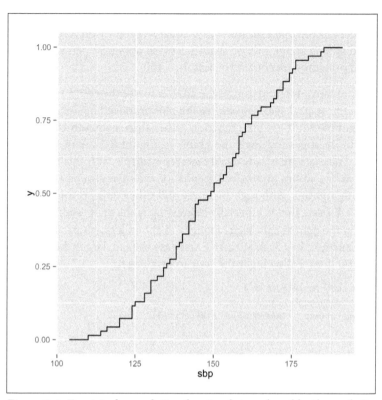

Figure 8-4. Empirical cumulative density plot produced by the ggplot2 package. The grid lines make this graph relatively easy to read.

Exercise 8-1

Continue the experiment of Figure 8-1. Choose a variety of band-widths and plot the resulting density-on-top-of-histogram graphs. Use some bandwidths close to those in Figure 8-1 and some wildly different. What did you learn?

Exercise 8-2

Based on Figure 8-4, what is the probability of selecting, at random, a person with a systolic blood pressure of 125 or less? What about 175 or greater? Finally, what is the probability of a blood pressure greater than or equal to 125, but less than or equal to 175?

# CHAPTER 9

Bar Plots (Bar Charts)

Basic Bar Plot

Let's revisit the Salaries dataset from Chapter 7. In Figure 7-5, we produced a display of six histograms, showing the distribution of faculty salaries in each of six combinations of rank and gender. Another interesting way of looking at the data would be to compare the counts of faculty members in each defined group. Let's begin with a simpler graph, representing just counts of the three faculty ranks. If we knew the counts in each rank, we could type them into a vector, such as in the following:

```
> ranknum = c(67,64,266)
```

then make a *bar plot* (also called a "bar chart") from the ranknum vector:

```
> barplot(ranknum)
```

If the counts are unknown, we can use the table() function to put these counts into a vector, and then have barplot() operate on that vector:

```
# preliminary to Fig. 9-1
install.packages("car")    # if you have not yet installed car
library(car)
attach(Salaries)
rankcount = table(rank) #get counts & save in vector rankcount
rankcount              # print results

rank
 AsstProf AssocProf     Prof
       67        64      266
```

The `barplot()` function shown in the code that follows uses bar height to represent the elements in a vector; in this case, it is the counts of each faculty rank. Thus, the graph will have three bars, the first two of nearly equal height, and the third one about four times the height of the other two:

```
# Fig. 9-1a
barplot(rankcount, ylab = "Count", col = "skyblue",
    main = "Faculty by Rank", sub = "a. Number in each rank")
```

Figure 9-1a shows this bar plot.

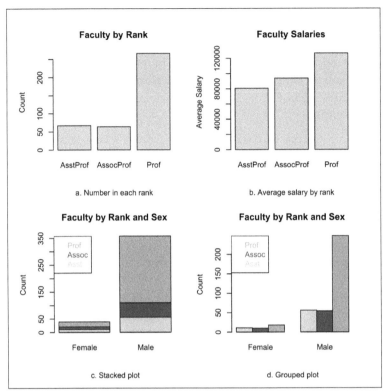

Figure 9-1. Bar plots of the number of professors in each category, of the average salary in each category, and counts by rank and sex.

Note that although the bar plot looks a little like a histogram, it is quite different. The bars in the histogram were defined by breaking a quantitative variable, ever increasing (or ever decreasing) along the axis, into sections. You could define the bars by different break-points, if desired. The bar chart uses discrete—or even categorical—definitions of the bars, so breakpoints are usually fixed and logically cannot be moved. The bars of a bar plot could be male/female or horse/cow/pig or mountain/seashore or gold/diamond/paper money, or any other categories that are mutually exclusive and not quantitative. Fitting a density plot makes sense over a histogram, but not usually over a bar plot.

In Figure 9-1a, the height of the bars represented a count of items in each bar. Although bar plots often are used for displaying counts, the height of the bar could represent anything; for example a measurement, a mean, income after taxes, and so on. Figure 9-1b illustrates such a bar plot that shows the average salary of each rank. To make such a graph, you must first put the average salaries in a vector by means of the `aggregate()` function and then call `barplot()` to operate on the newly created data. The expression `salary~rank` indicates that some operation will be performed on salary for each of the three ranks. `FUN = mean` shows that the operation will be finding the mean:

```
aver = aggregate(salary ~ rank, FUN = mean) # aver is new vector
aver    # see what is in aver
        rank    salary
1  AsstProf  80775.99
2 AssocProf  93876.44
3      Prof 126772.11

# Fig. 9-1b- bar height shows mean salary, names are ranks
barplot(aver$salary, ylab = "Average Salary",
   names.arg = aver$rank, col = "skyblue",
   main = "Faculty Salaries", sub = "b. Average salary by rank")
```

You can modify the bar plot to show the relationship between two variables. One way to accomplish this is the *stacked bar plot*, which you can see in Figure 9-1c. In this next example, two bars, showing numbers of male and female professors in the study, are each broken into smaller sections showing how many of each sex hold each rank. The first thing to do is to create a table, `rank2`, breaking down all the professors into groups of rank and sex:

```
rank2 = table(rank,sex)
rank2
            sex
rank        Female Male
   AsstProf     11   56
   AssocProf    10   54
   Prof         18  248
```

You can display the data in `rank2` by using `barplot()` (the result appears in Figure 9-1c):

```
# Fig. 9-1c
barplot(rank2, ylab = "Count", names.arg = c("Female","Male"),
   main = "Faculty by Rank and Sex",
   col = c("skyblue","skyblue4","burlywood"),
   sub = "c. Stacked plot")
legend("topleft", c("Prof","Assoc","Asst"),
   text.col = c("burlywood","skyblue4","skyblue"))
```

It is sometimes difficult to interpret a stacked bar plot, so you might want to consider another option. The various rectangles representing each combination of rank and sex can each become a separate bar and be grouped, in this case by putting all the bars for one sex together. You can see such a graph in Figure 9-1d. This requires one modification from the code used to create Figure 9-1c, which is to add the beside = T argument:

```
# Fig. 9-1d
barplot(rank2, ylab = "Count", names.arg = c("Female","Male"),
   main = "Faculty by Rank and Sex",
   col = c("skyblue","skyblue4","burlywood"),
   sub = "d. Grouped plot", beside = T)
legend("topleft", c("Prof","Assoc","Asst"),
   text.col = c("burlywood","skyblue4","skyblue"))
```

Note that the legend() function was added to the code for Figures 9-1c and 9-1d. This is to add extra text to the graph to explain the meaning of various colors and/or symbols. Depending on context, the legend can be essential or unnecessary, and sometimes even counterproductive. The legend can become clutter, so it is important to determine if it is needed. If it is, your next decision is where to place it for best effect. It is usually best to put the legend in a part of the graph that is relatively far away from important figures. Note that in Figure 9-1c and 9-1d, the legend is in the upper-left corner. This is done by using the "topleft" argument. The names in the legend correspond to the values of rank, and the color vector (col =) is exactly the same as the color vector in the barplot() command.

Spine Plot

We can improve the stacked bar plot that was a little difficult to read in Figure 9-1c by using a variation known as the *spine plot* (also called a *spinogram* or *proportional stacked bar graph*). The idea is that each of the six rectangles will be proportional in area to the number of professors in that combination, as they were in the stacked bar plot. However, in the bar plot both bars were the same width, and therefore the height was the sole indicator of the count within a particular sex/rank combination. This resulted in the height of some portions of bars being so small that they were difficult to compare to others. The spine plot takes a different approach. Both bars will be the same height, but they will be different widths. A scale located on the right side covers the interval from 0 to 1, making it easy to estimate the proportion of a rank within a given bar.

Compare the spine plot in Figure 9-2 to the stacked bar plot in Figure 9-1c. Which is more comprehensible?

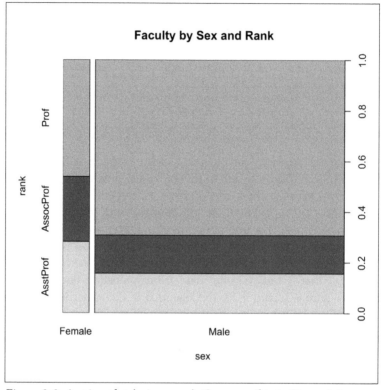

Figure 9-2. A spine plot (spinogram). Compare this to Figure 9-1c. Which of the two is easier to comprehend?

Here is the code that produces Figure 9-2:

```
# script for Figure 9-2
rank3 = table(sex, rank)
rank3
        rank
sex       AsstProf AssocProf Prof
  Female        11        10   18
  Male          56        54  248

spineplot(rank3, col = c("skyblue","skyblue4","burlywood"),
  main = "Faculty by Sex and Rank")
```

Bar Spacing and Orientation

The spacing and orientation of the bars in a chart are important to communicating the message. Consider the problem of comparing the salaries of the six combinations of sex and rank. The following script shows several ways to present the average salaries for each of the combinations:

```
# Script for Fig. 9-3
library(car)  # Fig. 9-3
attach(Salaries)
par(mfrow = c(2, 2))
grp.sal = aggregate(
  salary ~ sex * rank, FUN = mean) # mean of each group

# labels reused several times, can type vector name in commands
rankname = c(" Asst", " ", "  Assoc", " ", " Prof", "")
sexcol = c("blue", "maroon")
sexlab = c("Female", "Male")

# Fig. 9-3a
barplot(grp.sal$salary, ylab = "average salary",
  names.arg = rankname, col = sexcol,
  main = "Faculty Salaries",
  sub = "a. Default spacing between bars")
legend("topleft", sexlab, text.col = sexcol,
  text.font = 2, title = "Sex",
  title.col = "black", cex = 0.8)

# Fig. 9-3b
barplot(grp.sal$salary, ylab = "average salary",
  names.arg = rankname,  col = sexcol,
  main = "Faculty Salaries", space = 1.5,
  sub = "b. Wide space between, space = 1.5")
legend("topleft", sexlab, text.col = sexcol, text.font = 2,
  bty = "n")

# Fig. 9-3c
barplot(grp.sal$salary, ylab = "average salary",
  names.arg = rankname, col = sexcol,
  main = "Faculty Salaries", space = c(1, 0, 1, 0, 1, 0),
  sub = "c. Same rank together, space = c(1,0,1,0,1,0)")
legend("topleft", sexlab, text.col = sexcol,
  text.font = 2, bty = "n")

# Fig. 9-3d
barplot(grp.sal$salary, ylab = "average salary", col = sexcol,
  main = "Faculty Salaries", space = c(1, 0, 1, 0, 1, 0),
  horiz = T, sub = "d. Horizontal version of c. horiz=T",
  names.arg = rankname,
```

```
    cex.names = 0.8, las = 1)
legend("bottomright", sexlab, text.col = sexcol,
    text.font = 2, bty = "n")

detach(Salaries)
```

First, we get a vector of mean salaries, grp.mean, for each combination by using the aggregate() function. The expression salary ~ sex * rank indicates that some operation will be performed on salary in each of the six combinations of sex and rank. FUN = mean shows that the operation will be finding the mean. We will make several bar plots, showing different spacings between the bars and a change of vertical bars to horizontal ones. Such changes can make a difference in how we perceive the plots.

The next step is to define some character vectors, rankname, sexcol, and sexlab. This is not necessary, but it's a definite convenience: rather than typing out the character strings in each of the following calls of the barplot() function, you can substitute the relatively short vector names.

Figure 9-3 shows that there are four bar plots produced.

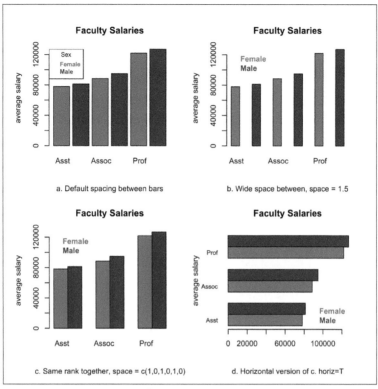

Figure 9-3. Four variants of the same graph, juxtaposing rank and sex.

Each plot command is followed by a legend() command, putting a legend on the previously produced bar plot. You could type all of the lines separately in the console; however, it is usually more convenient to put a group of commands for which you want to see the results on one screen, or one page, into a script. This way, if you make a mistake, you can simply correct the one error and run the entire batch of commands again without retyping all of it.

The four bar plots are quite similar, in terms of the groups examined, the colors, the labels, and the legends. The most important difference is the spacing between the bars, and in the last plot the orientation is different, too. In the first plot, Figure 9-3a, the space argument does not appear, so the default value is used to make the graph. In Figure 9-3b, the bars are widely separated because we used space = 1.5; that is, the spaces between bars are 1.5 times the width of the bars. In the last two bar plots, the male and female bars for each rank are adjacent, whereas the ranks are separated. This is accomplished by using the argument space = c(1, 0, 1, 0, 1, 0), which instructs R that there should be a space of size 1 before the first bar, size 0 before the second, and so on.

The legend() command for the first plot produces a very traditional legend with a title and a box around it. In this case, neither of those elements is really necessary, so the other plots leave out the title argument and add bty = "n", which deletes the box.

Compare the four bar plots in Figure 9-3. Notice that the legend in Figure 9-3a makes the graph look a little cluttered. The other graphs draw attention directly to the bars. If you examine the first two plots carefully, you will eventually notice that females have a lower average salary than males in every rank, but, especially in Figure 9-3b, this is obscured a bit by the wide separation of the bars. Conversely, in the last two graphs, the difference is obvious immediately! This demonstrates that just as you should carefully choose words to make your meaning clear, so too should you choose graphic devices to make your point as clear as possible.

Exercise 9-1

There is a little quirk in the legend in Figure 9-3d. The legend was fine for the first three graphs, but when the graph was made horizontal, the order in the legend should have been changed. Why? Try to fix it.

Exercise 9-2

This one is challenging, but will help you to see how much R you can do on your own. With the Salaries dataset used in this chapter, try to reproduce the graph in Figure 9-4, this time by using the pyramid() function in the epiDisplay package. Is this a bar plot or a histogram?

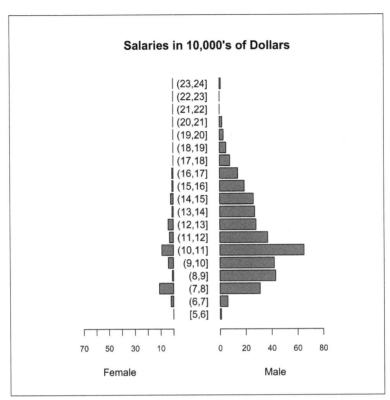

Figure 9-4. Salaries by sex.

Pie Charts

Ordinary Pie Chart

The *pie chart* is one of the most familiar types of graph. It would be difficult to imagine that you have not seen hundreds of them. One place where they seem to be taken for granted is in the realm of investment portfolios. Investment advisors recommend that their clients allocate their holdings to certain categories of investment, in specified amounts. Such recommendations are usually presented in the form of pie charts. Fund managers also report their holdings (at a point in time) in a similar way. Consider the following portfolio, allocated to "sectors" (this is not a recommendation, by the way):

- Domestic stocks—30 percent
- Foreign stocks—25 percent
- Bonds—28 percent
- Gold/precious metals—10 percent
- Cash equivalents—7 percent

We can make a vector out of the percentages and use the pie() function to produce the desired chart, as shown in the following script:

```
# Script for Figure 10-1
par(mfrow = c(2,2))

allocation = c(30,25,28,10,7)  # investment allocations

# sector & sectcol will be reused; we won't have to retype them
sector = c("Stock","For'n'","Bonds",
           "Gold","Cash") # names fit page
sectcol = c("burlywood","turquoise","firebrick",
            "gold3","green4")

# Figure 10-1 top left
pie(allocation, labels = sector, main = "pie, default colors")

# Figure 10-1  top right
pie(allocation, labels = sector, col = sectcol,
  main = "pie, choose colors")

# Figure 10-1 bottom left
install.packages("plotrix", dependencies = TRUE)
library(plotrix) # must have first installed plotrix
pie3D(allocation, labels = sector, col = sectcol, explode = .1,
  labelcex = .95, labelrad = 1.3, main = "pie3D")
# explode separates pieces/labelrad pushes labels away from edge

# Figure 10-1 bottom right
barplot(allocation, names.arg = sector, col = sectcol,
  main = "barplot")
```

Figure 10-1 shows the results of this script.

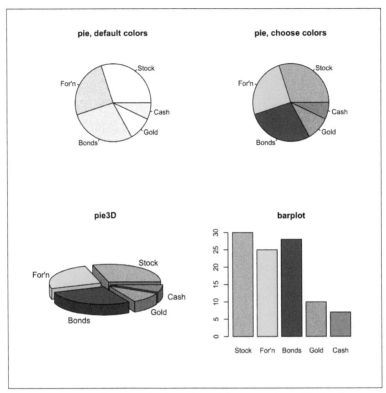

Figure 10-1. Pie charts and a bar plot of the same data. Notice how much easier it is to compare group sizes with the bar plot.

Figure 10-1 displays three pie charts: one with default colors, created by using the pie() function; one with the colors in the sectcol vector, also created by using the pie() function; and one sporting a three-dimensional view (which looks great!), created by using the pie3D() function. There is also a bar plot for comparison. Notice that in the pie charts, the largest three categories appear to be pretty much the same size. Likewise, the smaller categories, "Gold" and "Cash," seem to be equal. However, the bar plot, which was produced with exactly the same numbers, clearly shows there are differences. Thus, you may not be surprised to learn that pie charts get a lot of bad press from statisticians, and for good reason!

Despite the shortcomings of pie charts, there are times when they might be useful. When there are few categories, and the differences are pretty obvious, you might prefer to use this type of graph. Further, when you want to emphasize what part of the whole is represented by a single slice, the pie chart does this well. There are various ways in which you could organize data to make a pie chart. Working on the exercises for this chapter will help you to get a better understanding of this problem.

Fan Plot

An alternative to the pie chart is the *fan plot*, which you can see in Figure 10-2.

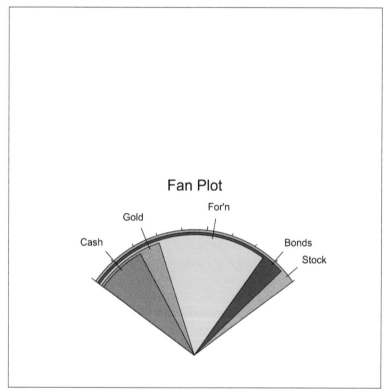

Figure 10-2. A fan plot.

This type of graph looks a little like a pie chart but fixes the most serious problem of that kind of graph. Here is the code to create Figure 10-2:

```
# Figure 10-2
library(plotrix)
allocation = c(30,25,28,10,7)  # investment allocations
# sector & sectcol will be reused; we won't have to retype them
```

```
sector = c("Stock","For'n","Bonds","Gold","Cash")
sectcol = c("burlywood","turquoise","firebrick","gold3",
  "green4")

fan.plot(allocation, labels = sector, col = sectcol,
  ticks = 30, main = "Fan Plot")
```

The fan plot in Figure 10-2 uses similar labels and the same colors as the pie charts in Figure 10-1. It is a little confusing, though, in that the sizes of the visible wedges do not represent the proportions of the portfolio given to the sectors named by the wedges. Rather, the allocations are represented by the arc in the color of each named wedge. So, you can see that the "Stock" portion is largest, "Bonds" is second largest, and so on. Another way to think about this graph is to imagine that the slices from the pie chart were laid down with the biggest on the bottom, the second largest on top of that, and so forth. Then, the visible part of the largest slice shows how much larger that slice is than the second largest. Likewise, we can easily see how much larger the second largest slice is than the next largest. If you understand how this plot works, it can be useful to you, but if you use it for presentation of your data, you will need to explain it carefully. Even so, there is a good chance that some people will not understand it, and will conclude, for instance, that the "foreign" sector is the largest in Figure 10-2. The fan plot is a very clever design, but long experience with the pie chart may be an impediment to its adoption. Be careful with this one.

Exercise 10-1

Make a pie chart of the causes of death of British soldiers during the Crimean War. You can find the data in the Nightingale dataset in the HistData package. You will need to install and load the package first. Notice how the dataset is structured; the three causes of death are three separate variables. You will need to create a new vector with three numbers: the sums of each of the variables. You can do it this way:

```
install.packages("HistData")
library(HistData)
attach(Nightingale)
deaths = c(sum(Disease), sum(Wounds), sum(Other))
```

Explain how this works. Is this a better use of the pie chart than the portfolio example? Why or why not?

Exercise 10-2

Make a pie chart of medium in the Nimrod dataset. You will need to create a vector containing the frequencies of each medium. The table() command will work for this. Make this chart a work of art!

# CHAPTER 11

Rug Plots

The Rug Plot

The *rug* is not really a separate plot. It is a one-dimensional display that you can add to existing plots to illuminate information that is sometimes lost in other types of graphs. Like a strip plot, it represents values of a variable by putting a symbol at various points along an axis. However, it uses short lines to represent points. You can place it at the bottom (the default) or top of a graph (side = 3). If appropriate—for example, if a box plot is vertical—the rug can be put on the left (side = 2) or right (side = 4) axis. When two observations have the same value, they are overprinted, so that the line is darker. Here are some examples:

```
# Script for Figure 11-1
library(multcomp)
par(mfrow = c(2,2))
stripchart(mtcars$drat,
  main="a. side = 3", method = "jitter",
  pch = 20, col = "sienna4")
rug(mtcars$drat, side = 3)

boxplot(mtcars$drat, main = "b. side = 2",
  col = "firebrick")
rug(mtcars$drat, col = "darkmagenta", side = 2)

hist(airquality$Ozone, main = "c. side = 1", col = "cyan4")
rug(airquality$Ozone, col = "cyan4")
```

```
boxplot(sbp$sbp,
  main = "d. side = 4", col = "darkorange3")
rug(sbp$sbp, side = 4, col = "cornsilk4")
```

The preceding script produces the plots in Figure 11-1.

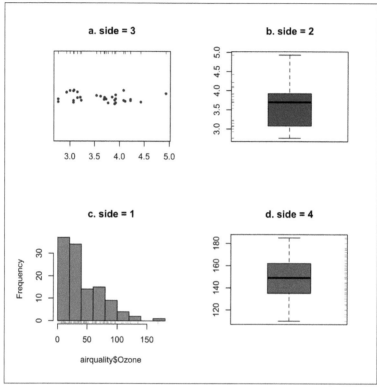

Figure 11-1. Uses of the rug plot.

Figure 11-1a shows that adding a rug is essentially like putting a strip chart at the bottom or top of another graph. This is not very useful on strip charts, because the rug is simply redundant. However, the rug can be helpful on other types of graphs to reveal information that might be lost in those displays. For example, in Figure 11-1b, the box plot shows a skewed distribution, but we could not possibly know from the box plot alone that the data is in several clumps, which is clearly shown in the rug. The long upper whisker, for example, might be the result of several dispersed points or simply one extreme value. The rug shows all the points and their placement, with one extreme value and a few points clumped just above the third quartile. Compare that to Figure 11-1d, in which the rug is nearly equally spaced throughout its range. The rug in Figure 11-1c again shows the data to be in clumps. This suggests that changing the bin size can change the shape of the histogram. By default, the rug is placed at the bottom of the graph, but you can place it at the top with the argument side = 3. For more information on the arguments that you can use, type **?rug**. The rug can sometimes be very helpful, but at other times it offers no real advantage.

Exercise 11-1

Add a rug plot to a density plot of time from the Nimrod dataset. Add a rug to a box plot of MathAchieve$SES (refer to Figure 5-2). Which of these is more helpful?

PART III

Two-Variable Graphs

It is natural to study the relationship between two variables. If we examine two quantitative variables, we might wonder if they are *associated* or *correlated*; that is, do they vary together? Or, put another way, does one become larger as the other grows in size? Or perhaps just the opposite: does one grow larger as the other becomes smaller? Is there some other kind of relationship? Or perhaps no relationship at all? Two-variable graphs enable us to address such questions as these.

# CHAPTER 12

Scatter Plots and Line Charts

Basic Scatter Plots

The *scatter plot* may be one of the most useful graphic tools that we have. We can easily study the associations between two variables—or lack thereof—on this familiar type of graph. Further, many other graph types are simply variants of the basic scatter plot.

Again, let's examine the `trees` dataset. Remember, the `head()` function prints out the first six rows. You can see the entire dataset by typing **trees**:

```
> head(trees)
  Girth Height Volume
1   8.3     70   10.3
2   8.6     65   10.3
3   8.8     63   10.2
4  10.5     72   16.4
5  10.7     81   18.8
6  10.8     83   19.7
```

There are probably strong relationships among the three variables, which we should be able to see on a scatter plot. We will use the `plot()` function to produce scatter plots. Its basic form is as follows:

plot(*x-variable, y-variable, arguments...*)

The following scripts produce several scatter plots of the **trees** data:

```
# 4 short scripts to produce the 4 graphs in Fig. 12-1
attach(trees)
par(mfrow = c(2,2), cex = .7)

# Fig. 12-1a: show just 2 points on the graph
trees2 = trees[1:2,] # trees2 a subset, only 1st 2 trees
                     # see sidebar
plot(trees2$Height, trees2$Girth,
  xlim = c(63,80),
  ylim = c(7.8,10),
  xlab = "Height",
  ylab = "Girth",
  main = "a. First two trees")

# text() allows annotation on the graph
text(72,8.1,labels = "(Height = 70, Girth = 8.3)",
  xlim = c(61,80),
  ylim = c(8,22))
text(65,8.8, labels = "(65, 8.6)",
  xlim = c(62,89),
  ylim = c(8,22))

# Fig. 12-1b: note that a basic plot requires very little
  coding!
plot(Height, Girth, main = "b. All trees")

# Fig. 12-1c /  see Table 3-1 for plot characters
plot(Height, Girth,
  main = "c. Change plot character, add grid",
  pch = 20,
  col = "deepskyblue")
grid(col = "gray70")

# Fig. 12-1d # abline puts linear regression line on plot
plot(Height, Girth,
  main = "d. Add regression line", pch = 20,
  col = "deepskyblue")
abline(lm(Girth ~ Height),
  col = "dodgerblue4",
  lty = 1,
  lwd = 2) # writes over last plot
grid(col = "gray70")
detach(trees)
```

Figure 12-1 displays the results.

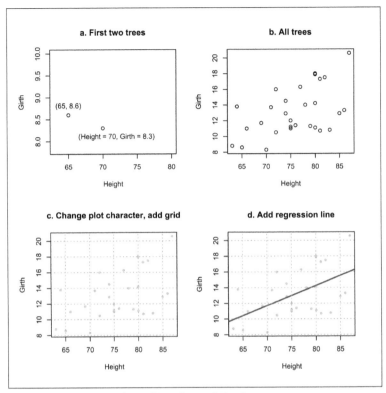

Figure 12-1. Scatter plots of Height and Girth.

Figure 12-1 shows several things about using scatter plots. Figure 12-1a shows how to interpret the points (little circles here), just in case it has been a long time since you did high school math. The very first tree in the dataset had a Height of 70 and Girth of 8.3. You can see how it is placed on the graph to correspond to those measurements.

Figure 12-1b takes the next step of plotting all the points (i.e., trees) on the graph. Note that there does seem to be a relationship between Height and Girth. As Height becomes bigger, so does Girth. It is not a perfect relationship, but it is not a random scatter, either.

Figure 12-1c takes the simple step of changing the plot characters. Not only does this look better, but it is a little easier to read, too. It also introduces a grid. The grid() function will add reference lines to the *active plot*, which is the last plot created if you have not issued a further command after you created the plot. By default, it draws the grid lines at the tick marks on the axis, but you can change this if desired. Type **?grid** to see how.

What Happened to All the Graphs I Made?

You might want to compare a number of graphs made during a single R session. If you simply type a command to make a graph, the previous one is normally wiped out—gone forever. It is possible, however, to keep the previous graphic window(s) open. In fact, you can have as many as 63 graphic windows open at one time. As with most tasks in R, there are several ways to do this. By the way, it might be useful to have a few windows open at the same time, but 63 is not recommended!

A method that works on all platforms is to type **dev.new()** before issuing the command to make the next graph. This creates a blank graphic window in which to display the next graph. All previously created graphic windows remain undisturbed. You can then reexamine any of the graphs you have made. You can click any window of interest to bring it to the foreground, but if there are several, finding the one you want can be quite tedious.

If you're using a Mac, a more convenient method is to open the Window menu and click New Quartz Device Window before issuing the command to make a new graph. As before, previous graphs are undisturbed. It is easy to move from one graph to another by opening the Window menu and then selecting Quartz2, Quartz5, and so on.

For Windows-based computers, after creating a new graphics window by using **dev.new()**, you can move from one graph to another by opening the Window menu and then choosing "R Graphics Device *n*."

Another approach is to create a graph and click its window. If you want to save it, open the File menu and then click Save As. In OS X, you can save the graph as a PDF file. In Windows, you will be given the choice of saving as any one of several different file types. (There is also another way to save in various formats, on either platform. For more information on how to do that, see the section "Exporting a Graph" on page 31.)

A more convenient method still, if your word processor (or presentation) program allows it, is to click the graph that you want, open the Edit menu, and then choose Copy. Then, click Paste to place it

---

into your word processor. Unfortunately, not all word-processor programs accommodate this. After you have examined all the graphs, just delete the ones that you do not want; the remaining ones are already in a document to which you can add text.

Figure 12-1d adds a regression line on top of the points. This was done by using the abline() function, which writes over the active plot. Linear regression is a method of finding the "best-fitting" straight line to the observed data. If you found the vertical distance from each point to the place on the line having the same x value, that distance is an "error"; in other words, it shows how far off the line was in predicting the value of that point. As a measure of how well any particular line fits, square all the errors and add them up. The "best fitting" of the infinite number of lines one could put on the graph is the one with the smallest sum of squared errors: the "least squares" line. R finds that line with the lm() function that you can see in the abline() command in the script of the trees data from earlier. If the points had fit even closer to the line, we would have concluded that the relationship between Height and Girth was even stronger than what we see in Figure 12-1d.

Recall the formula for a straight line, where Y is a point on the line:

```
Y = a + (b * X)
```

In the formula, a = the intercept (the point on the y-axis where the line crosses it), and b = the slope (the "rise over the run"; that is, the amount Y changes for every unit change of X).

Here's how you can get the values for intercept and slope:

```
lm(Girth ~ Height)

Call:
lm(formula = Girth ~ Height)

Coefficients:
(Intercept)      Height
    -6.1884      0.2557
```

So, the formula tells us that the line is determined by the equation:

```
Girth = -6.1884 + (0.2557 * Height)
```

Further, we could get relevant statistics for this model by using the following command:

```
summary(lm(Girth ~ Height))
```

Interpretation of that information, however, is beyond the scope of this book. In other situations, we might have seen a pattern in the data that was not close to a straight line, and might have attempted to fit a curve or have concluded that there was no association between the two variables. Although it is great to have the capability of adding regression lines to your plot, if you do not really understand what you are doing, you will be a bit like a child playing with matches, so be cautious!

Subsets

In Figure 12-1a, trees2 is a *subset*—a smaller dataset, extracted from trees. Subsets are useful for comparing a part to the whole, or two component parts to each other. Even though R offers several ways to make subsets, the method used in the script is elegant and economical, requiring little typing. The data frame/vector name is followed by two items in square brackets: an expression about rows, and an expression about columns.

The simplest use is finding a single element. For example, to find the element in the 3rd row and 2nd column:

```
> trees[3,2]
  [1] 63
```

Alternatively, you might want to create a new vector with that number in it:

```
> newrow = trees[3,2]
> newrow
  [1] 63
```

If the row expression or the column expression is left empty, the subset includes that entire row or column. If you wanted the entire 3rd row, you could use this:

```
> trees[3,]   # trees[-3,] for everything *but* the 3rd row

  Girth Height Volume
3   8.8     63   10.2
```

You can use a:b notation to get the elements beginning with a and ending with b. So, if you wanted all the rows from the 4th to the 6th, but only columns 2 and 3, you could do this:

```
> trees[4:6, 2:3]
```

```
     Height Volume
4       72   16.4
5       81   18.8
6       83   19.7
```

You can use vector notation to select noncontiguous rows or columns by number and/or by variable name:

```
> trees[,c("Girth","Volume")] #trees[,c(1,3)] does same thing

    Girth Volume
1    8.3   10.3
2    8.6   10.3
3    8.8   10.2
4   10.5   16.4
5   10.7   18.8
...
```

Here's how you can delete any rows with missing values:

```
> mysubset = na.omit(airquality)
```

To select only those observations with certain characteristics, the subset() function will probably be the best choice. For example:

```
> subset(trees, Height > 70) # only trees with Height > 70

    Girth Height Volume
4    10.5     72   16.4
5    10.7     81   18.8
6    10.8     83   19.7
8    11.0     75   18.2
...
```

Line Charts

A special case of the scatter plot that is very common and very useful is the *line chart* (also called "line graph" or "line plot"). In this type of graph, no two points have the same *x* value. Further, the points are connected by a line from the point with the lowest x value to the point with the next lowest *x*, and so on. It is also possible to display two or more line charts on the same set of axes. The plot() function, used for scatter plots, also produces line charts. Some examples of line charts are presented in Figure 12-2.

To create our charts, let's use the Nightingale dataset from the Hist Data package, which you first saw in "Exercise 10-1" on page 121. Load this package and take a look at the data:

```
# if not already done, must install HistData or the
# following won't work
# install.packages("HistData", dep = T)
library(HistData)
attach(Nightingale)
head(Nightingale)       # head() prints out the 1st 6 rows

        Date  Month Year  Army Disease Wounds Other
1 1854-04-01   Apr 1854  8571       1      0     5
2 1854-05-01   May 1854 23333      12      0     9
3 1854-06-01   Jun 1854 28333      11      0     6
4 1854-07-01   Jul 1854 28722     359      0    23
5 1854-08-01   Aug 1854 30246     828      1    30
6 1854-09-01   Sep 1854 30290     788     81    70
  Disease.rate Wounds.rate Other.rate
1          1.4         0.0        7.0
2          6.2         0.0        4.6
3          4.7         0.0        2.5
4        150.0         0.0        9.6
5        328.5         0.4       11.9
6        312.2        32.1       27.7
```

The data records the monthly deaths of British soldiers in the Crimean War. Each line of the data represents one month, with a number of variables such as the month and year, army size, and number of deaths from each of three causes. It is easy enough to plot the number of deaths from Disease for each Date, which would give an ordinary scatter plot. You might want to try it. The graph will give a much greater sense of order, however, if the dots are connected, from the first month to the second month, the second to the third, and so on. This is a basic line chart. You can create such a graph by adding the argument type = "b" to plot(). It is also necessary to add the argument lty = "solid" to specify the type of line. (The line could also be "dotted", "dashed", or other types; type ?par for more information.) The following script produces the line charts in Figure 12-2:

```
# Figure 12-2 - 4 graphs
par(mfrow = c(2,2)) # put 4 graphs on one page
library(HistData)
attach(Nightingale)

# Figure 12-2a
plot(Date, Disease,
  type = "b",
  pch = 20,
  lty = "solid",
  main = "a. Line chart of Disease")
```

```
# Figure 12-2b
plot(Date,Disease,
  type = "l",
  lty = "solid",
  main = "b. Line chart, Disease, Wounds, Other")
lines(Date,Wounds,
  lty = "dashed",
  col = "red",
  lwd = 2)
lines(Date, Other,
  lty = "dotted",
  col = "navyblue",
  lwd = 2)

# Figure 12-2c
plot(Date, Disease,
  type = "h",
  lty = "solid",
  lwd = 20,
  main = "c. Change Disease to histogram",col="gray67",
    lend="butt")
lines(Date,Wounds,
  lty = "solid",
  col = "red",
  lwd = 2)
lines(Date, Other,
  lty = "dotted",
  col = "navyblue",
  lwd = 2)

# Figure 12-2d
plot(Date, Disease,
  type = "h",
  lty = "solid",
  lwd = 20,
  main = "d. Add legend, remove box",col="gray67",
  lend ="butt",bty="l")
lines(Date, Wounds,
  lty = "solid",
  col = "red",
  lwd = 2)
lines(Date, Other,
  lty = "dotted",
  col = "navyblue",
  lwd = 2)
legend("topleft",
  c("Death from Disease","Death from Wounds","Other Deaths"),
  text.col = c("gray40", "red", "navyblue"),
  bty = "n",
```

```
     cex = .5)
     detach(Nightingale)
```

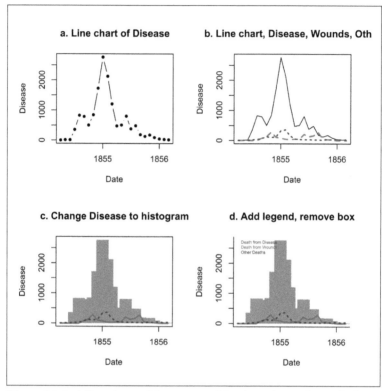

Figure 12-2. A line chart of the causes of death in the Nightingale dataset, in several transformations.

For the moment, take a look at Figure 12-2a. Another way to present this plot is to leave out the dots and have a completely connected line, which we can do by changing type = "b" to type = "l", as in Figure 12-2b. The lines() function has also been applied to Figure 12-2b to place two additional lines on the chart, the deaths due to Wounds and Other.

The differences in cause of death over the course of the war are stunning. Deaths from disease far outnumber deaths from wounds and other causes for much of the war. Although the effect is notable in Figure 12-2b, we can highlight it by a simple change in the graph . See Table 12-1 for type argument options. One of them is type = "h" for histogram, which is what we see in the plot in Figure

12-2c. It was also necessary to add lend = "butt" to make the histogram bars (line end or "lend") have square corners instead of rounded ones.

Figure 12-2c tells the story more dramatically, showing the gray bars of disease in the histogram, looming over the entire war. As if war were not tragic enough, disease, for which the British were not prepared, multiplied the catastrophe. The next step is to add a legend in which the colors of the various causes of death are identified, as is done in Figure 12-2d. (If you need to review the legend() function, refer to the section "Data Can Be Beautiful" on page 52.) Furthermore, Figure 12-2d removes the box around the plot by using the bty = "l" argument.

Table 12-1. Options for lines made with plot() or lines()

Argument	Line type
type = "p"	Points
type = "l"	Lines
type = "b"	Both lines and open points
type = "c"	Lines with spaces at the places points would be
type = "o"	Overplotted (i.e., lines with filled-in points)
type = "h"	Histogram-like vertical lines
type = "s"	Stair steps
type = "S"	Different stair steps
type = "n"	No plotting
lty = "blank"	
lty = "dotted"	
lty = "dashed"	
lty = "dotdash"	
lty = "longdash"	
lty = "solid"	
lty = "twodash"	
lwd = 1	Line width. The default is 1. Specify a greater number for a thicker line or a smaller number for a thinner line.

Finally, the next graph (see Figure 12-3) might seem a little "over the top" in terms of the amount of extra work it takes, but it is included here to make a point. We'll go over how to create it, but if you want, you can just skip to the last paragraph of this section.

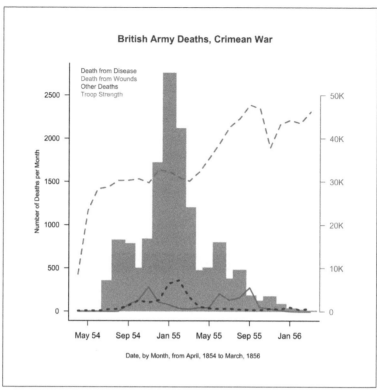

Figure 12-3. A completed line chart of the Nightingale dataset.

Here are several improvements that make the graph in Figure 12-3 more attractive and more complete:

Add a title by using the main argument in plot() as well as labels for the axes

I have chosen to make the already long plot command shorter by defining a vector, t, separately and then using main = t in plot(). Similarly, the vectors x and y have been created for labels.

Add another line to show the size of the army during each month

This is a little tricky because the size of the army is much larger than the number of deaths. Using the same scale would either send the Army data off the graph or make Wounds and Other so small and close to the horizontal axis that they would be barely noticeable. I decided to divide Army by 20 and plot the resulting new variable with a second vertical axis, on the right side, to show the scale for troop strength. Plotting a variable that is measured on a different scale can be confusing or misleading, so you need to take great care when doing it. In this case, I deliberately made the right axis quite different from the left axis, in terms of color, size of numbers, and line type so that it would be as clear as possible that two different scales are being presented.

Improve the presentation of the horizontal axis

Figure 12-4 shows only two points on the x-axis for the Date variable. I created a new variable, mon, with values from 1 to 24 for the 24 months during which the war took place. This variable will be on the x-axis. This works only because the dataset is sorted by month. In plot(), the argument xaxt = "n" suppresses the printing of x-axis labels so that a new axis can be created with the labels that will be specified for three months of each year, enough to give sufficient detail, but not so many that they run together and become unreadable. The at argument gives the values of months and the labels argument gives the names of the months.

The following is the script to create the enhanced Figure 12-3:

```
# Script for Figure 12-3
# if not already done, must:
# install.packages("HistData", dep = T)
library(HistData)
attach(Nightingale)
par(mar = c(6,6,5,5), cex = .8) # control size of plot window

Army2 = (Army)/20    # reduce size of Army so it fits on plot
t = "British Army Deaths, Crimean War" # make plot stmt shorter
x = "Date, by Month, from April, 1854 to March, 1856"
y = "Number of Deaths per Month"
mon = 1:24    # create new var, easier to work with than Date

plot(mon, Disease,
  type = "h",
  lwd = 22,
  col = "gray67",
  lend = "butt",
  main = t,
  col.main = "maroon",
  ylab = y,
  xlab = x,
  cex.lab = .8,
  las = 1,
  cex.axis = .9,
  bty = "l",
  xaxt = "n")
#xaxt = "n" suppresses x-axis labels; use axis() for custom axis
```

```
lines(mon,Wounds,
   pch = 18,
   col = "red",
   lty = "solid",
   lwd = 2)
lines(mon, Other,
   lty = "dotted",
   col = "navyblue",
   lwd = 3)
lines(mon, Army2,
   lty = "dashed",
   col = "seagreen4",
   lwd = 2)

# horizontal axis
axis(1, at = c(2,6,10,14,18,22),
   labels = c("May 54","Sep 54","Jan 55","May 55","Sep 55",
      "Jan 56"))
# right axis
axis(4, at = c(0,500,1000,1500,2000,2500),
   labels = c("0", "10K","20K","30K","40K","50K"),
   las = 1,
   tick = T,
   cex.lab = .6,
   col = "seagreen4",
   col.axis = "seagreen4",
   ylab = "Troop Strength")

legend("topleft", c("Death from Disease","Death from Wounds",
   "Other Deaths","Troop Strength"),
   text.col = c("gray40","red","navyblue","seagreen4"),
   bty = "n",
   cex = .8)

detach(Nightingale)
```

This section demonstrated the construction of a complex line chart.
As with some previous examples, constructing this graph involved
creating several layers, applied one-by-one to make a complex display that afforded us a great deal of control over the final product.
Maybe Figure 12-2b would have met your needs and you would not
have needed to go to all the trouble of producing a graph like that in
Figure 12-3. On the other hand, you might want a really eye-
catching display. Sometimes, you might need to do all the ugly work
to get one, but you can make really beautiful graphs. Other times,
you can take advantage of the work that the maker of a package has
already done, as we will see in the next section.

Templates

R produces fine basic scatter plots with little trouble. You can also customize your plots by taking advantage of the many arguments available with the plot() function. You can alter the axes; add titles; change the plot characters; change the colors of the background, titles, and points; and so on. This customization can sometimes be a lot of work, as it was in the preceding section. However, some package designers have included templates, or style types, in their packages to make a variety of styles easy to implement. One that I like is from the latticeExtra package, which imitates the style used for graphs in the *Economist* magazine. Figure 12-4 presents the plot from Figure 12-1b, redone with this style.

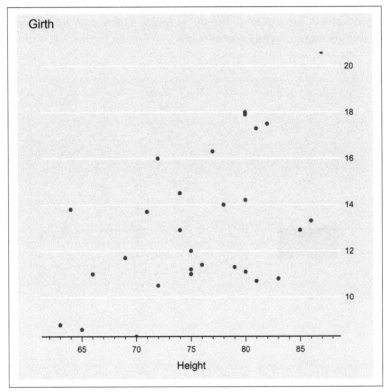

Figure 12-4. Plot of trees data as a lattice graph with asTheEconomist() function.

You get a very pretty graph with very little code:

```
# use a template to produce Fig. 12-4
# if not already done, must:
# install.packages("latticeExtra", dependencies = T)
library(latticeExtra)
attach(trees)
asTheEconomist(xyplot(Girth ~ Height), xlab = "Height",
  type = "p", with.bg = T)
detach(trees)
```

Another set of templates is provided in the epade package. The scat
ter.ade() function produces scatter plots. Using its wall argument,
you can choose from several output styles. The argument wall = 0
produces a graph similar to the plot() function, but arguments
from 1 to 6 create interesting alternatives. Each of the six fancy
graphs in Figure 12-5 required just one line of code. There are also
arguments for colors of points, text, background, and lines, as well
as arguments for legends, line types, point types, and so on. For
more information, type **?scatter.ade**.

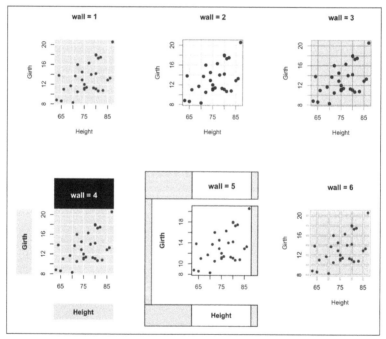

*Figure 12-5. Scatter plot styles produced by scatter.ade() function in
the epade package*

The script that follows shows how easy it was to produce the six graphs in Figure 12-5. You may or may not like the styles, but they will look quite different in color, as you will see later, in Figure 12-7:

```
# Figure 12-5
install.packages("epade") # if not already installed
library(epade)
attach(trees)
par(mfrow = c(2,3))
scatter.ade(Height, Girth, wall = 1, main = "wall = 1")
scatter.ade(Height, Girth, wall = 2, main = "wall = 2")
scatter.ade(Height, Girth, wall = 3, main = "wall = 3")
scatter.ade(Height, Girth, wall = 4, main = "wall = 4")
scatter.ade(Height, Girth, wall = 5, main = "wall = 5")
scatter.ade(Height, Girth, wall = 6, main = "wall = 6")
detach(trees)
```

Any of the styles in Figure 12-4 and Figure 12-5 would have taken quite a bit of effort to produce from scratch, and a lot of code. However, the package developers shared their efforts with us, and it was pretty easy to make graphs using the templates they provided. The epade package also provides similar templates for certain other functions. Although it can take a lot of time to search through the thousands of R packages, it is frequently time well spent.

Enhanced Scatter Plots

In addition to plot(), there are many other R functions for scatter plots. Some of them offer substantial enhancements. A good example is scatterplot() from the car package. Figure 12-6 shows a plot produced by this function including several extras:

- Box plots in the margins to show the distribution of each variable
- A regression line, in green
- A grid
- A smoother, in red, with a measure of spread, in dotted red

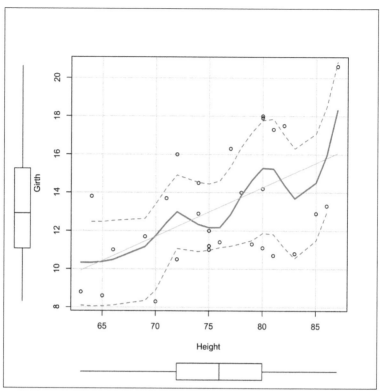

Figure 12-6. Scatter plot of Girth and Height produced by the scatter-plot() function in the car package.

A *smoother* is a tool for making patterns in scatter plot data a little easier to see. There are several types of smoothers, but they all show the center of the *y*'s at a given value of *x* (or several close *x*'s) and do it in such a way that the (usually curved) line formed by connecting all such points is relatively smooth. Figure 12-6 shows a scatter plot with a smoother, represented as a red line. You can use the smoother argument to select a smoothing method, but Figure 12-6 uses the default method, "loess," or locally weighted regression.

scatterplot() can also easily handle regression lines by groups, outlier identification, and other things that are beyond the scope of this book. For more information, type **?sp**. Here is the code to produce Figure 12-6:

```
# Figure 12-6
library(car)
attach(trees)
```

```
sp(Height, Girth)  # note the abbreviation "sp"
detach(trees)
```

Aside from the templates that we saw in the last section, the `scat
ter.ade()` function in the `epade` package has a few other notable
features. It can plot data by groups; it can plot points with size representing magnitude; or it can place linear regression, loess, or polynomial lines on a plot, and handle legends quite easily. Figure 12-7
shows an example of `scatter.ade()` plotting data by the groups
"treated" and "untreated." To get a little information about the
experiment from which the data came, you can type **?Puromycin**.

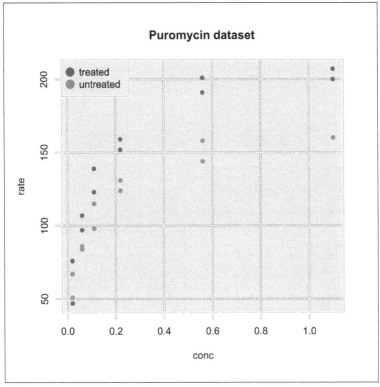

*Figure 12-7. Plot of Puromycin data by scatter.ade() in the epade pack-
age.*

Here is the code to produce Figure 12-7:

```
# Figure 12-7
library(epade)
attach(Puromycin)
scatter.ade(conc, rate, group=state,
  col = c("royalblue3", "sienna1"),
  legendon = "topleft", wall = 6,
  main = "Puromycin dataset")
detach(Puromycin)
```

The lattice package is designed to produce trellis plots, which were first mentioned in the section "lattice" on page 37. This might be a good time to go back and review that section. There is an example of a scatter plot trellis graph in Figure 2-3. Figure 12-8 shows the Puromycin data plotted by using lattice, with the treated and untreated subjects in different windows, or *panels*. Contrast this to Figure 12-7.

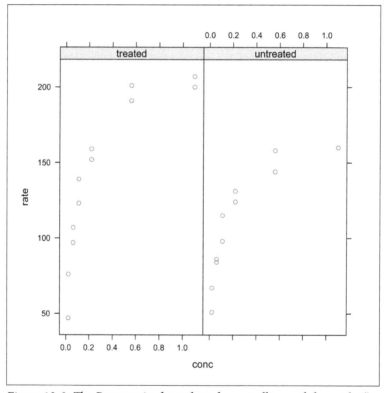

Figure 12-8. The Puromycin data plotted as a trellis graph by xyplot() in the lattice package.

Following is the code to create Figure 12-8:

```
# Figure 12-8
library(lattice)
attach(Puromycin)
xyplot(rate ~ conc | state)
detach(Puromycin)
```

The scatter plot is, perhaps, the most useful and most frequently used type of graph. Many other graphs, including several of the graphs in following chapters of this book, are based on the scatter plot. R provides many implementations of this graphic type, a few of which have been discussed in this chapter. Ponder for a moment that the varied scatter plots in this chapter are all "R." The plot functions in this chapter will probably serve you well, but there are more scatter plot functions to find in R, if you care to search for them.

---

x and y: Why?

Some functions that produce scatter plots, such as plot() and scatter.ade(), expect the variable names for x and y to be in a list, in the form *x, y*. Other functions, notably xyplot(), expect a *formula* of the form *y ~ x* or *y ~ x | z*, where *z* is a conditioning variable. Some functions, such as scatterplot(), accept the variable names in either format. Actually, plot() will also accept either, even though its help file doesn't say that. Many—perhaps most—R functions will accept one or both of these forms, or a close variant.

Exercise 12-1

If you saved the emissions dataset used in "Exercise 1-2" on page 15, you can retrieve it now by using the command:

```
> load("emiss.rda")
```

If you did not save it, enter part of the data now, as three vectors:

```
> Year   =  c(2004:2010)
> Europe = c(7.9, 7.9, 7.9, 7.8, 7.7, 7.1, 7.2)
> Eurasia = c(8.5, 8.5, 8.7, 8.6, 8.9, 8, 8.4)
```

Make a line chart showing emissions in both Europe and Eurasia over the seven-year period. Make the lines different, by color and/or line type. Include a legend. Your graph should look something like Figure 12-9.

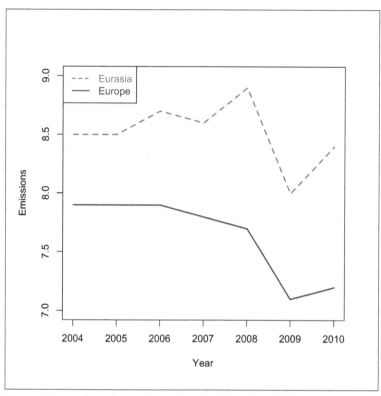

Figure 12-9. A line chart of emissions in Eurasia and Europe.

Exercise 12-2

Make a simple plot of the Velocity (x-axis) and Distance (y-axis) of the nebulae outside the Milky Way, which you can find in the case0701 dataset from the Sleuth2 package. What is the relationship between these two variables? Next, use a template of your own choosing to make a more interesting display of the data.

# CHAPTER 13

High-Density Plots

Working with Large Datasets

Sometimes a large dataset can be a challenge when applying techniques such as scatter plots. Let's consider one such dataset from the car package. Vocab contains more than 21,000 observations containing some basic demographic data and scores on a vocabulary test. Load the package and look at the data (be careful to use the head() command; you do not want to print the entire dataset!):

```
> library(car)
> attach(Vocab)
> head(Vocab)
```

```
            year     sex education vocabulary
20040001 2004 Female         9          3
20040002 2004 Female        14          6
20040003 2004   Male        14          9
20040005 2004 Female        17          8
20040008 2004   Male        14          1
20040010 2004   Male        14          7
```

It might be interesting to examine the relationship between vocabulary and education. Does it seem reasonable to expect that those with low education will have low vocabulary scores and that the scores will increase as amount of education increases? A scatter plot should make this clear. Here's how to create it:

```
# Figure 13-1
library(car)
attach(Vocab)
plot(education, vocabulary)
detach(Vocab)
```

The scatter plot in Figure 13-1 is anything but clear! There is not a simple line or band of points showing the relationship we thought we would see. There is a little whitespace at the upper left and the lower right, but every other place looks equally populated.

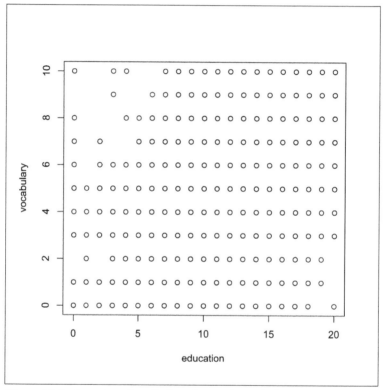

Figure 13-1. A scatter plot of education and vocabulary

The two variables are *discrete*; that is, even though they are numeric, not categorical, they take on only limited numbers of values over their numerical range. The amount of education is measured in number of complete years. Therefore, an individual might have completed 12 years of education, but not 12.4 or 10.75. Likewise, vocabulary is measured in number of correct answers. With vocabulary taking only 11 values, from 0 to 10, and education taking only

21 values, from 0 to 20, there are just 11 x 21 = 231 places on the graph where points can appear—yet there are more than 21,000 people in the survey. This means, of course, that there is a lot of overprinting. What can we do?

In Chapter 3, we used a clever trick called *jittering* to deal with a similar problem in a strip chart. This might work. However, if points are jittered up or down, it will look like the vocabulary scores are not whole numbers, suggesting a more precise test than it actually was. Let's try it, with `scatterplot()`, which has a `jitter` argument:

```
# Figure 13-2
library(car)
attach(Vocab)
sp(education, vocabulary, jitter = list(x = 2, y = 2),
    smoother  = F, spread = F, reg.line = F)
```

Figure 13-2 depicts the results.

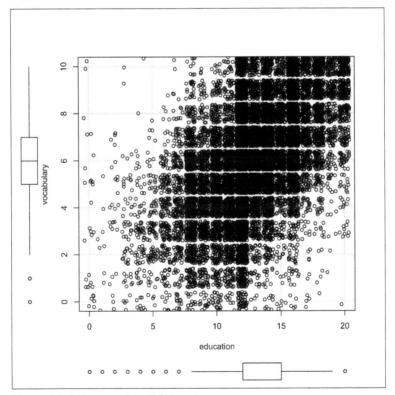

Figure 13-2. Scatter plot with jittering.

The scatter plot in Figure 13-2 shows a marked improvement over the first plot, and we can now discern a clear pattern. You can control the amount of jittering using the following argument:

```
jitter = list(x = 2, y = 2)
```

Try changing the jitter amount from 2 to other values to see what effect this has.

The other method we used earlier was to employ a smaller plot symbol, but that trick is no good in this situation. Here, it would not separate the points, it would only make them smaller. However, making smaller points and jittering at the same time could clear things up a little more. Try it.

Sunflower Plot

Another alternative method of plotting is the *sunflower plot*. This type of plot uses differing characters on a particular graph location, depending on how many points are coincident at that spot. Let's take a look:

```
# Figure 13-3
library(car)
attach(Vocab)
sunflowerplot(education, vocabulary,
    main = "Sunflower Plot",
    col.main = "deepskyblue3",
    family = "HersheySerif",
    font.lab = 3)    # x and y labels are in italic
detach(Vocab)
```

Figure 13-3 shows what this plot looks like.

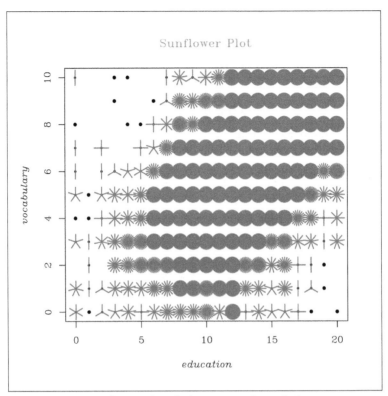

Figure 13-3. A sunflower plot of education and vocabulary

The sunflower plot in Figure 13-3 looks somewhat similar to the jittered scatter plot. Let's consider how the sunflower plot represents the data. Look at the point at the extreme upper left. It is a black dot with a red *petal* above the dot and another red petal below. This represents two observations (there were actually 2 of the 21,000 people in the survey who reported no education and a perfect score on the vocabulary test!). Likewise, at the lower left, there is one person with 20 years of education (PhD? MD? Two master's degrees?) who answered no questions correctly on the vocabulary test. Might this say something about the quality of the data? Are there mistakes here? If we go back to the upper left and move across the top of the graph, toward the right, we see the next two dots representing one observation each, another point with two petals, a point with nine petals (representing nine observations), the next with three petals, and so on. The solid red circles represent many observations; so many, in fact, that we can no longer count the petals.

Although this graph still does not offer ideal visual resolution, it does provide a pretty good indication of the density of points at any particular location on the graph. It seems that the expected relationship between years of education and vocabulary holds true.

Change Fonts?

Did you notice a change in the font types in Figure 13-3? A number of alternative fonts are available in R. You can request fonts by using the `family` argument in the `par()` command, which will affect any commands given thereafter until a new `par()` command is issued. Most commands for plotting will also accept the `family` argument for just the graph created by one command. For more information about available fonts, type **?Hershey** or **demo(Hershey)**.

In addition, you can specify font types by using the `font` argument (or `font.axis`, `font.lab`, `font.main`, or `font.sub`):

- 1 = plain text
- 2 = bold
- 3 = italic
- 4 = bold italic
- 5 = symbol font

Note that not all families include all font types (e.g., bold italic, extra bold, condensed). For more details, type **?Hershey**.

Smooth Scatter Plot

There are even better graphical tools in R to deal with this problem of high-density data. The `smoothScatter()` function takes a different approach:

```
# Figure 13-4
library(car)
attach(Vocab)
smoothScatter(education, vocabulary,
  las = 1,
  family = "HersheyGothicGerman",
  main = "Smooth Scatter Plot", font=3)
# las = 1 rotates numbers on y-axis
detach(Vocab)
```

Figure 13-4 shows the results of using `smoothScatter()`.

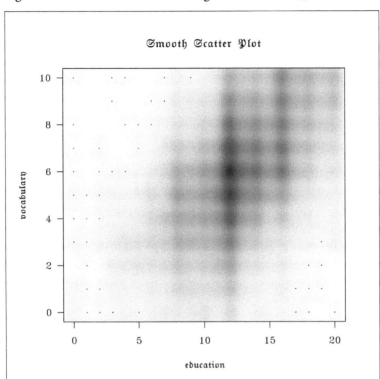

Figure 13-4. A smooth scatter plot of education and vocabulary.

The smooth scatter plot in Figure 13-4 uses hue and color intensity to show areas of high versus low density. This is not only more aesthetically pleasing than the sunflower plot, but it offers better resolution, too. Notice, for instance, a very dark spot for about 12 years of education (high school graduate) and vocabulary scores of about 5 to 7. There are other dark bands at about 14 years of education (community college) and 16 years of education (college graduate). No such thing was visible on the sunflower plot.

The sunflower plot shows the major trend quite well, perhaps even better than the smooth scatter plot. The smooth scatter plot, on the other hand, shows certain details that we would have missed entirely had we relied only on the sunflower plot. While exploring data, it is usually a good idea to look at the data in several different ways. Even though the smooth scatter might be our choice for a final presentation of this data, it will not always be the best choice.

Hexbin Plot

Another choice for such a large dataset is to do *binning*. This is rather like the sunflower plot, but provides counts in bins rather than simply varying shapes. This can be accomplished using the hex bin() function provided in the hexbin package; an example of the result appears in Figure 13-5. Several color gradients are available, as colramp = options. (For more information, type **?ColorRamps**.) The example shown uses the color gradient BTC. Note that there is a key on the right side, showing the number of counts represented by a particular color. A number of options are also possible, such as smoothing, trellis hexbins, adding a straight line, hexbin plot matrices, and others. For more information, type **?hexbin**.

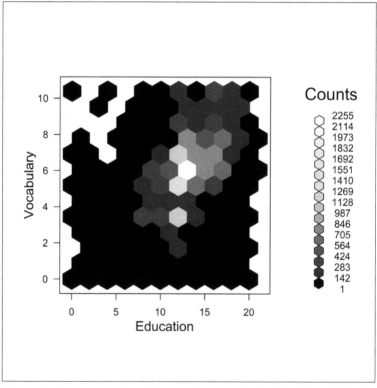

Figure 13-5. An example of binning by using the hexbin() function.

Here is the code to produce Figure 13-5:

```
# Figure 13-5 - hexbinning
install.packages("hexbin", dependencies = T)
library(car)
library(hexbin)
plot(hexbin(Vocab$education, Vocab$vocabulary, xbins = 10),
    xlab = "Education", ylab = "Vocabulary", colramp = BTC)
```

You do not always need the xbins argument. In this particular case, though, it is very useful. Try making this plot without the xbins argument to see what happens. The default value of xbins (the number of bins along the x-axis) is 30. The argument xbins = 10 makes the bins wide enough to fill up the empty space. A higher number puts smaller bins farther apart, and a lower number puts fatter bins closer together.

It would, perhaps, be more satisfying to see a smoother plot, but there are a couple of constraints that prevent this. First, the data is discrete, consisting only of whole numbers, so there can only be 11 levels of vocabulary and only 21 levels of education. Second, the color ramp is designed to have only so many levels that the progression from one color to the next is a "just detectable difference." Therefore, we can have no more than 16 levels of color.

The hexbin and smooth scatter plots are two types of *false-color plots*, which use color gradients to represent amounts or intensities. The *heat map* plot, discussed later in the book, is another type of false-color plot.

Exercise 13-1

Make a simple scatter plot of MathAch (y-axis) and SES (x-axis) from the MathAchieve dataset in the nlme package. Is there a clear trend? Can you get a better grasp of the relationship with another kind of plot? Try each of the plot types introduced in this chapter. Which type offered the most insight, and which offered the least?

CHAPTER 14

The Bland-Altman Plot

 If you are not interested in programming, you can skip this chapter with no loss of continuity.

Assessing Measurement Reliability

This chapter illustrates the flexibility of R. You cannot find the type of graph examined here in base R, and it can take a bit of effort to find such a specialized kind of plot among the thousands of available packages. I decided to write my own function to accomplish the task and have included it here. Since I wrote this function, I discovered that at least two packages include this plot; I'll introduce one of them here. There is a little more typing to do in this chapter than in most others, with a dataset to enter in a spreadsheet or text file and a relatively long R function to type. There is an alternate, shorter version of the function at the end of the chapter that you can use instead if you like.

The *Bland-Altman plot* is a tool used to assess the agreement between two measurement techniques, or the reliability/repeatability of a measurement. It is also known as the "Tukey mean-difference plot."

Bland and Altman (1986) give the data listed in Table 14-1 on measuring peak expiratory flow rate (PEFR), in liters/minute, with two different types of meters, a Wright flow meter and a Mini Wright flow meter. Two measurements were made with each meter, on each subject. The object here is to determine whether the Mini meter gives substantially the same readings as the Wright meter and could, therefore, be substituted for the standard measurement. Note that this is not a correlation problem. (A brief introduction to correlation appears in the section "Corrgram" on page 190.) Close association—even perfect correlation—of the two methods is not enough; the measurements themselves must be interchangeable. In other words, does one get the same results with both meters?

Table 14-1. Bland-Altman PEFR data

Subject	Wright1	Wright2	Mini1	Mini2
1	494	490	512	525
2	395	397	430	415
3	516	512	520	508
4	434	401	428	444
5	476	470	500	500
6	557	611	600	625
7	413	415	364	460
8	442	431	380	390
9	650	638	658	642
10	433	429	445	432
11	417	420	432	420
12	656	633	626	605
13	267	275	260	227
14	478	492	477	467
15	178	165	259	268
16	423	372	350	370
17	427	421	451	443

Enter the data in a spreadsheet and save it as a *.csv* file named *BlandAltmanPeakFlow.csv*. Read the data into an R data frame named Flow by using the following command:

```
Flow <- read.csv("BlandAltmanPeakFlow.csv", header=TRUE)
```

Use the following command to verify that the data is the same as in Table 14-1:

```
head(Flow)
```

The R function presented next will produce the Bland-Altman plot shown in Figure 14-1. It is basically a scatter plot of 17 points, one for each subject in the study. A point (x,y) on the graph is defined as $x =$ the average of the two measures for one subject, and $y =$ the difference between those same two measures. The function is defined as follows:

```
# result in Figure 14-1; shorter version at end of chapter
baplot <- function(meas1, meas2){

# calculate averages and differences
 ave = (meas1 + meas2)/2
    dif = meas1 - meas2

# calculate parameters for reference lines
    std = sd(dif)
    mdif = mean(dif)
    mdrnd = round(mdif,3)
    mxav = max(ave) - (max(ave) - min(ave))/12
    upperci = round((mdif + std*1.96), 3)
    lowerci = round((mdif - std*1.96), 3)
    maxx = 1.05*(max(ave))
    minx = 1.05*(min(ave))
    maxy = max(upperci,max(dif))
    miny = (min(lowerci,min(dif)))

# plot points
plot(ave,dif,
 pch = 16, col = "deepskyblue3",
 xlim = c(minx,maxx), ylim = c(1.1*miny, 1.1*maxy),
 main = "Bland-Altman Plot",
 col.main ="deepskyblue4",
 xlab ="Average of two methods",
 ylab ="Difference between two methods", las=1)

# draw reference lines
abline(h = mdif,
  lty = "solid", col = "grey75", lwd = 2)
abline(h = mdif + std*1.96,
  lty ="dotted", col = "grey75", lwd = 2)
abline(h = mdif - std*1.96,
  lty = "dotted", col = "grey75", lwd = 2)

# put text around reference lines
text(mxav, mdif,
  labels = "mean difference",
  pos = 3,
  cex = .7)
text(mxav, mdif,
  labels = mdrnd,
```

```
    pos = 1,
    cex = .7)
text(mxav, upperci,
    labels = "upper 95% limit of agreement",
    pos = 3,
    cex = .7)
text(mxav, upperci,
    labels = upperci,
    pos = 1,
    cex = .7)
text(mxav, lowerci,
    labels = "lower 95% limit of agreement",
    pos = 3,
    cex = .7)
text(mxav, lowerci,
    labels = lowerci,
    pos = 1,
    cex = .7)
}
```

Save the function to a file:

```
save("baplot",file = "baplot")
```

After you have typed and saved both the data and the function, you
can start an R session and make the graph of this data depicted in
Figure 14-1, comparing `wright1` to `mini1`. To do so, issue the following commands:

```
# Figure 14-1
Flow <- read.csv("BlandAltmanPeakFlow.csv", header = TRUE)
load("baplot")
baplot(Flow$wright1, Flow$mini1)
```

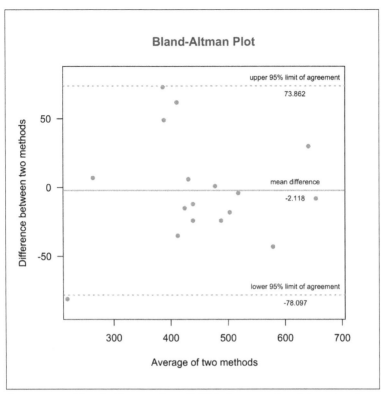

Figure 14-1. Bland-Altman plot of PEFR data, produced by using the baplot() function.

The plot shows one point for each subject. The point represents the subject's average of the two measurements (horizontal axis) against the difference between those same measurements (vertical axis). There are three reference lines. The solid line indicates mean difference (called *bias* in comparison studies). The dotted lines indicate the *limits of agreement*. The limits of agreement are calculated by first finding the mean of the differences (call it *m*) and the standard deviation of the differences (call it *s*). Thus, the upper and lower limits are:

```
m ± 1.96 * s
```

If you prefer a graph with reference lines but no labels, simply omit the text statements from the baplot() function.

The differences between the values in Figure 14-1 and the values in Bland and Altman (1986) are due to rounding error. The `baplot()` function carries more decimal places and uses the precise multiplier of 1.96 standard deviations rather than rounding to 2. In practice, these differences are trivial.

If there were no systematic bias, the points would cluster in a band around the reference line of the mean. The limits of agreement should be no larger than clinically acceptable error. In this case, the limits are quite large—up to nearly 80 l/min—and clinically unacceptable. Differences between the two methods might be related to the mean of the two measurements. Take note of the cluster of large differences, near to an average of 400, and the single extreme value at an average of about 200. The Mini meter appears to be an unacceptable substitute for the standard method. However, this is based on a very small sample. The apparent discrepancies might not be so apparent in a much larger sample.

Another use of this type of plot is to compare repeated measures on the same subject. For example, you could examine the reliability of the standard method of measurement by constructing the plot for the variables `wright1` and `wright2`. This is crucial. If the Wright meter measurements on the same subject do not agree with each other, there is little point in attempting to assess the agreement with the Mini meter. Here is the code to produce such a plot:

```
# Figure 14-2
baplot(Flow$wright1, Flow$wright2)
```

You can see the results of the repeated measure trial in Figure 14-2.

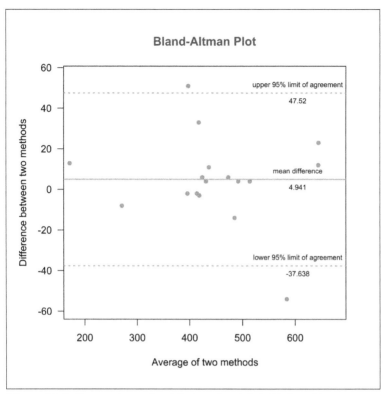

Figure 14-2. Comparison of wright1 and wright2. Each subject was measured twice with the same kind of meter.

Whereas most of the differences are pretty small, a couple of the 17 subjects displayed differences of about ±50. This outcome raises some questions about the reliability of flow measurements. Another study on a larger sample might be helpful.

The epade package provides several plotting tools, including one to produce a Bland-Altman plot quite similar to mine. This can be done using the following code:

```
# Figure 14-3
install.packages("epade") # if not already installed
library(epade)
Flow <- read.csv("BlandAltmanPeakFlow.csv", header = TRUE)
bland.altman.ade(Flow$wright1, Flow$mini1, fitline = 0)
```

Compare the result, which appears in Figure 14-3, to Figure 14-1. This function also allows for placing regression lines, either linear, polynomial, or loess, on the plot. To see the help file, type the following:

```
> library(help = epade)
```

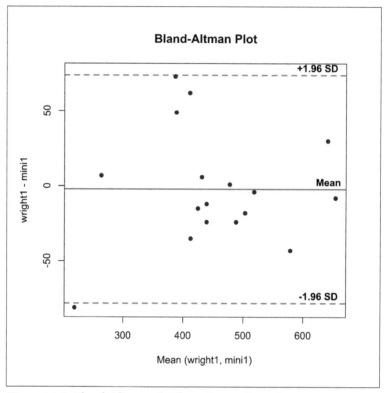

Figure 14-3. Bland-Altman plot from the epade package.

In this chapter, we have seen how to make a type of graph not provided in base R by writing a function to make such a graph. You can save this function and use it again. We also compared a similar but not identical graph provided in a package that you can download and add to R. This demonstrates the flexibility and extensibility of R and suggests that you need to take care in selecting the right tools for the job. Note that baplot() is a simple example presented to demonstrate how to write a function. It has limitations. For example, it does not work if there are missing values, and it does not offer any options such as placing regression lines on the plot. If you do not need more, it should be fine for your use. You might find it interesting to compare baplot() to a more complex function, such as the one in **epade**. You can view its code by typing the name of the function, without parentheses (assuming, of course, that you have previously installed and loaded **epade**):

```
bland.altman.ade  # displays code for this function
```

Exercise 14-1

Choose one of the Bland-Altman plots introduced in this chapter to plot the MFSV data from the ResearchMethods package. What is your conclusion? Are the two methods interchangeable?

A Shorter Version of baplot()

Here is a shorter version of `baplot()` without two of the reference lines. You might want to try a user-defined function, but with considerably less typing!

```
baplot <- function(meas1,meas2){
ave = (meas1 + meas2)/2
dif = meas1 - meas2
mdif = mean(dif)
plot(ave,dif,
  pch = 16,
  main = "Bland-Altman Plot",
  xlab = "Average of two methods",
  ylab = "Difference between two methods", las = 1)
abline(h = mdif,
  lty = "solid", col = "grey75", lwd = 2)
  }
```

CHAPTER 15

QQ Plots

Comparing Sets of Numbers

It can be quite useful to compare the distributions of two sets of numbers; for example, two variables or two vectors. The sets of numbers might both be sets of measurements, or one might be a theoretical distribution. For example, we might want to see how a particular variable compared to the theoretical "normal" distribution.

In the United States and many other parts of the world, it is customary for customers to leave a tip for people who perform services. Just how much to give is a topic of frequent discussion among patrons of restaurants. The reshape2 package includes a dataset, tips, that was compiled by a waiter about tips his own customers gave to him. Let's take a look inside this interesting dataset:

```
> library(reshape2)
> attach(tips)
> head(tips)
  total_bill  tip    sex smoker day   time size
1      16.99 1.01 Female     No Sun Dinner    2
2      10.34 1.66   Male     No Sun Dinner    3
3      21.01 3.50   Male     No Sun Dinner    3
4      23.68 3.31   Male     No Sun Dinner    2
5      24.59 3.61 Female     No Sun Dinner    4
6      25.29 4.71   Male     No Sun Dinner    4
```

Now, we'll try to learn more about the tip variable. First, how are the tips distributed? We could plot the density of tip to get an idea of that:

```
# Figure 15-1a
library(reshape2)
attach(tips)
par(mfrow = c(3,2))
plot(density(tip),
  main = "a. Density(tip)",
  col = "blue",
  lwd = 2)
```

The plot in Figure 15-1a shows that the distribution is quite skewed; that is, it has a long tail to the right. In other words, a few patrons give relatively large tips, but most others are clustered around $2 to $4. This is important because many methods of statistical analysis depend on the data being, at least approximately, "normally distributed," or nearly aligned with the bell-shaped curve.

Tips are usually based on the size of the bill. Treating the tips in this manner is the subject of one of the exercises at the end of the chapter.

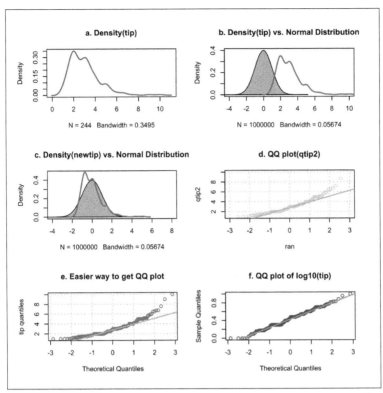

Figure 15-1. Comparing tip (and transformations of tip) to a normal distribution.

To get a better idea of how much the tip variable differs from the normal distribution, we could plot a normal distribution and the tip data on the same graph. To do this, use the rnorm() function to generate a large sample of numbers, which will be called ran, from a normal distribution. Then, plot the density of ran and fill in the curve with the polygon() function. This will make it stand out from the tip density. Finally, use the lines() function to plot the density of tip on the same graph:

```
# Figure 15-1b
ran = rnorm(1000000)  # a million random obs from a normal dist.
plot(density(ran),
  main = "b. Density(tip) vs. Normal Distribution",
  xlim = c(-4,10))
polygon(density(ran), col = "burlywood")
lines(density(tip),
  col = "blue",
  lwd = 2)
```

 The *aspect ratio* of a graph is the height of the graph divided by its length. This is important because changing this ratio can make it easier or more difficult for viewers to perceive the relationships between variables on the graph. Research in perceptual psychology has shown that lines with a slope close to 45° are optimum. Choosing an aspect ratio to achieve this optimum is called *banking*. R scatter plots, one per page, generally use an effective aspect ratio, although you can alter this by using arguments such as asp, mar, and ylim. Throughout this book, there are many examples of multiple graphs on one page. When the display is square —2 x 2 or 3 x 3—the aspect ratio of the various graphs on one page stays about the same as it would be in a single-page graph. (Try it yourself.) In Figure 15-1, which is a 3 x 2 display, the aspect ratio has been changed quite a bit. In this case, the advantage of having six graphs on one page for easy comparison was deemed more important than preserving the aspect ratio. Your audiences might not all agree. Be careful when you change aspect ratios!

Figure 15-1b shows the tip density plot superimposed on the normal distribution. This might be a little more informative than Figure 15-1a, but it would be easier to assess the differences if the plots coincided more closely. That is to say, we could compare the plots more readily if they had the same means. The vector ran was created by using the rnorm() function with the *default* options (what you get if you do not specify values) of mean = 0 and standard deviation = 1. Statisticians often *standardize* or *normalize* a variable to make it easy to compare with some distribution with known characteristics.

The `tip` variable can be standardized to have a mean of 0 and standard deviation of 1 by a simple procedure. First, find the mean and standard deviation of `tip`:

```
> mean(tip)
[1] 2.998279
> sd(tip)
[1] 1.383638
```

Next, create a new variable, `newtip`, by subtracting 2.998 (the mean) from every tip and dividing the resulting number by 1.384 (the standard deviation). This is an example of a *transformation* of the variable. A transformation is a replacement of the original variable with a function of the variable that keeps the essential information but makes the new variable easier to work with or more closely in compliance with the necessary assumptions underlying the statistical method in use. Here's the code to create the `newtip` variable:

```
> newtip = (tip-2.998)/1.384 # transform tip to have
# mean = 0 and sd = 1
```

Then, plot the two densities again:

```
# Figure 15-1c
newtip = (tip-2.998)/1.384 # transform tip to have
# mean=0 and sd=1
plot(density(ran),
  ylim = c(0,.48),
  main = "c. Density(newtip) vs. Normal Distribution",
  xlim = c(-4,8))
polygon(density(ran),
  col = "burlywood")
lines(density(newtip),
  col = "blue",
  lwd = 2)
```

Figure 15-1c shows the superimposition of the two densities in a much more informative way.

There are other ways to compare the two distributions, leading to different kinds of graphs. Consider first a numerical summary of the `tip` variable:

```
> summary(tip)
   Min. 1st Qu.  Median    Mean 3rd Qu.    Max.
  1.000   2.000   2.900   2.998   3.562  10.000
```

The `summary()` function gives quartiles—the 25th, 50th (median), and 75th percentiles—as is detailed in Chapter 1. We could divide the distribution of the `tip` variable into any groupings that we find useful, not just quartiles (four groups). For instance, we could break the variable into groups that were 10 percentage points apart. The breakpoints are called *quantiles*. There is a quantile() function that you can use to compute quantiles of a given variable, according to the requirements of the user. To see how this works, create a new variable, qtip, which contains the quantiles of tip, spaced every 10 percentage points apart. The quantiles must fall within the range of 0 to 1, so you need to use the seq() function to specify that the first and last points must be 0 and 1 and that the interval is 0.1. Then, print the values in qtip to see how it worked:

```
> qtip = quantile(tip, seq(0,1,.1))
> qtip
  0%    10%    20%    30%    40%
1.000  1.500  2.000  2.000  2.476
 50%    60%    70%    80%
2.900  3.016  3.480  4.000
 90%   100%
5.000 10.000
```

We can plot quantiles of the tip variable against quantiles of ran to determine how closely the two distributions conform. So, for instance, the value of the 10th quantile for qtip is plotted against the 10th quantile for ran, and so on. This type of display is called a *quantile-quantile plot*, or *QQ plot*. This kind of graph is usually easier to read, because comparing how close a group of dots comes to a straight line is more direct than comparing two curves. Figure 15-1d uses qtip2(), a function that makes the interval between the quantiles smaller than before. This creates more points on the graph. The plotting was done by using the qqplot() function and a reference line was added with the qqline() function. Finally, a grid was added to facilitate reading the axes. The code to produce Figure 15-1d follows:

```
# Figure 15-1d
qtip2 = quantile(tip, seq(0,1,.005))
qqplot(ran, qtip2,
  main = "d. QQ plot(qtip2)",
  xlim = c(-3,3),
  col = "skyblue2")
qqline(qtip2,
  col = "burlywood",
  lwd = 2)
grid(lty = "dotted",
  col = "gray75")
# required calculation of ran and qtip2 first
```

Figure 15-1d shows that even though tip is close to a normal distribution (as measured by the straight line) over much of its range, it is far off at both ends, and especially at the high end. This suggests that tip is not close to a normal distribution and that proceeding with an analysis that depends on such a distribution would be unwise.

This plot was used to show what QQ plots are. Now that you understand what they are, it is good to know that you can make virtually the same plot more easily, without first creating quantile variables (i.e., ran and qtip). The qqnorm() function, shown in the following code, can operate directly on the tip variable and produce the plot seen in Figure 15-1e:

```
# Figure 15-1e
qqnorm(tip,
    main = "e. Easier way to get QQ plot",
    col = "blue",
    ylab = "tip quantiles")
qqline(tip,
    col = "burlywood",
    lwd = 2)
grid(lty = "dotted",
    col = "gray75")
```

Because tip seems not to be normally distributed, we might see if there is a transformation of tip that is. Recall that the idea behind a transformation is that if the original data does not meet the assumptions required for the analysis to give valid results, sometimes applying a function of the data (i.e., a transformation) can produce data that does meet the assumptions. If so, the analysis can be performed on the transformed data. Conclusions will then necessarily be about the transformed data, not the original data. Although there are many things that could be tried, a log transform is often successful at reducing or removing skewness (the degree of asymmetry of a distribution). The following code produces Figure 15-1f, which shows that the log (common or base 10) transformation works very well:

```
# Figure 15-1f
logtip = log10(tip)
qqnorm(logtip,
    main = "f. QQ plot of log10(tip)",
    col = "blue4")
qqline(logtip,
    col = "burlywood3",
    lwd = 2)
```

So far, we have used QQ plots to compare a variable's distribution to that of a theoretical distribution. You can also use QQ plots to compare the distributions of two variables. This could be two variables such as `tip` and `size` in the `tips` dataset. In this particular dataset, however, it might be much more interesting to compare tips given by men and women, or at lunch and dinner, and so on. To do this, you could form appropriate subsets of the data and make QQ plots of the groups. The `lattice` package makes it very easy to compare two groups when there are exactly two levels of a variable, such as `sex` in the `tips` dataset. Use the qq function:

```
qq(y ~ x)
```

In this case, *y* has exactly two levels and *x* is quantitative:

```
# Figure 15-2,left
library(lattice)
qq(sex ~ tip,
  main = "Tips given by men and women")
```

Figure 15-2 shows the results, on the left.

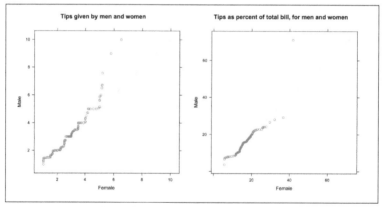

Figure 15-2. QQ plots of tip for men and women (left) and ratio [i.e., 100*(tip/total_bill)] (right). These plots were produced by using the lattice package.

The graph on the left in Figure 15-2 shows that the distribution of tips given by males and females is pretty similar for tips below about five dollars. Tips higher than five dollars, however, are more likely to be from males. We can confirm that with a numerical summary:

```
> summary(tip[sex == "Male"])  # subset containing only males
  Min. 1st Qu.  Median   Mean 3rd Qu.   Max.
  1.00    2.00    3.00    3.09    3.76   10.00
```

```
> summary(tip[sex == "Female"]) # subset containing only females
   Min. 1st Qu. Median   Mean 3rd Qu.   Max.
  1.000   2.000  2.750  2.833  3.500  6.500
```

We have learned some interesting things about the distribution of tips, but perhaps it would make more sense to study not the tips, but the tip as a percentage of the total bill. After all, most guidelines about tipping suggest something like "15 percent of the bill." We can compute a new variable by multiplying the ratio of tip to total bill by 100. Then, we can make a QQ plot of that variable for males and females:

```
# Figure 15-2, right
tips$ratio = 100*(tip/total_bill)
qq(sex ~ tips$ratio,
   main = "Tips as percent of total bill, for men and women")
```

The graph on the right in Figure 15-2 shows males and females as equally generous up to about 25 percent, but then females become more generous, with the exception of one very big extreme. Maybe this guy was trying to impress his girlfriend? Maybe the decimal point was inadvertently moved? Problems like this occur in real data analysis pretty frequently. You'll need to recheck the data to see if it is right. Further, you will need to decide whether to include or exclude that one point, or analyze the data both ways and report both results. Things like this make life interesting!

Exercise 15-1

Continue analyzing the tips dataset. Use the variable ratio instead of tip. Are other factors related to the size of tips? Do apparent relationships make sense? Could other factors be misleading you?

Exercise 15-2

Take another look at the Vocab dataset in the car package. Are the variables vocabulary and education "normally distributed"? Are vocabulary scores equally distributed for males and females?

## PART IV

Multivariable Graphs

Sometimes, we need to examine relationships among three or more variables—but the media we usually have available for graphs, such as paper or computer screens, are only two-dimensional objects. Although this presents challenges, a number of clever ways of visualizing higher-dimensional data have been devised. Some of these methods involve looking at pairs of variables at a time, usually with other pairs on the same page, so that we can readily make comparisons, whereas others attempt to display three or more variables in one plot. The next section examines a few promising graphical methods for multivariable visualization.

# CHAPTER 16

Scatter Plot Matrices and Corrgrams

Scatter plot Matrix

When faced with many quantitative variables, it sometimes helps to look at the relationships of each of the possible pairs of variables first. To avoid making you type a plot() command for each of the combinations, R provides a shortcut command, pairs(), which will do the same thing. Furthermore, pairs() puts all the plots on the same page so that they can be compared quite easily. The result is called a *scatter plot matrix*. We will use the scatter plot matrix to study the relationships among member characteristics of various church groups.

A long line of research on American religious life has shown that weekly attendance and membership seem to be related to a church's strictness. Iannaccone (1994) discusses this research and gives an interesting dataset showing several variables for each of 18 religious denominations. You can find the data in ex1713 from the Sleuth2 package. Let's take a look:

```
> library(Sleuth2)
> attach(ex1713)
> head(ex1713)
```

```
            Denomination Distinct Attend NonChurch StrongPct AnnInc
1       American Baptist     2.5   25.6      1.01      50.6  24000
2      Assemblies of God     4.8   35.4      0.68      58.6  27100
3               Catholic     3.0   26.4      1.43      40.0  32900
4     Disciples of Christ    2.1   24.3      2.58      47.0  28600
5              Episcopal     1.1   17.3      1.93      32.0  39000
6   Evangelical Lutheran     2.7   23.0      1.71      41.5  33700
```

To see the codebook for this data, type:

```
> ?ex1713
```

Here's a brief summary of the codebook:

Distinct
> The distinctiveness/strictness of discipline, on a seven-point scale

Attend
> The average percentage of weekly attendance

NonChurch
> The average number of secular organizations to which members belong

StrongPct
> The average percentage of members who consider themselves strong church members

AnnInc
> The average annual income

The scatter plot matrix shown in Figure 16-1 was produced by using the pairs() function. Note that the variable names are typed as a formula, beginning with the ~ symbol, followed by the variable names in the order in which they will appear on the graph, separated by the + symbol. Further, you can add any of a number of special arguments for this function, as well as par() arguments. For the code to produce Figure 16-1, only the pch and col arguments have been used:

```
# Figure 16-1: produce scatter plot matrix of denomination data
library(Sleuth2)
attach(ex1713)
pairs(~ Distinct + Attend + NonChurch + StrongPct + AnnInc,
```

```
pch = 16,
col = "deepskyblue")
```

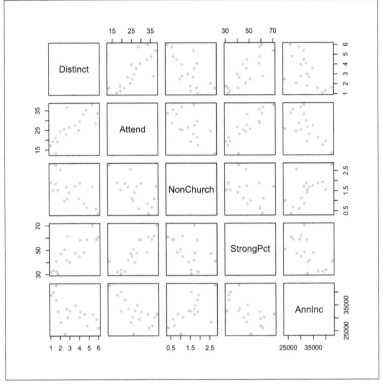

Figure 16-1. A scatter plot matrix of the church denomination data.

In the scatter plot matrix in Figure 16-1, each variable is plotted against every other variable, twice. In each pair, a given variable is once the *x*-variable and once the *y*-variable. For example, in the second row, the variable `Attend` is the *y*-variable in each of the four scatter plots, and each of the other four variables is the *x*-variable once. In the second column, `Attend` is the *x*-variable in each of the four scatter plots, and each of the other variables is the *y*-variable one time.

Looking across the second row, we can see that `Attend` has a positive association with `Distinct`; that is, as one of these increases, the other does also. Likewise, there is a positive association between `Attend` and `StrongPct`. In contrast, `Attend` has negative associations with `NonChurch` and `AnnInc`; as one increases, the other decreases.

However, these negative associations are not as strong as the positive ones. In other words, the points in the negative associations do not hug a straight line as tightly as the positive association plots do. This is clearer in Figure 16-3, in which least-squares lines are placed on each scatter plot. Of course, associations, even strong ones, do not imply causation—or, put another way, knowing that greater strictness and higher attendance usually go together does not prove that one causes the other. It does, however, suggest that this relationship might be an interesting one to study further.

The `car` package has a function called `scatterplotMatrix()` that adds some useful features to the scatter plot matrix. First, it is easy to plot the distribution of each of the variables on the diagonal of the matrix as a histogram, density plot, box plot, QQ plot, or 1D (diagonal) strip chart. In addition, you can easily add a least-squares line to each plot.

Smoothers are also available for each plot. As we saw in Chapter 12, a smoother is a tool for making patterns in scatter plot data a little easier to see. There are several types of smoothers, but they all show the center of the y's at a given value of x (or several close x's) and do it in such a way that the (usually curved) line formed by connecting all such points is relatively smooth. Figure 16-2 shows a scatter plot matrix with smoothers, represented as red lines. You can use the `smoother` argument to select a smoothing method, but Figure 16-2 uses the default method, "loess," or locally weighted regression.

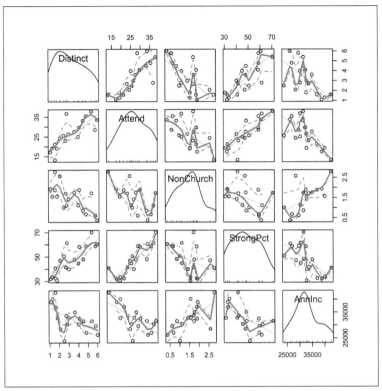

Figure 16-2. A scatter plot matrix produced by scatterplotMatrix() in the car package. The default options add kernel density plots and rug plots in the diagonal as well as least-squares lines and smoothers in each of the plot windows.

Here is the code to produce Figure 16-2:

```
#Fig 16-2: scatter plot matrix w/ smoother & diagonal density
library(car)
library(Sleuth2)
attach(ex1713)
scatterplotMatrix(~Distinct + Attend + NonChurch + StrongPct +
   AnnInc)
```

The lines produced by the smoother in Figure 16-2 show some interesting things. The associations between Attend and Distinct and between Attend and StrongPct are close to straight lines and suggest that these relationships may be described as simple linear correlations. Certain other associations that looked close to linear on the simple scatter plot—for example, that between Attend and

AnnInc—now appear more complex. It should be noted, however, that this dataset only has 18 denominations in it, which is a rather small number from which to draw conclusions about the shape of the relation between any two variables. This example is merely an illustration of the features available in the package. In most cases, you will probably find it useful to look at a display like Figure 16-1 first; after getting a feel for the data, you might find some of the other features helpful.

You can customize the matrix produced by scatterplot() quite a bit. You can omit the smoother by using the smoother = NULL argument, as shown in the code that follows. Likewise, you could remove the regression line by using the reg.line = F argument. It is also possible to change the type of graph on the diagonals by using the diagonal argument. To see the options, type **?scatterplotMatrix**.

Figure 16-3 illustrates the customized scatterplot() matrix created by the following code:

```
# Figure 16-3: scatter plot matrix w/out smoother & with
  histograms
scatterplotMatrix(~Distinct + Attend + NonChurch + StrongPct
  + AnnInc, diagonal = "histogram",
  smoother = NULL)
```

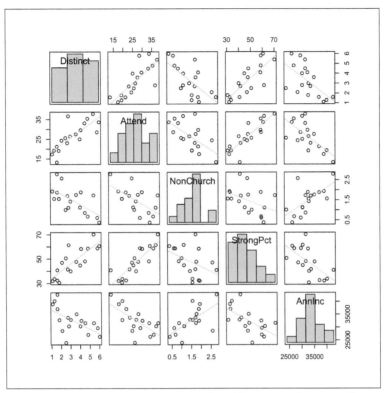

Figure 16-3. A scatter plot matrix produced by scatterplotMatrix() in the car package. Smoothers have been left out and the diagonal density plots replaced with histograms.

Figure 16-3 shows a matrix with diagonal histograms. This might be a better choice than the density plots that are produced by default, at least in this instance, given that the sample size is only 18. The distribution of a couple of variables, Attend and NonChurch, is less smooth than the density plots might lead us to think. Further, the two especially large values of NonChurch can cause the relationship between that variable and Attend to appear stronger and more linear than it really is. You can probably see that by looking carefully at the scatter plot of those two variables, but you might have missed it had not the histogram flagged the plot first.

When examining a scatter plot matrix, it is important to remember that you are actually being presented with many separate plots. Do not let yourself become overwhelmed by the amount of information on the page. Look at each plot by itself. After you have done this for many of the plots, you will probably find it enlightening to compare them.

Corrgram

The *corrgram* (sometimes called "correlogram," although this term actually refers to something else) is a type of graph related to the scatter plot matrix. In this type of graph, the individual scatter plots are replaced by symbols that represent numbers measuring the amount of linear correlation between two quantitative variables. The *Pearson correlation coefficient*, usually denoted as r, can vary between -1 and 1. A perfect positive correlation is 1, meaning that all the points on the scatter plot of two quantitative variables lie exactly on an ascending straight line. A perfect negative correlation is -1, indicating that all points lie exactly on a descending straight line. Values near 0 indicate little or no association between two variables. Take note that the correlation coefficient is not a measure of the steepness of a line's slope. It is, instead, a measure of the total deviation of the points from a straight line. Figure 16-4 illustrates the meaning of the correlation coefficient. A further caution: the correlation coefficient is useful only if the relationship between the variables is linear; that is to say, if the points fall on a straight line. In other situations, the correlation coefficient can be misleading or even deceptive.

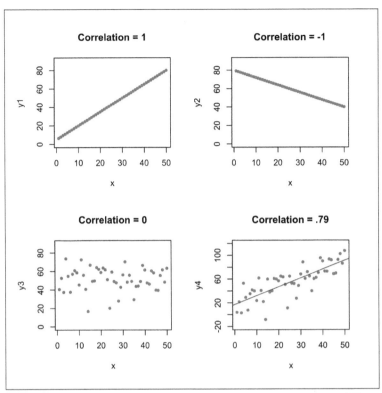

Figure 16-4. A perfect positive correlation of 1 has all the points falling exactly on an upward-sloping line. A perfect negative correlation of –1 has all the points falling exactly on a downward-sloping line. A correlation of 0 shows no discernible pattern. A positive correlation of .79 shows points falling "close" to a straight line.

To make a corrgram, it is first necessary to make a *correlation matrix* —a matrix containing the correlation coefficients of all the variable pairs in the dataset. This is accomplished by using the cor() function:

```
> library(Sleuth2)
> attach(ex1713)
> y = cor(ex1713[, 2:6]) # use all rows and columns 2-6
> y
              Distinct      Attend  NonChurch   StrongPct      AnnInc
Distinct     1.0000000   0.7891067 -0.6585883   0.8127124  -0.6003892
Attend       0.7891067   1.0000000 -0.6107342   0.8649691  -0.6766143
NonChurch   -0.6585883  -0.6107342  1.0000000  -0.4218525   0.6458747
StrongPct    0.8127124   0.8649691 -0.4218525   1.0000000  -0.6146261
AnnInc      -0.6003892  -0.6766143  0.6458747  -0.6146261   1.0000000
```

When the correlation matrix has been produced, you can use the corrplot() function from the corrplot package to make several types of corrgram. Some examples appear in Figure 16-5. All of the examples use color to depict size of correlation. You can also use size of object, orientation of object, or numbers to show how large the correlation of a given pair of variables is.

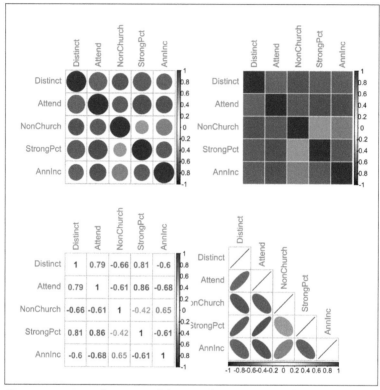

Figure 16-5. Visualizations of the correlation matrix. This is a type of summary, or approximation, of the scatter plot matrix, produced by the corrplot() function in the corrplot package. Upper left: method = "circle"; upper right: method = "color"; lower left: method="number"; lower right: method= "ellipse", type="lower"

The correlation between variables A and B is the same as the correlation between B and A, so the complete corrgram is redundant. That is to say, the correlations in the upper half are exactly the same as the correlations in the lower half. For this reason, some prefer to display only the upper half or only the lower half of the matrix. An example of this appears in the lower-right corner of Figure 16-5. You can do this by using the argument `type = "lower"`. The code to produce the corrgrams in Figure 16-5 follows:

```
# Figure 16-5: various corrgrams
library(corrplot)
library(Sleuth2)
attach(ex1713)
y = cor(ex1713[, 2:6])
par(mfrow = c(2,2))
corrplot(y)  # default method is "circle"
corrplot(y, method = "color")
corrplot(y, method = "number")
corrplot(y, method = "ellipse", type = "lower")
```

Despite all the warnings about correlation coefficients, the corrgram can be an effective way to present and screen data, *if* you take the time to look at the scatter plots (and possibly smoothers), first, to see if correlation coefficients make sense. Compare the corrgrams in Figure 16-5 to the scatter plot matrices in earlier figures in this chapter to see how consistent the conclusions from these varied displays may be. Corrgrams are also available through the `cor.plot()` function in the `psych` package.

All of the plots in Figure 16-5 use color to indicate the strength of the correlation, with a color gradient either on the right or the bottom to show the color meanings. Shades of blue show a positive relationship, with darker colors being stronger (i.e., closer to 1). Shades of red show a negative correlation, with darker colors being closer to −1. In two graphs (the upper-left corner and the lower-right corner), size also indicates strength, but in opposite ways. In the upper-left graph, larger size shows larger absolute value. In the lower-right graph, orientation indicates positive or negative correlation, with narrow ovals showing points close to a line (i.e., strong correlation). Fat ovals indicate a lot of variation around a line, or weaker correlation. You probably picked this up without my telling you, but it feels better to have your suspicions confirmed, right?

It is also possible to combine the scatter plot matrix with the corrgram by putting one of these graphs in the lower half of the matrix, and the other in the upper half. The `ggscatmat()` function in the `GGally` package does exactly that:

```
# Figure 16-6
library(GGally)
library(Sleuth2)
ggscatmat(ex1713, columns = 2:6)
```

Figure 16-6 shows the results.

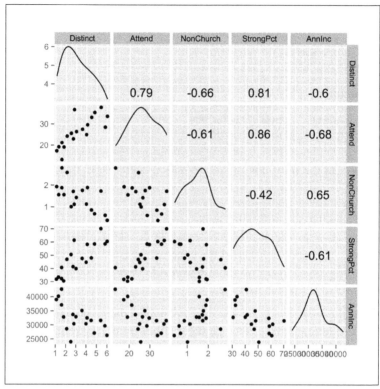

Figure 16-6. A combination of scatter plot matrix and corrgram pro-duced by the ggscatmat() function in the GGally package. Note the overprinting on the x-axis in the lower-right corner. This can be fixed!

Note a small problem in Figure 16-6. The x-axis values in the lower-right corner are overprinting because the numbers are too big to fit in a small space. There is a pretty simple fix for this. Change the scale of the values of AnnInc from dollars to thousands of dollars, and redo the graph with this new variable. Accomplishing this will require one new command and a small change in another one. First, create a new variable, Inc, that is AnnInc divided by one thousand. This new variable becomes the seventh column of the data frame. Next, modify the ggscatmat() command to include the desired columns, leaving out AnnInc and including Inc:

```
# Figure 16-7: fix a bug in Figure 16-6
library(GGally)
library(Sleuth2)
```

```
ex1713$Inc = ex1713$AnnInc/1000
ggscatmat(ex1713, columns = c(2:5,7))
```

Take a look at Figure 16-7 to see how that resolved the overprinting problem.

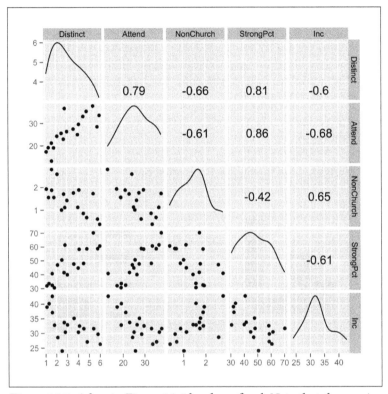

Figure 16-7. A bug in Figure 16-6 has been fixed. Note that the x-axis in the lower-right corner is now readable.

Generalized Pairs Matrix with Mixed Quantitative and Categorical Variables

Datasets with both quantitative and categorical variables are quite common. In such cases, although scatter plots do not work with categorical variables, it is still possible to produce a meaningful display of all the pairwise plots of variables. It simply means that the display will include several types of plots, each appropriate for the variable types included. This type of graphical display is illustrated in the code example that follows with `ggpairs()` from the `GGally` package and `gpairs()` from the `gpairs` package.

Consider again the `Nimrod` dataset. This dataset has one quantitative variable, `time`, and two categorical variables, `level` and `medium`. The variable `performer`, simply being the names, will not give us any useful insight and will make the page more crowded, so we'll leave it out. We can do this by using a subset of the dataset (see the section "Basic Scatter Plots" on page 129, in Chapter 12 to review this concept). The subset we want is `Nimrod[, 2:4]`; that is, all the rows, but only columns 2 through 4:

```
# Figure 16-8
library(GGally)
ggpairs(Nimrod[,2:4])
```

Look at Figure 16-8 to see how that comes out.

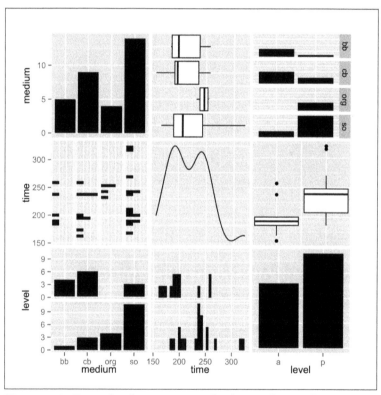

Figure 16-8. Generalized pairs matrix, for data with mixed quantitative and categorical variables. This was produced by using ggpairs() in the GGally package.

There are some familiar types of graphs in Figure 16-8. The diagonal displays bar charts for the two categorical variables and a density plot for the quantitative variable. There are also some box plots, for pairs including one quantitative and one categorical variable.

Additionally, there are some plots that we have not seen yet. The lower-left corner and the upper-right corner are plots of the same two categorical variables. In each case, the square is broken up into multiple bar charts. In the lower left, there are bar charts of medium for each of the two values of level. In the upper-right square, there are bar charts of level for each of the values of medium.

Finally, there are *barcode plots* in some squares plotting a categorical and a quantitative variable. For instance, the middle square in the lefthand column presents the data as something that looks rather like a barcode stamped on a book cover or other item. Each point is represented by a small bar. The bars are arranged as four strip charts, one for each value of medium. When there are ties, the second bar is not simply overprinted, but placed next to the one already in the location that it shares. In other words, these bars are jittered, but in a very orderly manner. The middle square of the bottom row is also a barcode plot, but this time it contains two strip charts of level, amateur and professional.

One last observation about this figure. Note that when there is a quantitative and a categorical variable, the two displays of that pair are presented as two different types of graph. Each of those two displays gives, perhaps, a slightly different insight about the relationship. There are a number of options available. For more information about them, type **?ggpairs**.

The gpairs() function shown in the code that follows gives a similar overview of the pairwise comparisons but introduces one additional type of plot, the *mosaic plot*. Chapter 20 is devoted to this type of plot, so I will not discuss it here. After you have read about the mosaic plot, it might be worth your time to come back to this example and compare Figure 16-8 and Figure 16-9 again. The code to produce Figure 16-9 is:

```
# Figure 16-9
install.packages("gpairs") # if not already installed
library(gpairs)
gpairs(Nimrod[,2:4])
```

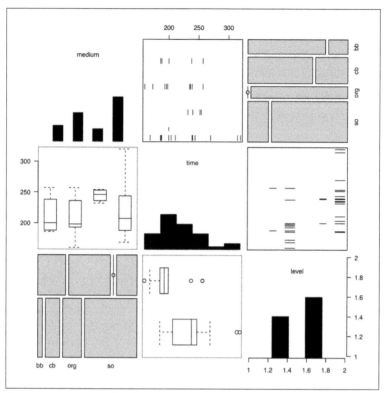

Figure 16-9. Generalized pairs matrix, for data with mixed quantitative and categorical variables. This was produced by using gpairs() in the gpairs package.

Look closely at Figure 16-9. The diagonal mixes the bar plot and the histogram. Which is which? Why? If you are not sure, review Chapter 7 and Chapter 9. To see the options available for gpairs(), type **?** **gpairs**.

Exercise 16-1

Use the tools introduced in this chapter to study the Ginzberg data from the car package—just the first three variables. Do you find some interesting relationships? Are they linear?

# CHAPTER 17

Three-Dimensional Plots

3D Scatter plots

The trees dataset has three quantitative variables. We looked at the distribution of one of them, Volume, in a strip chart and the relationship of two of them, Height and Girth, in a scatter plot. It is possible to visualize all three at once in an extension of the scatter plot, a graph commonly called a *3D scatter plot*. Several packages have functions to create 3D scatter plots, including lattice, scatter plot3d, rgl, plot3D, car, and probably others.

In this section, the scatterplot3d package is emphasized because its syntax is very much like that of the plot() function in base R. It is also relatively easy to work with and quite versatile. Finally, many of the tricks that you can use to make 3D plots comprehensible are easily demonstrated with this package. A couple of other functions will also be introduced and compared.

The scatterplot3d() function has a basic syntax of either:

```
scatterplot3d(x, optional arguments)
```

where x is a data frame or matrix,

or:

```
scatterplot3d(x, y, z, optional arguments)
```

where x, y, and z are vectors.

Although the first option is usually more convenient, the second is often preferable because it gives you the ability to decide upon the order of the variables or to select a subset of variables. Variable *x* is plotted on the horizontal axis, *y* on the diagonal axis, and *z* on the vertical axis. In the example script that follows, *x*, *y*, and *z* are Height, Girth, and Volume.

```
# script for Figure 17-1
library(scatterplot3d)
attach(trees)
par(mfrow = c(2,2),
  cex.main = .9,
  las = 1)

scatterplot3d(Height, Girth, Volume,
  main="a. 3D scatter plot of trees data")
# you could substitute: scatterplot3d(trees)
# to see what happens...

scatterplot3d(Height,Girth,Volume,
  pch = 16,
  highlight.3d = T,
  main = "b. 3D scatter plot with highlighting",
  cex.axis = .5)

scatterplot3d(Height,Girth,Volume,
  pch = 16,
  highlight.3d = T,
  type = "h",
  main = "c. 3D scatter plot with lines and highlighting",
  cex.axis = .5)

scatterplot3d(Height, Girth, Volume,
  pch = 15, type = "h",
  lwd = 5,
  color = "cyan4",
  main = "d. 3D bar plot without box",
  box = F,
  cex.axis = .5)
```

Figure 17-2 shows the result of this script.

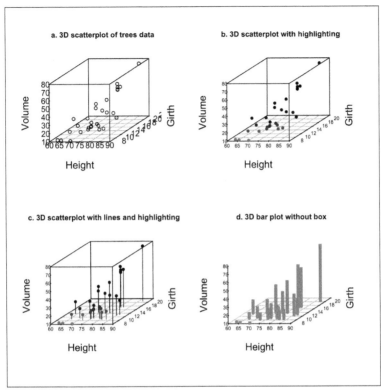

Figure 17-1. The basic scatterplot3d() output and several improvements.

Figure 17-1a shows a basic 3D scatter plot. A grid in the base of the box surrounding the graph helps a little to suggest a three-dimensional space on a two-dimensional surface. It is still pretty difficult to reckon the coordinates of a given point from the picture, however.

Figure 17-1b shows an improvement. Specifying the argument highlight.3d=T adds color to the points in such a way that points "out front" (those with lower *y* values) are bright red and the color becomes darker as the *y* values grow larger. The pch=16 argument fills in the circles and thereby strengthens the color effect a bit.

Figure 17-1c makes a further improvement by adding vertical lines from each point to the grid on the base. This is done by using the type="h" argument, making it much easier to discern the precise *x* and *y* values.

Finally, Figure 17-1d turns the plot with lines into a bar plot by changing the plot characters to squares and increasing the width of the vertical lines to match the width of the squares. The plot characters are changed by using the pch=15 argument and the line width with lwd=5. Finding the right line width often takes some trial and error. The box around the graph was removed by using box=F. Decide for yourself: which of these plots is easiest to read?

Another way to help the viewer make sense of a 3D plot is to place a *reference surface* on the graph. This could be a plane or a curved surface. Figure 17-2 shows one possibility, a prediction plane defined by a linear model. If you do not already know about multiple regression, you can skip this example.

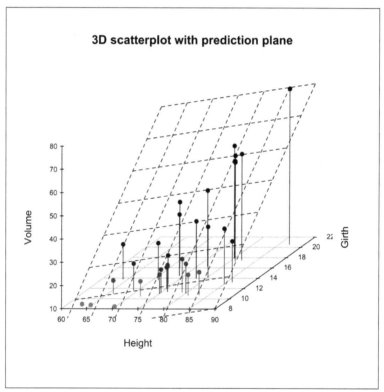

Figure 17-2. A 3D scatter plot with a prediction plane/reference surface, made by using scatterplot3d()

Here is the code to produce Figure 17-2:

```
# Figure 17-2
library(scatterplot3d)
attach(trees)
par(mfrow=c(1,1), las = 1)
# put plot results in an object, sp3
sp3 = scatterplot3d(Height, Girth, Volume, pch = 16,
  highlight.3d = T,
  type = "h",
  main = "3D scatter plot with prediction plane",
  cex.axis = .7,
  box= F)
model = lm(Volume ~ Height  +Girth) # fit linear model, named
  "model" sp3$plane(model)  # draw the plane created by the
                            # model
```

The plot in Figure 17-2 is a little confusing because it is very hard to gauge whether a particular point lies above or below the reference plane. We can generate a better image by using the scatter3d() function in the car package. The graph displayed in Figure 17-3 is similar, but the plane is colored to give it more substance and the points are colored differently depending on whether they lie above or below the plane.

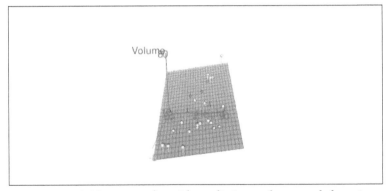

Figure 17-3. A 3D scatter plot with prediction a plane, made by using scatter3d() in the car package.

In contrast to scatterplot3d(), scatter3d() puts *y* on the vertical axis, so to make a graph that can easily be compared to the one produced by scatterplot3d(), you must change the order of the variables. Furthermore, the orientation of the *z* variable is opposite, so the variable Girth has been multiplied by –1 to make the plot comparable to Figure 17-2. This is one of those things that is not clear until you experiment with your code. Following is the code to produce Figure 17-3:

```
# Figure 17-3
library(car)
library(rgl)
attach(trees)
scatter3d(Height, Volume, -1*Girth)
rgl.snapshot("ch17.3.png", fmt = "png") # save to working dir
```

Figure 17-3 is clearly an improvement, but it is still difficult to get a
good view of all the points. One approach to this problem is to look
at the plot from a different angle, which you can accomplish easily
by changing the order of the variables, as demonstrated in
Figure 17-4.Even better, by adding the argument revolutions = *n*,
as shown in the code that follows, we can make the graph spin
around *n* times on the screen, enabling a good view from all sides.
Try it!

```
# Figure 17-4
library(car)
library(rgl)
attach(trees)

scatter3d(Girth, Volume, Height, revolutions = 2)
rgl.snapshot("ch17.4.png", fmt = "png") # save to working dir
```

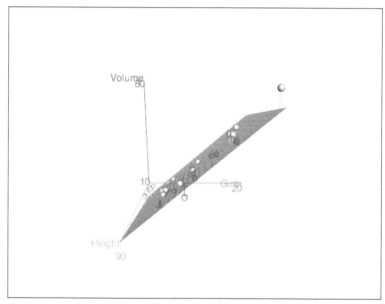

*Figure 17-4. The plot from Figure 17-3, but viewed from a different
angle. The revolutions = 2 argument makes it spin around twice on the
screen.*

There are many options to customize `scatter3d()`, such as colors, lines on the surface grid, speed of revolution, and more. For more information, type **?scatter3d**.

False Color Plots

3D scatter plots represent three dimensions as horizontal, vertical, and diagonal. This is sometimes successful, but other times it is confusing. A different approach to representing the third dimension is to use gradations in color to give a sense of depth. Called a *false-color plot*, this type of 3D plot is implemented in the `levelplot()` function in the `lattice` package. Figure 17-5 shows an example of such a plot with two variables represented spatially and the third by color intensity. The dataset plotted here is the `coalash` dataset from Gomez and Hazen (1970), found in the `sm` package.

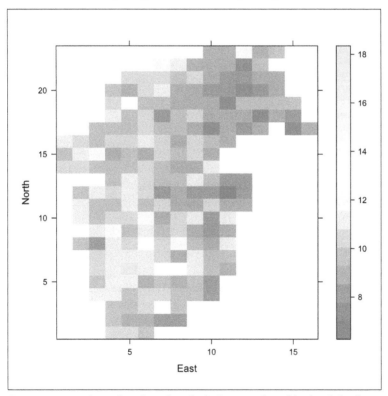

Figure 17-5. False-color plot of coalash data produced by levelplot() in the lattice package. The amount of coal ash, at any point, is represented by color gradient.

The axes represent northerly and easterly directions, whereas the color gradient represents amount of coal ash. It is easy to see how high the concentrations are and the precise locations of each. Following is the code to produce this plot:

```
# Figure 17-5
library(lattice)
library(sm)
data(coalash)
attach(coalash)
levelplot(Percent ~ East*North)
```

Bubble Plots

Yet another way to represent three-dimensional data is the *bubble plot*. In this type of graph, two variables are plotted on the x- and y-axes, and the third variable is represented by the area of the circle, or "bubble," on the plot. The `symbols()` function in base R can create bubble plots, but I find `PlotBubble()`, which you can find in the `DescTools` package, easier to use. Here is its syntax:

```
PlotBubble(x = x-variable, y = y-variable,
    area = var represented by bubble,
    col = bubble color,
    border = color of bubble border,
    inches = diameter of largest bubble)
```

The arguments x, y, area, and col are all required. Note that, because the area of a circle is proportional to the square of the radius, it is necessary to make the `area` variable proportional to the *square root* of the variable represented by the bubble. Otherwise, the larger bubbles will be too big, relative to the smaller ones. Another way of thinking about this is that the variable's size should be represented by the bubble's area, not by the bubble's diameter. Fortunately, `PlotBubble()` does this automatically. Had we used `symbols()`, an adjustment to `Volume` would have been necessary. I had to run several problems with each of the two functions and measure the bubbles to convince myself that this is true. You might find it useful to do the same.

First, consider the `trees` data, with `Volume` as the variable represented by the bubbles. The code that follows (for Figure 17-6) shows that `Volume` has been assigned to the `area` argument. The bubble plot of the `trees` data might be a bit clearer than other 3D plots of the same data. This is true because the amount of data is small, and with the inches argument set at an appropriate size, there is relatively little overlap of bubbles (try setting inches at various sizes and see what you get):

```
# Figure 17-6
library(DescTools)
attach(trees)
PlotBubble(x = Height, y = Girth, area = Volume,
  col="steelblue", border = "burlywood",
  inches = .25,
  xlab = "Height", ylab = "Girth",
  main = "Tree volume, proportional to circle area",
  family = "HersheySerif", font.main = 4,
  col.main = "maroon")
```

Figure 17-6 shows the bubble plot created by this script.

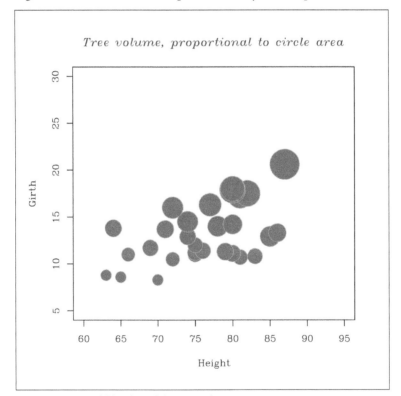

Figure 17-6. Bubble plot of the trees data.

To illustrate another use of the bubble plot we'll consider a much larger dataset, ex0923 from the Sleuth3 package. The data is taken from a study of male and female incomes, accounting for amount of education and IQ. Our goal is to produce a plot that shows the three quantitative variables, Educ, AFQT, and Income2005, and distinguishes the points by Gender. That is to say, the plot will show four variables! In PlotBubble(), the argument area operates on Income2005, but this particular dataset presents a problem because a few of the income values are very high—more than half a million dollars. PlotBubble() apparently overadjusts by leaving too much empty space on the graph and pushing all the points together. To correct this, make an adjustment in the data by dividing all the incomes by 1,000. This leaves all the relationships between individual incomes intact but prevents the crowding problem:

```
# Figure 17-7
library(DescTools)
library(Sleuth3)
attach(ex0923)
PlotBubble( x= Educ, y = AFQT, area = Income2005/1000,
  col = SetAlpha(as.numeric(Gender)), border = "burlywood",
  inches = .5, xlab = "Education", ylab = "AFQT test score")
title(main = "Income, proportional to circle area")
legend("left", c("Female","Male"),
  text.col = c(1:2), cex =.9, bty = "n")
```

The argument col = SetAlpha(as.numeric(Gender)) enables the two values of Gender to have different colors. The argument inches = .5 makes the largest bubble a half-inch wide and scales all the others to be the correct size relative to the largest. In the legend() command, the two values of Gender are in alphabetical order, ensuring that the right names are assigned to the colors.

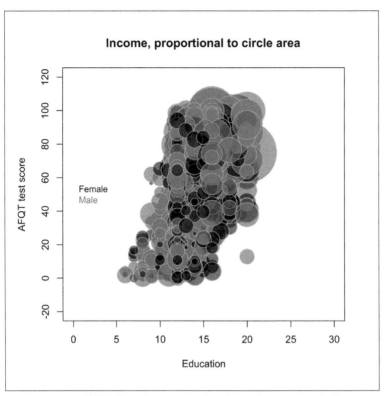

Figure 17-7. Bubble plot of incomes related to education and IQ.

The bubble plot shows that Educ and AFQT are related, but it is difficult to make a determination about income because there are so
many overlapping circles. Making inches larger would make things
worse, whereas making it smaller might help. Try setting inches at
various sizes to see what you get. You probably won't find a value
that helps very much, as bubble plots rarely work well for a large
amount of data. To see what effect sample size has, let's take a random sample of the dataset and make a new bubble plot. We'll pare
the dataset down from more than 2,500 observations to just 100.
Our approach to this problem is to use the sample() function to
pick a random sample of 100 row numbers. After that, we use the [ ]
method (see the section "Basic Scatter Plots" on page 129 to review
this method) to find a subset of the complete dataset, keeping only
the rows from our random sample, but keeping all columns. Note
that the resulting subset is a random sample of the larger dataset,

because the rows in `samp = ex0923[s,]` came from a random sample. Here's the entire script:

```
# Figure 17-8
library(DescTools)
library(Sleuth3)
attach(ex0923)

# take random sample from ex0923
set.seed(3)                  # get the same random sample each time
s = sample(nrow(ex0923), 100) # random sample of 100 row IDs
samp = ex0923[s,]            # all rows in s; all columns in ex0923

detach(ex0923)           # R will not use the full dataset, ex0923
attach(samp)                  # R will use the subset data
PlotBubble( x= Educ, y = AFQT, area = Income2005/1000,
  col = SetAlpha(as.numeric(Gender) +3), border = "burlywood",
  inches = .25, xlab = "Education", ylab = "AFQT test score")
title(main = "Income, proportional to circle area")
legend("left", c("Female","Male"),
  text.col = c(1:2)+3, cex =.9, bty = "n")
```

You can see the result in Figure 17-8.

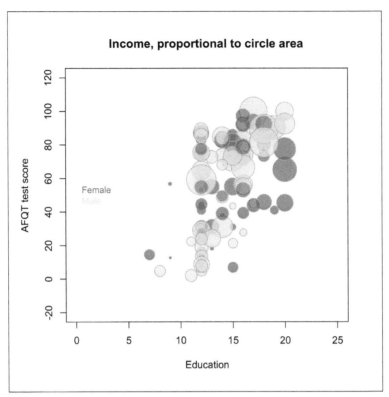

Figure 17-8. Bubble plot relating education, IQ, income, and gender, in a random sample of the ex0923 dataset.

The argument `col = SetAlpha(as.numeric(Gender) +3)` makes the two values of `Gender` have different colors and sets the colors three steps along the color scale that can be seen by issuing the following command(s):

```
> library(DescTools)
> PlotPar()
```

Therefore, instead of using the default colors 1 = black and 2 = red, used in Figure 17-6, the colors are 1+3 = dark blue and 2+3 = light blue. Note that it is also necessary to adjust the `text.col` argument with +3 to make the legend colors match the circles on the plot. There are other color palettes that you could choose, as well. To see other color options, type **?hblue**.

Figure 17-8 is much easier to read than the very dense plot in Figure 17-7. We can clearly see that incomes rise with increasing education and IQ. It is also easy to compare the incomes of males and females. In most cases, when other factors are about equal the bubbles for males are bigger, meaning higher income.

Exercise 17-1

Use 3D scatter plots to examine the relationship between deaths, smoke, and SO2 in the SO2 dataset in the epiDisplay package. Plot deaths on the vertical axis and explain its relationship to the other variables.

Exercise 17-2

Using the same data as in the previous exercise, make deaths the false-color variable in a false-color plot. What do you conclude from the graph?

# CHAPTER 18

Coplots (Conditioning Plots)

The Coplot

Sometimes, the apparent relationship between two variables can be quite misleading. This may well be due to a strong association that one or both variables have to a third variable. Consider the States dataset from the car package. This is data about the SAT exam, a test that many students in the United States take as part of the college admissions process. States also contains several other variables about secondary education on the state level in 1992. Each of the 51 observations in this dataset represents one state, or the District of Columbia. Figure 18-1 shows a scatter plot of average scores on the SATM, the math subtest of the SAT, against the amount of money (in thousands of dollars per student) spent on public education in each state.

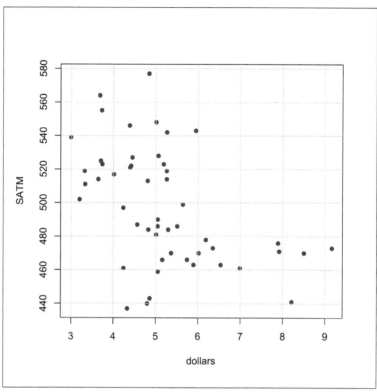

Figure 18-1. A scatter plot of the state average SATM scores and the average amount of state spending on public education, per student, in thousands of dollars. There are 51 points, one for each state and the District of Columbia.

Here is the code to produce Figure 18-1:

```
# Figure 18-1
library(car)
attach(States)
plot(dollars,SATM,
  pch = 16,
  col = "maroon")
grid(lty = "solid")
```

Figure 18-1 seems to indicate that states that spent relatively little on education had high SATM scores, whereas higher-spending states had relatively low scores. This is completely counterintuitive! We would expect—or at least hope—that spending more on education leads to better results. Could it be that some other factor is influencing outcomes?

The dataset includes a variable called `percent`, which is the percentage of graduating seniors who take the SAT. Are test averages different in states where few students take the SAT and those states where most students take the test? Might it be that in states where few take the test, only the higher-performing students are included? Perhaps in states where nearly everyone takes the test, the less talented or less motivated students bring the state average down. We can study this theory with a type of graph called a *conditioning plot*, or *coplot*. The idea is to slice the data into pieces so that we can look at several scatter plots of `SATM` by `dollars`, each at a different value of `percent`, the conditioning variable. If all of the scatter plots look the same, or very similar, this indicates that `percent` did not influence the outcome. If the plots look quite different, however, this shows that `per cent` did influence the relationship between `SATM` and `dollars`. The `coplot()` function takes a formula of the following form:

y ~ x | z

Here, *y* is the vertical axis, *x* is the horizontal axis, and *z* is the conditioning variable. It is also possible to condition with two variables, *a* and *b*, in which case the formula is *y ~ x | a * b*. The following script produces the coplot in Figure 18-2:

```
# Figure 18-2
library(car)
attach(States)
coplot(SATM ~ dollars | percent,
 pch = 16,
 col = "royalblue",
 bar.bg = c(num = "goldenrod2"))
```

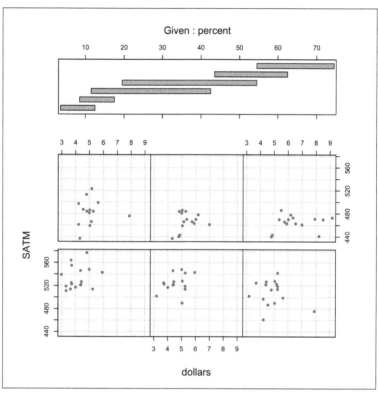

Figure 18-2. Coplot of SATM by dollars with percent as the conditioning variable.

Figure 18-2 shows six scatter plots, each of them for a "slice," or subset, of the data with a particular range of values of percent. The box at the top of the display shows a group of six bars, each bar indicating what range of percents are included in one of the scatter plots. The bar in the lower-left corner indicates that the plot at the lower left includes states with a percent of up to about 12 percent. The next bar up from the bottom shows that the second plot in the lower row includes states with percent scores of about 8 to about 16. The bar at the top of the pile shows that the plot at the upper right includes states with percent scores of about 54 and higher. The coplot seems to be consistent with the hypothesis expressed earlier: states with the smallest percentage of students taking the test had the highest scores, and vice versa. Furthermore, in none of the six plots does there seem to be any notable association between SATM and dollars!

The bars in Figure 18-2 are overlapping. This means that some states are represented in two, or even three, plots. R does this by default to ensure that there are sufficient points in each plot to make a useful graph. Notice that there are about 15 to 17 points in each plot. If each of the plots were to be nonoverlapping, there would only be about 8 or 9 points in each (51 divided by 6), or possibly a few more or less depending on just where the cut points were. In this case, the defaults chosen by R seem to have done what we had hoped for, but this might not always be true.

It is possible to control how many slices there will be by using the number argument. You can control how much individual slices overlap by using the overlap argument, as is demonstrated in the following example:

```
# Figure 18-3
library(car)
attach(States)
coplot(SATM ~ dollars | percent,
  pch = 16,
  col = "royalblue",
  bar.bg = c(num = "seagreen"),
  overlap = 0,
  number = 5)
```

As you can see in Figure 18-3, there are only five slices now, and they do not overlap. Notice that R chose where the cut points would be, creating the slices in such a way that the number of points would be about equal in all the plots.

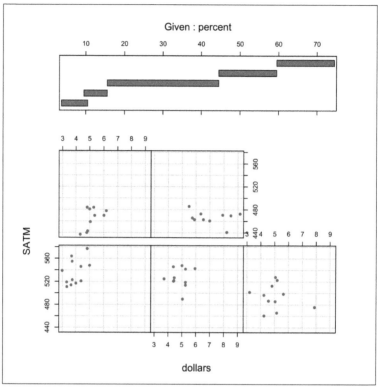

Figure 18-3. Coplot of SATM by dollars with percent as the condition-ing variable. The user specified five slices, with no overlap.

The results in Figure 18-3 still look pretty good, even though we surrendered control of the cut points to R. There might be circum-stances in which we want to pick the exact cut points without avail-ing ourselves of R's sage wisdom, though. It is possible, but it takes a little bit of effort. Suppose that we want to have four nonoverlapping plots and to pick the precise cut points. We need to create a matrix with four rows, one for each plot. Each row will have two numbers: the lowest percent in the plot and the highest. The name of the matrix will be supplied to the given.values argument. The matrix will look like this:

```
 0   19.9
20   39.9
40   59.9
60   75
```

For more information about creating a matrix, type **?matrix**.

Figure 18-4 has four slices with exactly equal widths of percent (except the highest one), but very different numbers of points in each plot. The script to create it follows:

```
# Figure 18-4
library(car)
attach(States)
mat = matrix(c(0,19.9,20,39.9,40,59.9,60,75),
  byrow = T,
  nrow = 4,
  ncol = 2)
coplot(SATM ~ dollars |percent,
  pch = 16,
  col = "royalblue",
  bar.bg = c(num = "maroon"),
  given.values = mat)
```

Figure 18-4 shows you the results.

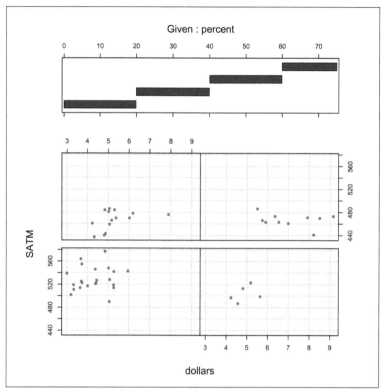

Figure 18-4. Coplot of SATM by dollars with percent as the conditioning variable. The user has specified four slices with precise cut points.

The extent of the relationship of percent with SATM is still so strong that our conclusion is unchanged. In this case, there were no fewer than five points in a panel. However, there could be instances where one or more panels contain zero, one, or two points, making those panels of little value or difficult to interpret. Thus, R defaults to the overlapping bars we saw in Figure 18-2, thereby avoiding empty or nearly empty panels. We always have the option to create a coplot with panels that do not overlap. When given a sufficiently large number of points, this will often be easier to interpret.

Exercise 18-1

Does pollution kill? Examine the relationship between mortality and air pollution in the ex1123 dataset from the Sleuth2 package. Could other factors explain the apparent connection?

# CHAPTER 19

Clustering: Dendrograms and Heat Maps

Clustering

Clustering refers to a number of related methods for exploring multivariate data. There are dozens of clustering functions available in R. We will focus on just one of them in this chapter: the hclust() function in base R. This function performs *hierarchical clustering*, which is one of the most commonly used clustering techniques and will be a good introduction to clustering in general. The idea is to put observations into clusters, or groups, in which the members of a single cluster are similar to each other and different from observations in other clusters. Further, a particular cluster may be judged to be similar, in varying degrees, to other clusters. We will use a graph called the *dendrogram*—which looks like an inverted tree—to understand the relationships of clusters to one another. Figure 19-2, later in this chapter, presents an example of a dendrogram.)

Consider the mtcars dataset from *Motor Trend Magazine*'s 1974 report on the characteristics of a number of new models for that year. Let's take a look at the first six rows of this dataset by using the head() function:

```
> head(mtcars)
                   mpg cyl disp  hp drat    wt  qsec vs am
Mazda RX4         21.0   6  160 110 3.90 2.620 16.46  0  1
Mazda RX4 Wag     21.0   6  160 110 3.90 2.875 17.02  0  1
Datsun 710        22.8   4  108  93 3.85 2.320 18.61  1  1
Hornet 4 Drive    21.4   6  258 110 3.08 3.215 19.44  1  0
Hornet Sportabout 18.7   8  360 175 3.15 3.440 17.02  0  0
Valiant           18.1   6  225 105 2.76 3.460 20.22  1  0
                  gear carb
Mazda RX4            4    4
Mazda RX4 Wag        4    4
Datsun 710           4    1
Hornet 4 Drive       3    1
Hornet Sportabout    3    2
Valiant              3    1
```

We would like to put the various models into clusters, such that similar cars are in the same cluster. There are two ways to do this. The *agglomerative* method begins by making a cluster of the most closely matched pair, then making a cluster of the next most closely matched of either a pair of single observations or a pair of a single observation and an existing cluster, and so on, until all the observations are in one big cluster. The other approach, the *divisive method*, breaks the total group into subgroups, those subgroups into further subgroups, and so on. The hclust() function uses agglomeration, but there are several methods available. We will use the default method, "complete."

How should we measure the similarity, or distance, between two observations? This involves finding a measure—combining all the available information—to determine the "distance" between one car model and another. If we had only one variable to consider, the absolute difference between the values of that variable for each car model would be the obvious choice. In our example, however, there are 11 variables, so we would like to have a distance measure that takes all 11 into account. Let's begin with a simpler example. Suppose that there are two cars, Car-1 and Car-2, each with measurements on two variables, x and y. So, Car-1 is a point $(x1,y1)$ and Car-2 is a point $(x2,y2)$. These two points are represented in the graph in the upper left of Figure 19-1. The shortest distance between the points is displayed by the solid line in Figure 19-1, in the graph in the upper-right corner.

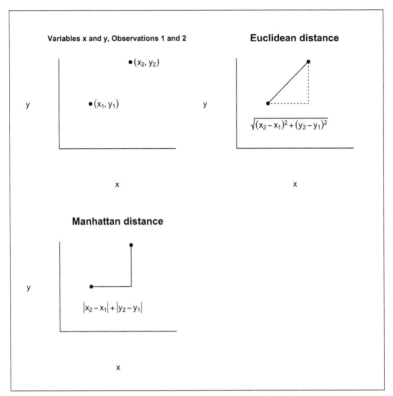

Figure 19-1. Measuring distances in two-dimensional space.

Note that this line is the hypotenuse of a right triangle, so it is easy to calculate the distance:

```
distance = sqrt[(x2 - x1)^2 + (y2 - y1)^2]
```

Remember that the square of the hypotenuse equals the sum of the squares of the two sides. This distance, "as the crow flies," is called the *Euclidean distance*; it is the default distance measure used by the `dist()` function in R. There are several other ways to measure distance. One of them is shown in the graph in the lower left of Figure 19-1. This is the *Manhattan* option, also called "taxi cab" or "city block" distance. Depending on the particular problem you are solving, this measure might be more appropriate. R makes this option available as well as several others, but we will stick with Euclidean distance for this problem. If there are three variables, you can extend the Euclidean method as follows:

```
Euclidean distance = sqrt[(x2 - x1)^2 + (y2 - y1)^2 +
    (z2 - z1)^2]
```

Likewise, you can extend the measure to as many variables as
needed.

Putting Mathematical Expressions in Graphs

There are times when a mathematical formula or expression greatly
enhances a graph. Fortunately, R accommodates adding such
expressions by using expression as an argument to any of the
functions text(), mtext(), axis(), and legend(). The following
script produced Figure 19-1 with mathematical expressions in the
text() commands:

```
# script for Figure 19-1
par(mfrow = c(2,2))
x = c(2,5)
y = c(3,6)
yp = c(0,6)
xp = c(0,8)

plot(x,y, pch = 16, xlim = xp, ylim = yp,
    xaxt ="n", yaxt = "n", bty ="l",
    main="Variables x and y, Observations 1 and 2",
    cex.main = .9,
    ylab = "")
text(x = 3.2, y = 3,
    labels = expression(group("(", list(x[1], y[1]), ")")))
text(x = 6.2, y = 6,
    labels = expression(group("(", list(x[2], y[2]), ")")))
mtext(text = "y",
    side = 2, las = 1,
    cex = .8, line = 3)
plot(x, y, pch = 16, type = "o", xlim = xp, ylim = yp,
    main = "Euclidean distance",
    xaxt = "n", yaxt = "n", bty = "l", ylab = "")
text(3.6, 1.5, labels =
    expression(sqrt((x[2] - x[1])^2 + (y[2] - y[1])^2)))
lines(x, y, type = "s", lty = "dotted")
mtext(text = "y", side = 2, las = 1, cex = .8, line = 3)

plot(x,y,
    pch = 16, xlim = xp, ylim = yp,
    main = "Manhattan distance",
    xaxt = "n", yaxt = "n", bty = "l", ylab = "")
lines(x,y,type="s" )
text(3.6, 1.5,
    labels = expression(group("|", x[2] - x[1],"|") +
```

```
        group("|",y[2] - y [1],"|")))
      mtext(text = "y", side = 2, las = 1,cex = .8, line = 3)
```

For usage details, refer to the plotmath help file.

Notice that the values of the variables in mtcars vary widely. For example, disp has values well in excess of 100, but cyl is all in single digits. This means that disp will play a much more important role in determining the distance than cyl will, if only because of the scale on which it is measured. Imagine that two variables were measurements of length but one was expressed in inches, whereas the other was in feet. The exact same distance would be noted in very different numbers, giving the one with a higher number more influence on the Euclidean distance. For this reason, it makes sense to convert all the variables to a comparable measurement scale.

We can *normalize* (or "standardize") the data by applying a simple transformation. We will make each variable have a mean of 0 and a standard deviation of 1. Let's try this with mpg. First get the mean and standard deviation of mpg:

```
> mean(mpg)
[1] 20.09062
> sd(mpg)
[1] 6.026948
```

If we subtract the mean from each value of mpg and divide that by the standard deviation, we will have an mpg variable that has a mean of 0 and standard deviation of 1:

```
> mpg2 = (mpg - 20.09)/6.026948
> mean(mpg2)
[1] 0.0001037009       # tiny round-off error!
> sd(mpg2)
[1] 1
```

This kind of process of normalization happens so frequently that R provides a function that makes it a one-step operation:

```
> mpg3 = scale(mpg)
> mean(mpg3)
[1] 7.112366e-17   #tiny, tiny; for all practical purposes = 0
> sd(mpg3)
[1] 1
```

Fortunately, we do not need to scale each variable: we can do an entire matrix at once. Let's now convert the data frame to a matrix, make the distance measurements on a scaled matrix, compute the clusters, and plot the dendrogram:

```
# Figure 19-2
attach(mtcars)
cars = as.matrix(mtcars)  # convert to matrix- dist requires it
h = dist(scale(cars)) # scale cars matrix & compute dist matrix
h2 = hclust(h)                  # compute clusters
plot(h2)                # plot dendrogram
```

The dendrogram in Figure 19-2 shows the results of the clustering procedure.

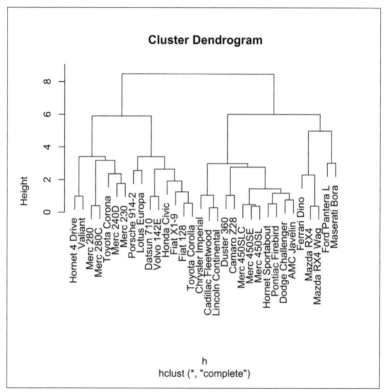

Figure 19-2. Dendrogram of clusters in mtcars dataset.

The vertical scale, called "Height," will help us to understand what has happened. The figures that look rather like staples connect observations in the same cluster. The lower down on the Height scale the horizontal part of the staple is, the earlier that cluster was formed. Thus, the staples that have a Height near zero were the first ones formed and therefore are the closest in Euclidean distance.

Conversely, clusters with a Height of close to eight were among the last formed and thus are relatively far apart. Clusters that are next to each other are not necessarily close! For example, look at the right-hand side of the graph. The two Mazda models are very close, having formed a cluster at a height of about 1. The Ford Pantera, which is next to the Mazda cluster, is not especially close to the Mazdas, because it did not become part of a cluster with them until a height of about 5.

It is also possible to cluster the variables, rather than the observations, by *transposing* the cars matrix; that is, making the first row become the first column, the first column become the first row, and so on:

```
newcars = t(cars)  # newcars is the transpose of cars
h = dist(scale(newcars))
h2 = hclust(h)
plot(h2)
```

Heat Maps

Another way to get an overview of all the numbers in the mtcars dataset is to look at a *heat map*. In this kind of visualization, every number in the standardized matrix is transformed into a colored rectangle. This is done in a systematic way so that a color represents the approximate value, or intensity, of the number. For instance, one possible range of colors we might use runs from dark red for very low numbers, through ever lighter shades of red, orange, yellow, and finally white as the numbers become higher. This range of colors is the default for the image() function, but many other color sets are possible. A simple heat map on scaled values in the mtcars dataset appears in Figure 19-3. The code that produced it follows:

```
# Figure 19-3
attach(mtcars)
cars = as.matrix(mtcars)
image(scale(cars))    # simple heat map
```

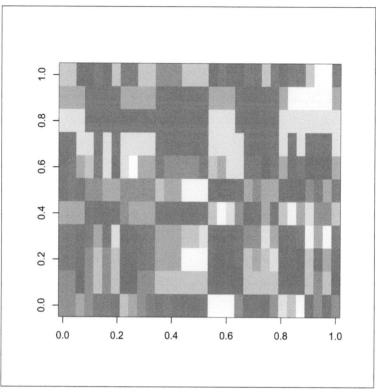

Figure 19-3. Heat map of mtcars dataset in default colors

The col = rainbow() argument controls the color range in the image() function. Another reasonable color scheme is a range of blues, from very dark to very light. The following command shows how to invoke the blue range of colors:

```
# Figure 19-4
image(scale(cars), col = rainbow(256, start = .5, end = .6))
# heat map with range of blues
```

The result appears in Figure 19-4.

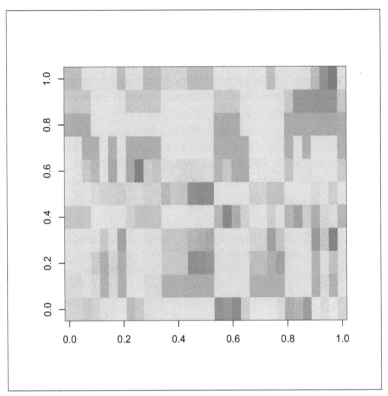

Figure 19-4. Heat map of mtcars dataset in a range of blue colors.

Not all color sets are easily interpreted. If you used all possible colors, it would be difficult to know whether, for instance, dark green was more positive or more negative than dark blue. The color schemes in Figure 19-3 and Figure 19-4, however, are relatively easy for most people to grasp. Each of the values start and end in the rainbow argument must be 0 or larger but no larger than 1, and the two values must be different. You might experiment with different values and see if you find a combination that works as well for you as the two demonstrated here. For more information, type **?rain bow**.

The heat map in Figure 19-3 (also Figure 19-4) is turned on its side, as if the data matrix fell to the left. If you count, you can find 11 rows and 32 columns, instead of the 11 columns and 32 rows in the original dataset. Even though the colors show a wide range of values, with many dark red (low) values and some pale yellow and white (high) values, there does not seem to be any obvious pattern in the graph.

We would like to find patterns in the data, just as we did with the cluster analysis. It is actually possible to combine the dendrogram and the heat map into one visual display to aid in understanding the relationships among the variables and particular car models. The heatmap() function can both perform clustering and make a heat map at the same time. Rows and/or columns are reordered to put like items together, and cells are colored appropriately. The command that follows produced Figure 19-5, using the default options:

```
> heatmap(scale(cars))  # Figure 19-5
```

 See the help file for more information about the many options available, such as whether to include a row and/or column dendrogram, methods for measuring distances, how to weight rows and columns, and more.

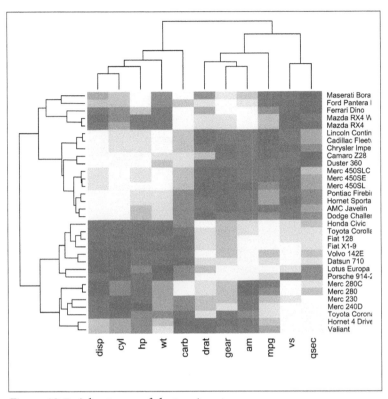

Figure 19-5. A heat map of clusters in mtcars

You can see some striking patterns in Figure 19-5. Notice how the colors set off some groups of car models from others. Compare those clusters to the ones indicated by the dendrogram on the left-hand side. We can see not only that certain models are in the same clusters, but that models within clusters—especially in the ones that were among the earliest formed—have similar color patterns among the variables.

A similar heat map is shown in Figure 19-6.

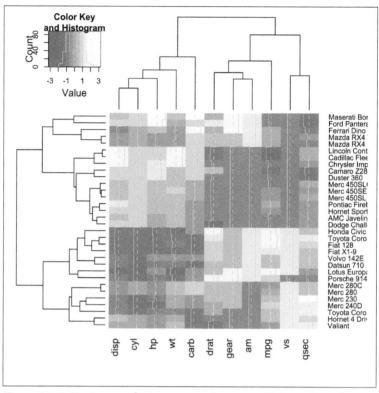

Figure 19-6. Heat map of mtcars, using heatmap.2() from the gplots package.

Figure 19-6 was made by using the function heatmap.2() from the gplots package. There are a couple of extra features provided by heatmap.2() that make interpretation of the map a bit easier. First, there is a key in the upper-left corner that shows the relation of the colors to variable values. Second, there is a system of vertical lines running through each of the columns. The dotted line represents the value 0. The solid line shows how much the value in a particular cell varies, positively or negatively, from 0. This reinforces the key, giving a confirmation in each cell. The code to produce this figure follows:

```
# Figure 19-6
library(gplots)
heatmap.2(scale(cars))
```

Clustering is not an exact science; rather, it is a way of searching for order in complex data. Clustering algorithms, dendrograms, and heat maps are tools we use in that search. Like other tools, they can help us reach our goals, or they can scrape, cut, or burn, if we are not careful! The foregoing discussion is far from a complete explanation of clustering, but more of a teaser, perhaps inspiring you to go ahead and learn more. There are many other clustering and heat map functions provided in R.

Exercise 19-1

Create a new dendrogram for the mtcars data by using a different agglomerative method. Use the help function (?hclust) to see what methods are available. How different are the results? The alternate methods will not necessarily give the same answers. You might find one method works very well on one problem, but not well on another problem. Furthermore, you can try a different method of measuring distance. Type ?dist to see the methods available.

Exercise 19-2

Make alternate heat maps of the mtcars data by using each of these color schemes:

```
heat.colors
cm.colors
terrain.colors
topo.colors
rainbow.colors
```

Are some easier to read than others? Which ones do you think you will continue to use? Are there any that you will not use?

Exercise 19-3

Recall that the airquality dataset we examined in Chapter 1 had a number of missing values. The missmap() function in the Amelia package uses a simple type of heat map to look for missing values. Install and load Amelia and find the missing values in airquality. In what way is this heat map simpler than the ones discussed in this chapter? How does this graphic help you to understand the dataset? Compare it to the output provided by the missiogram() function in the epade package.

# CHAPTER 20

Mosaic Plots

Graphing Categorical Data

Most of the graphs we have studied so far have been of quantitative variables. In a few cases, we have mixed quantitative and categorical variables, usually by making the distinct values of the categorical variable(s) define groups, each one having its own graph. Sometimes, however, all of the variables of interest are categorical. This requires special graphical methods.

Let's consider a dataset in the epiDisplay package. You will need to install this package, as well as vcd, which includes some functions for working with categorical variables. Here's how to do that:

```
> install.packages("epiDisplay")
> install.packages("vcd")
> library(epiDisplay)
> library(vcd)
```

We will be looking at the ANCdata dataset. You'll need to get some information about this dataset:

```
> ?ANCdata
```

This data is from a study of the types of care given to women with high-risk pregnancies in two clinics. There are three variables, all categorical, and each has only two values, or levels. We would like to know if perinatal mortality (i.e., a stillborn fetus or death of newborn within seven days) is related to the type of treatment or the clinic in which care was received. Let's first look at the relationship between death and anc (treatment). The table() command shown in the following script will count the number of observations in each combination of the two variables:

```
# Table 20-1
library(epiDisplay)
library(vcd)
attach(ANCdata)
xtab1 = table(death,anc)   # make this table an object, "xtab1"
xtab1    # show the values in xtab1
```

Table 20-1. Frequencies of expectant mothers by treatment and infant mortality

```
       anc
death old new
   no  373 316
  yes   46  20
```

This table shows that of the women receiving the "old" treatment, 373 of their babies survived and 46 died. Of those women receiving the "new" treatment, 20 lost their babies and 316 did not. This is a small table, yet it might take a little while to process mentally. Which treatment had better results? The answer might be more obvious with a visual presentation of this summarized data. We will use a *mosaic plot*, which represents the number in each *cell* (each count) by the size of the area of a rectangle. Notice that the following `mosaic()` command takes information from the table in the object `xtab1`:

```
> mosaic(xtab1) # command operates on table, not original cases
```

Alternatively, the `mosaic()` command can take an argument as a *formula*. So, the following two commands are equivalent:

```
> mosaic(xtab1)
> mosaic(~death+anc)
```

The entire set of commands to produce Figure 20-1 includes the following:

```
# Figure 20-1
library(epiDisplay)
library(vcd)
attach(ANCdata)
xtab1 = table(death,anc)
mosaic(xtab1)    # or mosaic(~death+anc)
```

What if the Only Data I Have Is a Table of Frequencies?

An article in a scientific journal, report, or presentation might give a table of frequencies, similar to the one we've produced for the ANCdata dataset (Table 20-1). Perhaps you want to continue the analysis, but do not have access to the original data. Do not despair! Create a short script, including the frequency data, and you can produce all the graphs in this chapter, plus more. This involves creating a type of data structure we have not yet discussed: an *array*. Here is the basic form of the array() command:

array(*data*, dim = length(*data*), *dimnames* = list())

Here, *data* is a vector, *dim* is a vector of table dimensions, and *dim names* gives the names of the possible variable outcomes. To create Table 20-1, we could use a command like this:

```
xtab1 = array(c(373, 46, 316, 20), c(2,2),
   list(c("no", "yes"), c("old", "new")))
```

The object, xtab1, is essentially the same as the xtab1 produced by table(). Alternatively, you can use the following equivalent, in a script, which breaks the long array() command into smaller pieces (which some people find easier to read):

```
# enter table of ANC frequencies, rather than read ANCdata
# two-way table - data from Table 20-1
library(vcd)
counts = c(373, 46, 316, 20)  # enter 1st col, 2nd col
death = c("no", "yes")
anc = c("old", "new")
xtab1 = array(counts, c(2,2), list(death, anc))
names(dimnames(xtab1))  = c("death", "anc")
xtab1            # prints Table 20-1
mosaic(xtab1)    # produces Figure 20-1

# three-way table - data from Table 20-2
library(vcd)
cnts = c(176, 197, 12, 34, 293, 23, 16, 4)
clinic = c("A", "B")
death = c("no", "yes")
anc = c("old", "new")
xtab2 = array(cnts, c(2,2,2), list(clinic, death, anc))
names(dimnames(xtab2)) = c("clinic", "death", "anc")
xtab2          # Table 20-2
mosaic(xtab2)  # Figure 20-2
# use appropriate mosaic() command for any other plot in
# chapter
```

The plot in Figure 20-1 shows slightly more women received the old treatment, because the block under "old" is bigger than that under "new." Deaths among those receiving the old treatment are disproportionately high. Notice that the "yes" rectangle under the "old" treatment column extends under the "new" treatment column, and not by just a little bit. This shows that the two variables, death and anc, are *associated* or *correlated*; that is, the proportion of deaths in the old treatment group is greater than the proportion of deaths in the new treatment group. As we have pointed out earlier, however, correlation does not prove causation. It makes sense to look at the other variable we have available to see if there might be a more complex relationship among all the variables.

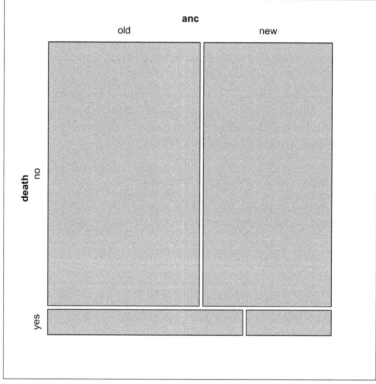

Figure 20-1. Mosaic plot of death by anc (treatment).

Mosaic plots are helpful for examining two categorical variables but will illuminate even more when studying three variables. Next, we'll create the three-way table so that we can examine the frequencies and then make the frequencies into a mosaic plot:

```
# Table 20-2
xtab2 = table(clinic,death,anc)
xtab2 # produces the following table
```

Table 20-2. Frequencies of patients by treatment and mortality and clinic

```
, , anc = old

       death
clinic  no yes
     A 176  12
     B 197  34

, , anc = new

       death
clinic  no yes
     A 293  16
     B  23   4
```

Running the following code produces Figure 20-2:

```
# Figure 20-2
xtab2 = table(clinic,death,anc)
mosaic(xtab2)
```

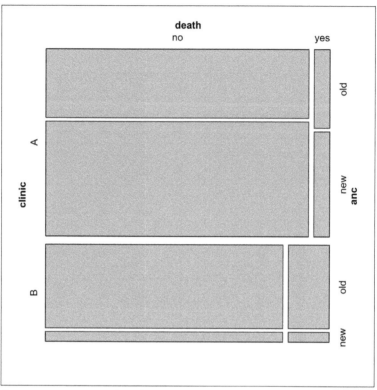

Figure 20-2. Mosaic plot of clinic,death,anc.

Figure 20-2 shows some quite interesting relationships. First, the plot is broken into an upper part, representing clinic A, and a lower part, representing clinic B. Take a look at each part separately for a moment. The relationship we saw in the two-way table (Figure 20-1) between treatment type and deaths still exists in clinic A, but not in clinic B. Considering the entire plot, it is quite striking that the death rate is much higher in clinic B, as a whole, than in clinic A. Also worth noting is that, whereas more women in clinic A received the new treatment, in clinic B patients overwhelmingly received the old treatment.

There are several ways that we can modify the plot to make certain relationships stand out. For instance, suppose that we wanted to highlight the fact that the distribution of treatments was far different in the two clinics. We could add one more argument to the mosaic() command:

```
# Figure 20-3
# make treatment groups (anc) obvious
mosaic(xtab2, highlighting = "anc")
```

This returns Figure 20-3.

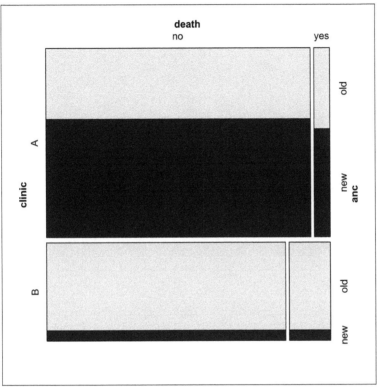

Figure 20-3. Mosaic plot of clinic,death,anc, with anc highlighted.

We might also highlight a variable that is considered a *response variable*; in other words, a variable that is the consequence of the condition of the other variables. In this case, the response variable is death. We could add a vector of colors as well to make the plot more interesting (you may well find that the relationships are more striking when the tiles are in contrasting colors):

```
# Figure 20-4
mosaic(table(clinic,anc,death),
  highlighting = 'death',
  highlighting_fill = c('royal blue', 'gold'))
```

Figure 20-4 shows the results.

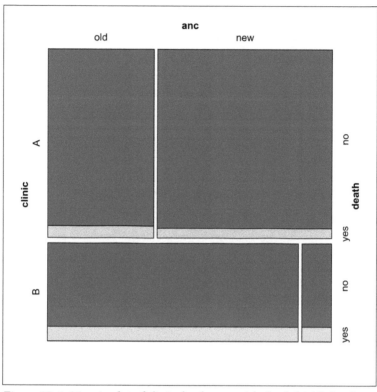

Figure 20-4. Mosaic plot of clinic,death,anc, with death highlighted and color added.

Sometimes changing the orientation of the table can make certain associations stand out or be hidden. Try highlighting a different variable and see how it might change the ease of interpreting the outcome:

```
# Figure 20-5
mosaic(table(death,anc,clinic),
   highlighting = 'clinic',
   highlighting_fill = c('royal blue', 'gold'))
```

Figure 20-5 shows the results.

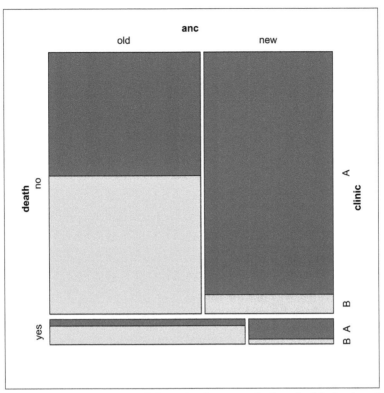

Figure 20-5. Mosaic plot of clinic,death,anc, with clinic highlighted and color added.

Another approach to interpretation of the mosaic plot is a *residual analysis*. If there is no association between the variables in the table —that is to say, the variables are *independent*—we would expect that the cells would be of a certain number. The differences between the actual frequencies in the table and the expected values are called *residuals*. The following shows the process of calculating expected values for the two-way table:

Table 20-3. Actual values from Table 20-1 and calculated totals, expected values, and residuals

```
        anc
death old new        Totals
  no   373 316       689 = 91.3% of 755
  yes  46  20        66  =  8.7% of 755

Expected values
      old                   new
no    382.5 (91.3% of 419)  306.6 (91.3% of 336)
yes   36.5 (8.7% of 419)    29.4  (8.7% of 336)

Residuals
      old                   new
no    373 - 382.5 = -9.5    316 - 306.6 = 9.4
yes   46 - 36.5  = 9.5      20 - 29.4  = -9.4
```

The idea is the same for the three-way table, but we will not do the calculation here, because it is a little messier and it is not necessary for our purposes. The mosaic plot can use the information about residuals to show us where the discrepancies between the actual frequencies and the expected frequencies (under the assumption of independence) are. To get the residual plot, add the argument shade=TRUE to the mosaic() command. To have an explanation of the meaning of the various colors and shades on the graph, add the argument legend=TRUE:

```
# Figure 20-6
mosaic(xtab2, shade = TRUE, legend=TRUE)
```

You can see the resulting plot in Figure 20-6. The blue-colored tiles represent cells that have large positive residuals, whereas the red tiles represent cells that have large negative residuals. The gray tiles indicate that the corresponding cells were close to their expected values. If you compare the four tiles in clinic A to their corresponding tiles in clinic B, you will see a pattern of stark differences between the two clinics.

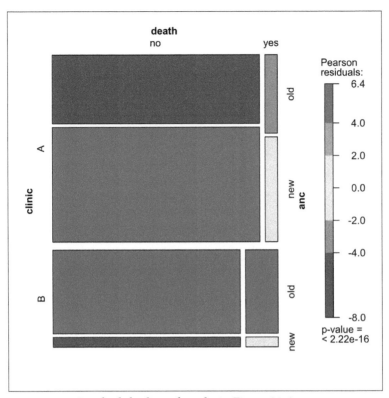

Figure 20-6. Residual shading of results in Figure 20-3.

Exercise 20-1

The well-known tragic sinking of the *Titanic* has been the topic of much study. A dataset concerning the characteristics of survivors and nonsurvivors comes with the base R installation and is called, appropriately, Titanic. Use the mosaic plot technique to determine which factors are related to survival. When you are done, search the Internet to find at least two other analyses of this same dataset to which you can compare your analysis. It should not be hard to find several other studies.

PART V
What Now?

We have covered a lot of ground, but if you have interesting data to study, you may yet have lots of unanswered questions. Fortunately, this book is not the last word on graphics and R. *Graphing Data with R* has prepared you to move on to more advanced resources, such as the ones introduced in this last section.

CHAPTER 21

Resources for Extending Your Knowledge of Things Graphical and R Fluency

Art is never finished, only abandoned.
—attributed to
Leonardo da Vinci

This book will never be finished, but there comes a time when it should be turned over to those who can benefit from the knowledge accumulated thus far, incomplete though it may be. I am astounded by the ingenuity of the countless people who have devised useful ways to visualize data and by those who have contributed their implementations of graphical methods to R. It would take many more years than I have left to thoroughly describe them all. Long before I could ever finish with the methods presently available, many more will have appeared. Recognizing the futility of completing this quest, I hand the further search for graphical wisdom and R truth over to you.

Having read this book, you now have a basic knowledge of making graphic displays of data by using R. There are many ways to apply your newfound skills, and no doubt you will find outlets for putting these skills to work. It is also very likely that you will encounter problems for which you are, at present, unprepared. Although I hope that you will find this book a handy reference tool that will help you solve many of those problems, there are also a number of excellent materials for further self-study readily available. What follows is far from a comprehensive list, but it includes materials that I have found helpful and feel comfortable recommending to you. For full references, see Appendix A.

R Graphics

The Comprehensive R Archive Network (CRAN) is part of the R Project. CRAN Task Views, at *http://cran.r-project.org/web/views/*, gives an overview of R packages, broken down by categories. If you click Graphics, you will see a general discussion of graphics packages with some mention of specific packages and their strengths as well as links to documentation for many graphics packages. What you will not find here is information about packages that might have some useful graphic features but are not primarily graphics packages. If you have a very specialized interest, take a look at the corresponding category: say, the Survival category if you are interested in survival curves, TimeSeries if you are interested in plotting time-series data, SpacioTemporal if you are interested in geography, and so on.

If you want to delve into the `lattice` package, look at the very readable book by the creator of this package, Sarkar (2008). Likewise, Wickham (2009) is the package creator's approachable book on `ggplot2`. Chang (2013) is a "cookbook" with lots of recipes for making graphs in R, mostly with `ggplot2`. This book is especially appropriate if you know beforehand the basics of R and a bit about various types of graphs—but, of course, now you do!

General Principles of Graphics

Tufte (1983) is probably one of the most cited books on data graphics. The author covers centuries of graphics and deduces a number of principles of effective display. There are many great—and poor—examples from which to learn what makes a good graph.

The books by Cleveland (1985, 1993) are masterworks of clear and logical thought. They do require a bit of math for complete understanding, but will give most readers—even those without advanced math backgrounds—a much better grasp of graphic principles. The graphs look a little plain compared to the colorful displays now possible, but the design of Cleveland's graphs surpasses most others anyway. Much of lattice derives from these two books.

Learning More About R

R is becoming enormously popular, and there are now a large number of books on the market devoted to it. I cannot tell you which is the best, but my favorite for general data analysis with R is Kabacoff (2011). An expanded second edition has just been published, but I have not seen it yet. To get the most out of this book, you should understand basic statistics.

If you want to know more about R as a programming language, see Matloff (2011). You might now know most of what you wanted to learn about graphics. There are, however, lots of issues with data handling, simulations, text strings, and a host of other subjects that you probably cannot imagine yet that Matloff deals with.

Statistics with R

If you did not have any background in statistics before reading this book, you might want to learn something about this subject now. There are several basic textbooks on statistics that incorporate R. One that I can suggest to you is Diez et al. (2012). In keeping with the open source philosophy of R, this book is free and you can download it at www.openintro.org. A paper copy is offered at Amazon for a very low cost. The datasets used in the book are in the open intro package.

There you have it. I believe this book works as a prerequisite to most of the resources discussed in this chapter, which is one of the reasons that I felt it needed to be written. I hope you will find your new expertise in R graphics just what you were looking for.

Exercise 21-1

Here is a real test of how much you have learned: reproduce Figure 1-3.

References

Bland, J. M. and Altman, D. G. 1986. "Statistical methods for assessing agreement between two methods of clinical measurement." *Lancet*, 327(8476) i: 307–10.

Boslaugh, Sarah. 2013. *Statistics in a Nutshell*, 2nd ed. Sebastopol, CA: O'Reilly.

Chang, Winston. 2013. *R Graphics Cookbook*. Sebastopol, CA: O'Reilly.

Cleveland, William S. 1985. *The Elements of Graphing Data*. Monteray, CA: Wadsworth.

———. 1993. *Visualizing Data*. Summit, NJ: Hobart Press.

de Vries, Andrie and Meys, Joris. 2012. *R for Dummies*. Chichester, England: John Wiley & Sons.

Deng, Henry and Wickham, Hadley. 2011. "Density estimation in R." *http://vita.had.co.nz/papers/density-estimation.pdf*.

Diez, David M., Barr, Christopher D., and Çetinkaya-Rundel, Mine. 2012. *OpenIntro Statistics*, 2nd ed. www.openintro.org.

Few, Stephen. 2009. *Now You See It*. Oakland, CA: Analytics Press.

Fox, John. 2005. "The R Commander: A Basic-Statistics Graphical User Interface to R." *Journal of Statistical Software*, 14(9): 1–42.

Gomez, M. and Hazen, K. 1970. "Evaluating sulfur and ash distribution in coal seams by statistical response surface regression analysis." Report RI 7377, US Bureau of Mines, Washington, DC.

Hanneman, S. K. 2008. "Design, Analysis and Interpretation of Method-Comparison Studies." *AACN Advanced Critical Care*, 19(2): 223–34.

Iannaccone, L. R. 1994. "Why Strict Churches Are Strong." *American Journal of Sociology*, 99(5): 1180–211.

James, Gareth, Witten, Daniela, Hastie, Trevor, and Tibshirani, Robert. 2013. *An Introduction to Statistical Learning: with Applications in R*. New York: Springer.

Janert, Philipp K. 2011. *Data Analysis with Open Source Tools*. Sebastopol, CA: O'Reilly.

Kabacoff, Robert I. 2011. *R in Action*. Shelter Island, NY: Manning.

Kleinman, Ken and Horton, Nicholas J. 2014. *SAS and R: Data Management, Statistical Analysis and Graphics*, 2nd ed. Boca Raton, London, New York: CRC Press.

Ligges, U. and Maechler, M. 2003. "3D Scatter plots: an R Package for Visualizing Multivariate Data." *Journal of Statistical Software* 8(11): 1-20.

Matloff, Norman. 2011. *The Art of R Programming*. San Francisco, CA: No Starch Press.

Murrell, Paul. 2011. *R Graphics*, 2nd ed. Boca Raton, FL: Chapman and Hall.

Ramsey, Fred and Schafer, Daniel. 2001. *Statistical Sleuth*, 2nd ed. Pacific Grove, CA: Brooks/Cole.

Sarkar, Deepayan. 2008. *Lattice: Multivariate Data Visualization with R*. New York, NY: Springer.

Tufte, Edward R. 1983. *The Visual Display of Quantitative Information*. Chesire, CT: Graphics Press.

Tukey, John W. 1977. *Exploratory Data Analysis*. Reading, MA: Addison-Wesley.

Wainer, Howard. 1984. "How to Display Data Badly." *American Statistician*, 38(2): 137–47.

Wickham, Hadley. 2009. *ggplot2: Elegant Graphics for Data Analysis.* New York: Springer.

Wilk, M. B. and Gnanadesikan, R. 1968. "Probability plotting methods for the analysis of data," *Biometrika,* 55(1): 1–17.

Wilkinson, Leland and Friendly, Michael. 2009. "The History of the Cluster Heat Map." *American Statistician,* 63(2): 179–84.

Wong, Dona M. 2010. *The Wall Street Journal Guide to Information Graphics.* New York: W. W. Norton.

Yau, Nathan. 2011. *Visualize This.* Indianapolis, IN: John Wiley & Sons.

Yau, Nathan. 2013. *Data Points: Visualization That Means Something.* Indianapolis, IN: John Wiley & Sons.

R Colors

You can obtain a display of 657 named R colors by using the following command:

```
> demo(colors)
```

For a list of the color names, use this command:

```
> colors()
```

The following script produced the color table shown in Figure B-1 (I included it here so that you can reproduce if it you want to print your own copy):

```
# Script to produce color chart
par(col.axis="white",col.lab="white", mar=c(0.1,0.1,0.4,0.1),
  xaxt="n",yaxt="n")

n = c(0:656)  # a number for each color
n2 = (n %%73)  # each color has a number (1 to 73) in its column
cc = t(colors())  # color names
k = (2:9)  # a number for each column
x=rep(c(1),times=73)

for(i in k) {
r = rep(c(i),times=73)
x = (c(x,r))
}

# print, at (x,n2), color rectangle
plot(x,n2,col=cc,pch=15,
xlim=c(0,10),
ylim=c(0,73),
bty="n",
```

```
main="Named colors available in R",cex.main=.65)

x1 = x+ 0.5
text(x1,n2,cc,cex=.4)  # print (at x1,n2), the color name vector
```

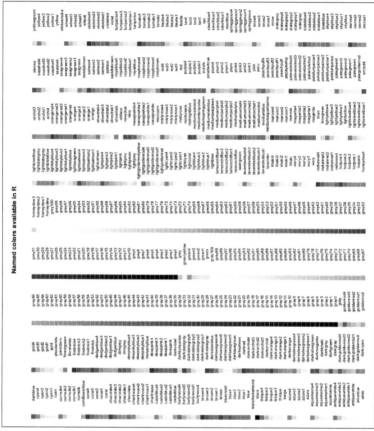

Figure B-1. 657 named colors.

A nice R color chart by Professor Tian Zheng of Columbia University is available on the Internet at *http://www.stat.columbia.edu/~tzheng/files/Rcolor.pdf.*

The R Commander Graphical User Interface

Some people just do not like the command-line interface of R and would prefer to work in a graphical user interface (GUI; a.k.a. point-and-click) environment. If you do not work with R on a regular basis, it can be hard to remember the R commands; or you might find that you make a lot of mistakes when typing, or that it can be painfully slow to make some simple graphs. Using R Commander could make your life a little more pleasant, with the caveat that you will not have access to the full range of R capabilities with the point-and-click interface.

If you want to try R Commander, you first must install it by using the following command:

```
> install.packages("Rcmdr", dependencies=TRUE)
```

After you've installed it, you won't need to do it again, but you must load it during each session for which you want to use it. Here's the command to do that:

```
> library(Rcmdr)
```

The R Commander window appears in Figure C-1. You will probably find that you can produce routine graphs/tables/analyses more quickly by using R Commander, but some highly customized graphs will not be possible. The console will stay open and you can go back and forth between the two windows if you want to use both the GUI and the command-line interface. Alternatively, you can type a command into the R Script window of R Commander and select it. To select a command, click the beginning of the line, drag across the line to the end, and release the mouse button. The line will now be highlighted. Click the Submit button, and R will execute the command.

Figure C-1. The R Commander GUI interface for R.

Try working through the strip chart problems in Chapter 3 using R Commander. At the top of the screen, on the menu bar, click Data. On the menu that opens, choose "Data in packages" and "Read dataset from an attached package." Figure C-2 shows the window that opens, in which you can select the trees data set. Click OK.

Figure C-2. Selecting a dataset in R Commander for analysis with R.

Below the menu bar, you will see that trees is now the active dataset. Continue by selecting "strip chart" from the Graphs window. Compare your result to the first chart in Chapter 3. Next, try to duplicate the second chart, the one that demonstrates jittering. (Hint: after you open the strip chart window, click "options.") You will not be able to replicate the other charts in that chapter by using only the GUI. If you want to produce the third graph, you can submit a command line to R in the R Script window. The easiest way to do this is to edit the command line produced when you made the previous graph. Just add the pch=20 parameter and edit the xlab argument (see Figure C-3). When you have the command the way you want it, select it and then click Submit.

Figure C-3. Using the R Script window to submit a command line to R.

If you like R Commander, try to replicate some other examples from the book with this GUI. In many cases, it will not be hard to figure out what to do if you know how the graph should look. For more complex graphs, you will need to type a command.

It is possible to extend R Commander (i.e., add more commands). You can do this by using a *plug-in*. As I write this, 36 plug-ins are available to be installed, just the way you would install other packages. Most of them add many new commands. It is also possible to write your own. For more information, click Help on the menu bar, or see the R Commander web page at *http://www.rcommander.com*, the author's web page at *http://socserv.mcmaster.ca/jfox/Misc/ Rcmdr/*, or the complete list of R packages at *http://cran.r-project.org/web/packages/available_packages_by_name.html*. Scroll down to the entries that begin with "RcmdrPlugin."

Many of the plug-ins have one or more graphical functions. To see how plug-ins work, install *RcmdrPlugin.HH*. The package HH contains a number of useful graphic functions. The plug-in makes these functions available from R Commander. First, install the package:

```
> install.packages("RcmdrPlugin.HH", dependencies=TRUE)
```

Next, start R Commander:

```
> library(Rcmdr)
```

When the R Commander screen opens, on the menu bar, click Graphs. Get a sense of how many options there are without the plug-in. To load the plug-in, click the Tools option on the Menu bar and select "Load Rcmdr plug-ins." On the menu that follows, select the plug-in name. Now, look at the Graphs option again: you will notice many more choices than before, all in the bottom half of the menu. Some of these add really useful options. For example, the *Scatterplot.HH* plug-in offers much greater control of output (such as type and size of plot character), several kinds of lines to put on the graph, and even the ability to click a point and have it identified.

Several other plug-ins include nice graphic functions, too. Unlike *RcmdrPlug.HH*, some of them will add a new menu to the menu bar. Among the ones that add interesting graphs are *RcmdrPlugin.KMggplot2*, *RcmdrPlugin.NMBU*, *RcmdrPlugin.EZR*, and others.

Packages Used/Referenced

Package	Authors	Description
Amelia	James Honaker Gary King Matthew Blackwell	Program for missing data
aplpack	Hans Peter Wolf Uni Bielefeld	Another Plot PACKage: adds stem.leaf(), bagplot(), faces(), spin3R(), plot summary(), plothulls(), and some slider functions
car	John Fox Sanford Weisberg	Companion to Applied Regression
corrplot	Taiyun Wei	Visualization of a correlation matrix
DescTools	Andri Signorell Other contributors	Tools for descriptive statistics
epade	Andreas Schulz	Easy Plots
epiDisplay	Virasakdi Chongsuvivatwong	Epidemiological calculator
foreign	R Core Team	Read data stored by Minitab, S, SAS, SPSS, Stata, Systat, Weka, dBase...

Package	Authors	Description
GGally	Barret Schloerke Jason Crowley Di Cook Heike Hofmann Hadley Wickham Francois Briatte Moritz Marbach Edwin Thoen	Extension to ggplot2
ggplot2	Hadley Wickham Winston Chang	An implementation of the Grammar of Graphics
gmodels	Gregory R. Warnes other contributors	Various R programming tools for model fitting
gpairs	John W. Emerson Walton A. Green	Produces a generalized pairs (gpairs) plot
gplots	Gregory R. Warnes Ben Bolker Lodewijk Bonebakker Robert Gentleman Wolfgang Huber Andy Liaw Thomas Lumley Martin Maechler Arni Magnusson Steffen Moeller Marc Schwartz Bill Venables	Various R programming tools for plotting data
grid	Paul Murrell	The Grid Graphics Package
hexbin	Dan Carr Other contributors	Hexagonal Binning Routines
HistData	Michael Friendly Stephane Dray Hadley Wickham James Hanley Dennis Murphy	Datasets from the history of statistics and data visualization
Hmisc	Frank E. Harrell Jr, Other contributors	Harrell Miscellaneous
lattice	Deepayan Sarkar	Lattice Graphics
latticeExtra	Deepayan Sarkar Felix Andrews	Extra Graphical Utilities Based on Lattice
multcomp	Torston Hothorn Frank Bretz Peter Westfall Other contributors	Simultaneous Inference in General Parametric Models

Package	Authors	Description
ncdf	David Pierce	Interface to Unidata netCDF data files
nlme	Jose Pinheiro Douglas Bates Other contributors	Linear and Nonlinear Mixed Effects Models
plotrix	Jim Lemon, Ben Bolker, Sander Oom, Eduardo Klein, Barry Rowlingson, Hadley Wickham, Anupam Tyagi, Olivier Eterradossi, Gabor Grothendieck, Michael Toews, John Kane, Rolf Turner, Carl Witthoft, Julian Stander, Thomas Petzoldt, Remko Duursma, Elisa Biancotto, Ofir Levy, Christophe Dutang, Peter Solymos, Robby Engelmann, Michael Hecker, Felix Steinbeck, Hans Borchers, Henrik Singmann, Ted Toal, Derek Ogle	Various plotting functions
psych	William Revelle	Procedures for Psychological, Psychometric, and Personality Research
Quandl	Raymond McTaggart Gergely Daroczi	Quandl Data Connection
Rcmdr	John Fox Milan Bouchet-Valat Other contributors	A platform-independent basic-statistics GUI (graphical user interface) for R, based on the tcltk package
RcmdrMisc	John Fox Other contributors	R Commander Miscellaneous Functions
RcmdrPlugin.EZR	Yoshinobu Kanda	R Commander Plug-in for the EZR (Easy R) Package
RcmdrPlugin.HH	Richard M. Heiberger Contributions from Burt Holland	Rcmdr support for the HH package
RcmdrPlugin.KMggplot2	Triad sou Kengo Nagashima	Rcmdr Plug-in for Kaplan-Meier Plots and Other Plots by Using the ggplot2 Package
RcmdrPlugin.NMBU	Kristian Hovde Liland Solve Sæbø	R Commander Plug-in for Statistics at NMBU

Package	Authors	Description
ResearchMethods	Mohamed Abdolell Sam Stewart	Using GUIs to help teach statistics to non-statistics students
	Hadley Wickham	Flexibly reshape data: a reboot of the reshape package
rgl	Daniel Adler Duncan Murdoch Other contributors	3D Visualization Using OpenGL
scatterplot3d	Uwe Ligges Martin Maechler Sarah Schnackenberg	3D Scatter Plot
RCurl	Duncan Temple Lang	General network (HTTP/FTP/...) client interface for R
Sleuth2	F. L. Ramsey D. W. Schafer Other contributors	Data sets from Ramsey and Schafer (2001)
sm	Adrian Bowman Adelchi Azzalini	Smoothing methods for nonparametric regression and density estimation
vcd	David Meyer Achim Zeileis Kurt Hornik Other contributors	Visualizing Categorical Data
XLConnect	Mirai Solutions GmbH Martin Studer Other contributors	Excel Connector for R
XML	Duncan Temple Lang	Reading and creating XML (and HTML) documents

Importing Data from Outside of R

Some Useful Internet Data Repositories

There are many websites from which you can download datasets and to analyze with R. A few sources are presented in the list that follows, as examples of the vast universe of shared data. In many cases, it is necessary to register to use the datasets and/or agree to terms of use. Carefully read the requirements of any provider from whom you plan to acquire data. Datasets from the following sources are frequently offered in Excel or CSV format, which have already been discussed in the section "Reading from an External File" on page 16; some examples in other formats follow:

Open Access Directory (http://oad.simmons.edu/oadwiki/Main_Page)
This site provides links to downloadable data from many sources on diverse subjects, especially the sciences. Many of the datasets are free; some you must purchase. Scroll down the table of contents to "Data repositories" to see the variety of topics covered.

FedStats (http://fedstats.sites.usa.gov/)
This is a repository of many kinds of United States federal government data freely available to the public. This page has links to various government agencies sharing data.

DATA.GOV (http://catalog.data.gov/dataset)
This is another repository of federal data.

Quandl (http://www.quandl.com)

This is a repository of more than 10 million datasets that are available for free download in several formats, including R data frames. Compared to many other sources, Quandl is easy to work with. Install and load the Quandl package:

```
> install.packages("Quandl")
> library(Quandl)
```

Browse the Quandl web page until you find a file that you want. For example, suppose that you chose the FBI "Crimes by State" file for Pennsylvania at *http://www.quandl.com/FBI_UCR/ USCRIME_STATE_PENNSYLVANIA*. You can load it into an R data frame, penn.crime, with one command:

```
> penn.crime = Quandl("FBI_UCR/USCRIME_STATE_PENNSYLVANIA")
```

Importing Data of Various Types into R

R can read data in many different formats. Importing data from some of the most important ones is discussed in this section.

CSV

Our first example is a simple CSV file from the National Science Foundation. Note that it looks very much like the example in the section "Reading from an External File" on page 16; however, because this file is not in a working directory on your computer, you must include the entire URL in quotes—identifying the web page from which it comes—as shown here:

```
> nsf2011 = read.csv(
  "http://www.nsf.gov/statistics/ffrdc/data/exp2011.csv",
    header=TRUE)
```

Statistical Packages (SPSS, SAS, Etc.)

I found an interesting dataset at the Association of Religion Data Archives (http://www.t (*http://www.thearda.com*)hearda.com (*http:// www.thearda.com*)). After reading about ARDA, click Data Archive on the Menu bar at the top of the page to see what datasets are available. Datasets come in many different formats. As an example, you can download "The Gravestone Index," collected by Wilbur Zelinsky, at *http://www.thearda.com/Archive/Files/Downloads/ CEMFILE_DL.asp* in any of three versions. Two formats, SPSS and

Stata, were designed for rival statistical software packages. An R package called `foreign` can translate either of these formats into an R data frame. Here's how to install and load the package:

```
> install.packages("foreign", dependencies=TRUE)
> library(foreign)
```

After downloading the SPSS file to your working directory, you can read it into an R data frame named `stone` by using the following commands:

```
> stone=read.spss("The Gravestone Index.SAV",to.data.frame=TRUE)
> fix(stone)  # look at the data in the editor
```

The `foreign` package can also read and write other data formats, such as Minitab, SAS, Octave, and Systat. You can learn more about the `foreign` package by using this command:

```
> library(help=foreign)
```

ASCII

The Gravestone file is also available as an ASCII file with *fixed-width format*. This means that the data falls into fixed positions on a line, without a space or other separator between data points. The first few lines and last few lines look like this:

```
11862  8   11820000000000000000000000000000000000
11868  8   11820000000000010000000000000000000000
11875  8   11820000000000000000000000000000000000
11910  8   11820000000000000000000000000000000000
11885  8   11820000000000000000000000000000000000
11861  8   11820000000000010000000000000000000000
11864  8   11820000000000010000000000000000000000

52003 18   64120000     0 110   0 00000001 0 0000000000 0
52003 18   64120000     0 1 0   0 00000000 0 0000000000 0
52007 18   64120000     0 0 0   0 0000000010 0010000000 0
52003 18   64120000     0 0 0   0 00000000 0 0000000000 0
51990 18   64120000     0 0 0   0 00000000 0 0000000000 0
```

The first part of the codebook looks like this:

```
1) BOOKNUM: 1
2) YBIRTH: 2-5
3) CEMNAME: 6-8
4) YEAREST: 9-10
5) CITYCEM: 11-12
6) COUNTRY: 13
7) COLLYEAR: 14
8) GOTHICW: 15
```

```
9) MARRIAG: 16
10) HEART: 17
11) HEARTSS: 18
12) MILITAR: 19
13) SECMESS: 20
14) OCCUPAT: 21
```

You can read the data by using the read.fwf() (read fixed-width format) command. Notice that there is no header information. Including the header=TRUE argument would give misleading information to R, which would try to assign variable names according to the numbers in the first row. This would result in an error message. It will be necessary to include the widths argument, followed by a vector giving the column widths of each of the variables, as indicated in the codebook. The first variable, BOOKNUM, is one column; the second variable, YBIRTH, four columns (2 through 5); the third variable, CEMNAME, is three columns (6 through 8); and so on. The following command reads the ASCII file, which has been copied to the working directory:

```
gs = read.fwf("The Gravestone Index.DAT",widths = c(1,4,3,2,2,1,
1,1,1,1,1,1,1,1,1,1,1,1,1,1,1,1,1,1,1,1,1,1,1,1,1,1,1,1,1,1,1,1,1,
1,1,1,1,1,1,1,1,1))
```

Alternatively, instead of typing 42 1s, you can use the rep() function to accomplish the same thing:

```
> gs = read.fwf("The Gravestone Index.DAT",
    widths = c(1,4,3,2,2,rep(1,42)))
```

The SPSS datafile of this same data had variable names, but the ASCII file comes without names and the variables are assigned names of V1, V2, V3, and so on. We can give the variables real names by creating a new vector with the names from the codebook:

```
vars = c("BOOKNUM", "YBIRTH", "CEMNAME", "YEAREST", "CITYCEM",
"COUNTRY", "COLLYEAR", "GOTHICW", "MARRIAG", "HEART", "HEARTSS",
"MILITAR", "SECMESS", "OCCUPAT", "PICTORIA", "DECEAEL",
"PHOTODEC", "RELMES", "SYMBOL", "ANGEL", "SYMBOOK", "SYMDEATH",
"DOVE", "FISH", "FINGERS", "SYMDIVIN", "GATES", "HANDSIP",
"IHSE", "HANDS", "LAMB", "SYMCROSS", "STATUE", "STAANGEL",
"STABOOK", "STADIVIN", "STALAMB", "STACROSS", "EFFIGY",
"WEEPWIL", "SECULAR", "SYMCHURC", "HANDSCIP", "CROWN",
"STADOVE", "PICCHURC", "STADEATH")
```

Then we can give the variables of gs the names in the vars vector:

```
> names(gs) = vars
```

XML

XML (Extensible Markup Language) is a text format used for exchange of data. Because there are so many different formats for data, some of which are proprietary or even secret, it becomes virtually impossible to translate every format to every other one. XML, which is transparent and open, is a common means for sharing data among different computer systems and applications. There is an XML package for R, making it possible for R users to read and create XML documents. You can find the documentation for this package at *http://www.omegahat.net/RSXML/*. XML files can be considerably more complex than the simple flat files we have looked at so far. There will usually be some exploration of the XML file required—to learn its structure—before converting it to an R data frame. Following is an example of converting a relatively simple XML file to a data frame. This is the Federal Election Commission 2009–10 Candidate Summary File, which you can find at *http://catalog.data.gov/dataset/2009-2010-candidate-summary-file*.

You can do the conversion after you install and load the XML package:

```
> install.packages("XML",dependencies=TRUE)
> library(XML)
> cand = xmlToDataFrame("CandidateSummaryAction.xml")
```

netCDF

You can find the following dataset in the data repositories list on the National Snow and Ice Data Center (http://nsidc.org). I have chosen it to demonstrate another data type, the netCDF (Network Common Data Form) file. This format has become popular for storing large arrays of scientific data, especially geophysical data. Like XML, datasets in this format can be complex. Download the dataset by FTP from *http://bit.ly/1jO6Ir9* and and save it your to your working directory. Install and load the ncdf package to work with this data in R:

```
> install.packages("ncdf")
> library(ncdf)
```

This dataset is a rather complex list of objects, each of which is itself a list of objects. In netCDF parlance, each of the main lists is a "variable." To use the data in R, it is necessary make a subset of the data that will include the list of items associated with one variable. You can accomplish this as follows:

```
> ice = open.ncdf("seaice_conc_monthly_nh_f08_198707_v02r00.nc")
> # creates an R object named "ice"
> str(ice) # shows that ice is a list comprised of other lists
> icedata = get.var.ncdf(ice,"seaice_conc_monthly_cdr")
> close.ncdf(ice)
```

The names of the variables were discovered in the results of the str(ice) command, and seaice_conc_monthly_cdr was selected for the sake of this example. In most cases, you will need to know more about the data in order to select a variable name.

Web Scraping

It is also possible to copy data contained within web pages. This is commonly known as *web scraping*. A thorough discussion of the topic is beyond the scope of this book, but should you have a need to extract web data, a good place to start would be the help files for download.file() and readLines(). There are some packages that might be useful, such as RCurl, XML, and several others.

Solutions to Chapter Exercises

A solution is provided for each exercise in the book. Do not look at the solution until you have made a serious effort to solve the exercise! For many problems, there will be several possible solutions in R. If you come up with a solution different from the one provided, try to see if the two solutions are equivalent—do you get the same answer? Why or why not?

Exercises 1-1 Through 1-4

Solutions provided in the chapter.

Exercise 3-1

```
attach(mtcars)
stripchart(mpg ~ cyl, method = "jitter")
```

This helps to separate the cars a bit. Now we can see how many cars are in each group.

Not surprisingly, cars with fewer cylinders get better gas mileage.

Exercise 3-2

```
install.packages("plotrix", dependencies=TRUE)
library(plotrix)
attach(trees)
dotplot.mtb(Volume)
```

A type of jittering is automatic. Even so, some values that are very close still run together. One way to deal with this is to make the plot character smaller:

```
dotplot.mtb(Volume, pch = 20) # or
dotplot.mtb(Volume, pch = ".") # too small!
dotplot.mtb(Volume, pch = "/")  # Hmm...
detach(trees)
```

Exercise 4-1

```
dotchart(USArrests$Murder, labels = row.names(USArrests))
```

The state names are so big, they overwrite and become illegible!

Exercise 4-2

```
load("Nimrod.rda") # .rda shows it was saved as an R data frame
dotchart(Nimrod$time)
```

Good!

```
dotchart(Nimrod$time, labels = Nimrod$performer, cex = .5)
```

Better!

```
Nimrod2 = Nimrod[order(Nimrod$time),]
dotchart(Nimrod2$time, labels = Nimrod2$performer, cex = .5)
```

Yeah!

Exercise 5-1

```
# print results to screen
library(nlme)
attach(MathAchieve)
boxplot(SES ~ Minority * Sex)

# graph to file
pdf("SES.pdf") # opens a device
library(nlme)
attach(MathAchieve)
boxplot(SES ~ Minority * Sex)
dev.off() # closes and saves file
```

Insert the file *SES.pdf* into a word processor document.

It looks like SES has the same relationship to Minority and Sex that MathAch has.

Exercise 5-2

```
par(mfrow = c(1,2)) # show 2 graphs side-by-side
attach(mtcars)
boxplot(mpg ~ cyl)
library(plotrix)
ehplot(mpg, cyl)
detach(mtcars)
par(mfrow=c(1,1)) # reset to one graph/page
```

The box plot shows reference points (i.e., quartiles); the EH-Plot shows actual points, including jittering.

You can add a box and whiskers to the EH-Plot: ehplot(mpg, cyl, box = T).

Exercise 6-1

```
library(multcomp)
stem(sbp$sbp, scale = .5)
stem(sbp$sbp, scale = 3)
stem(sbp$sbp, scale = 4)
```

A scale choice larger than 3 seems to give us worthless charts! This will not necessarily be true for all datasets.

Exercise 6-2

```
install.packages("aplpack", dependencies = T)
library(aplpack)
attach(trees)
stem.leaf.backback(Height, Volume)
detach(trees)
```

The units of measurement are different. What happens if you standardize the units?

```
library(car)
attach(Baumann)
stem.leaf.backback(pretest.1, post.test.1)
```

It appears that the posttest scores are higher.

Exercise 7-1

```
library(Sleuth2)
attach(case0302)
par(mfrow = c(2,2)) # show 4 graphs on one page
hist(Dioxin)
```

```
hist(Dioxin, breaks = 20)
hist(Dioxin, breaks = 30)
hist(Dioxin, breaks = 40)
par(mfrow = c(1,1)) # reset to one graph/page
```

The distributional shape changes a great deal. With no breaks specified, it looks like most points are clustered around zero. With many
breaks, it looks like a nearly symmetrical distribution with a few
extreme values added to it. The strip chart emphasizes this idea. It
appears that just two points are atypical. Why are they so different?
Are they mistakes? Should they be included?

Exercise 7-2

library(Hmisc) library(car) attach(Burt) histbackback(IQbio, IQfoster)
detach(Burt)
The two histograms look fairly similar, except that the IQbio group
has a few more higher-end IQs.

Studying the salaries of males and females in the Salary dataset is a
little trickier than the previous problem, because there are not separate vectors for "male salary" and "female salary." So, to use hist
backback(), we must create such vectors. There are several ways to
do this. Here is one of them:

```
attach(Salaries)
m = subset(Salaries, sex == "Male") # contains only male data
f = subset(Salaries, sex == "Female") # contains female data
histbackback(m$salary, f$salary)
detach(Salaries)
```

Exercise 8-1

```
library(multcomp)
eq2 = density(sbp$sbp, bw = 4) # Figure 8-1c
hist (sbp$sbp,
  main="c. Histogram + Kernel Density, bw = 4",
  col = "maroon", las = 1, cex.axis = .8,
  freq = F) #freq=F: prob. densities
lines(eq2,lwd = 2) # Plot density curve on existing histogram
```

This gives us sharper bends than when bw = 5.

```
eq2 = density(sbp$sbp, bw = 2) # Figure 8-1-c
hist (sbp$sbp,
  main="c. Histogram + Kernel Density, bw = 2",
```

```
   col = "maroon", las = 1, cex.axis = .8,
   freq = F) #freq=F: prob. densities
lines(eq2,lwd = 2) # Plot density curve on existing histogram
```

This produces about a dozen bends; further detail does not really fit the histogram better, but then, the histogram is a very rough approximation.

```
eq2 = density(sbp$sbp, bw = 20) # Figure 8-1c
hist (sbp$sbp,
   main="c. Histogram + Kernel Density, bw = 20",
   col = "maroon", las = 1, cex.axis = .8,
   freq = F) #freq=F: prob. densities
lines(eq2,lwd = 2) # Plot density curve on existing histogram
```

This line is flatter than bw = 10, but not a radical change.

Exercise 8-2

The sbp of 125 has a *y*-coordinate about halfway between 0 and 0.25, or about 0.125. That is to say, the probability of selecting a patient with systolic blood pressure of 125 or less is about 0.125, or 12.5 percent.

By a similar process, we can determine that the probability of a systolic blood pressure less than or equal to 175 is about 90 percent. The probability of selecting a person with systolic blood pressure of 175 or greater is 1 – prob[175 or less] = 1 – 0.9 = 0.1, or 10 percent.

The probability of falling between 125 and 175 is prob[175 or less] – prob[125 or less] = 90% – 12.5% = 77.5%.

Exercise 9-1

The Male bars are on top in each group, but the legend is reversed in order, making the chart confusing to read. Change sexlab to c("Male", "Female") in legend().

Exercise 9-2

```
library(car)
attach(Salaries)
library(epiDisplay)
salK=salary/10000
pyramid(salK,sex, binwidth = 1,
   col = "seagreen",
```

```
        main = "Salaries in 10,000s of Dollars",
        cex.bar.value =.4, cex.axis = .8)
```

Compare this to the result from "Exercise 7-2" on page 94.

Exercise 10-1

```
install.packages("HistData")
library(HistData)
attach(Nightingale)
deaths = c(sum(Disease), sum(Wounds), sum(Other))
pie(deaths, labels=c("Disease","Wounds","Other"))
```

The deaths command found the totals in each of the columns Dis
ease, Wounds, and Other. Those totals were used to make the pie
chart. The difference between Disease and the other causes was
very obvious, but the difference between the other variables is not
easy to see.

Exercise 10-2

```
load("Nimrod.rda")
x = table(Nimrod$medium)
x
pie(x, labels = c("Brass band","Concert band","Organ",
                  "Orchestra"),
  col = c("gold3","deepskyblue","peachpuff3","magenta"))
```

Exercise 11-1

```
load("Nimrod.rda")
den = density(Nimrod$time)
plot(den)
rug(Nimrod$time)

library(nlme)
boxplot(MathAchieve$SES,main="Socioeconomic Status", ylab="SES
  score")
rug(MathAchieve$SES)
```

The first of these is probably more helpful. The second one is so
dense that we cannot see a separation of points over most of the
range of the data.

Exercise 12-1

```
Year   = c(2004:2010)
Europe = c(7.9, 7.9, 7.9, 7.8, 7.7, 7.1, 7.2)
Eurasia = c(8.5, 8.5, 8.7, 8.6, 8.9, 8, 8.4)

plot(Year, Europe, type = "l",
  col = "maroon", ylim = c(7,9),
  ylab = "Emissions", lwd = 2)
# ylim makes graph big enough for Eurasia with values > 7.9

lines(Year, Eurasia,
  lty = "dashed",
  col = "steelblue", lwd = 2)
legend("topleft", c("Eurasia", "Europe"),
  text.col = c("steelblue","maroon"),
  lty = c("dashed","solid"))
```

Exercise 12-2

```
library(Sleuth2)
library(epade)
attach(case0701)
plot(Velocity, Distance)
```

As expected, distance is greater with greater velocity.

```
scatter.ade(Velocity, Distance, wall = 3,
  main = "The Big Bang", col="red")
```

Very cool!

Exercise 13-1

```
library(nlme)
attach(MathAchieve)
plot(SES, MathAch)
```

There may be a near-linear relationship, but it is hard to be sure.

```
library(nlme)
attach(MathAchieve)
sunflowerplot(SES, MathAch)
```

The sunflower plot does not help very much.

```
library(nlme)
attach(MathAchieve)
library(hexbin)
plot(hexbin(SES, MathAch), colramp = heat.ob)
```

The relationship is much clearer, nearly vertical; that is to say, there is a similar wide range of math scores for all SES scores from −1 to about 1.5.

```
detach(MathAchieve)
```

Exercise 14-1

```
library(ResearchMethods)
load("baplot") # if you saved baplot!
data(MFSV)
attach(MFSV)
baplot(MF,SV)
```

There is no obvious pattern, but we don't know, based on the information given in the help file, what the clinically acceptable difference is.

Exercise 15-1

```
library(reshape2)
library(car)
attach(tips)
tips$ratio = 100*(tip/total_bill)
attach(tips)
qqnorm(ratio)
qqline(ratio)
```

ratio is not normally distributed; it is skewed at the upper end.

```
qq(time ~ ratio)
```

lunch and dinner are very different distributions.

```
qq(smoker ~ ratio)
```

smoker and nonsmoker are also very different.

Exercise 15-2

```
library(reshape2)
library(car)
attach(Vocab)
qqnorm(vocabulary)
qqline(vocabulary)
```

vocabulary does not seem to be normally distributed.

```
qqnorm(education)
qqline(education)
```

education is not, either.

```
qq(sex ~ vocabulary)
```

It is predominantly `female` through most of the range, and `male` at the upper extreme.

Exercise 16-1

```
library(car)
attach(Ginzberg)
head(Ginzberg)
pairs(~ simplicity + fatalism + depression)

scatterplotMatrix(~ simplicity + fatalism + depression)

library(corrplot)
corrplot(y)

library(GGally)
ggscatmat(Ginzberg, columns = 1:3)
```

Exercise 17-1

```
library(scatterplot3d)
library(epiDisplay)
data(SO2)
scatterplot3d(SO2$smoke, SO2$SO2, SO2$deaths,
  highlight.3d = T,
  type = "h")
```

This is a tricky dataset to work with, because the dataset and a variable have the same name. If you try `attach(SO2)` and `scatter plot3d(smoke, SO2, deaths)`, it won't work! Therefore, use the `SO2$smoke` name instead. Deaths seem to be positively related to both of the other variables.

Exercise 17-2

```
library(lattice)
library(epiDisplay)
data(SO2)
levelplot(SO2$deaths ~ SO2$smoke + SO2$SO2)
```

Exercise 18-1

```
library(Sleuth2)
attach(ex1123)
plot(SO2, Mort)
```

There appears to be a strong relationship between SO2 and mortality, with the exception of a single, high-mortality point.

```
coplot(Mort ~ SO2 | Educ)
```

The coplot shows that there is little SO2, and lower mortality, in cities where education levels are highest! Perhaps there are fewer smokestacks in cities with major financial businesses or research centers.

Exercise 19-1

```
attach(mtcars)
cars = as.matrix(mtcars)
h = dist(scale(cars))
h2 = hclust(h, method = "single")
plot(h2)

h = dist(scale(cars), method = "manhattan")
h2 = hclust(h, method = "single")
plot(h2)
```

Exercise 19-2

```
cars = as.matrix(mtcars)
image(scale(cars), col = cm.colors(256))
image(scale(cars), col = rainbow(100))
image(scale(cars), col = terrain.colors(16))
```

And so on. The number after `colors` tells how many colors are in the range.

Exercise 19-3

```
install.packages("Amelia", dependencies = T)
library(Amelia)
missmap(airquality)

library(epade)
missiogram.ade(airquality)
```

Exercise 20-1

The Wikipedia article on mosaic plots (*https://en.wikipedia.org/wiki/Mosaic_plot*) includes a demonstration of the `Titanic` dataset. You can also find a mosaic plot of this data at *http://bit.ly/1VDPbmp* in a different orientation. You can find another one at *http://bit.ly/1jdkQKr*.

Exercise 21-1

```
attach(Nimrod)
par(bg = "white", mfrow = c(2,2))

# graph 1
x = table(medium)
barplot(x, horiz = T,
  main = "Number of ensembles of each medium",
  names = c("Brass band", "Concert band", "Organ","Orchestra"),
  las = 1, cex.names = .8, col = "turquoise", space = 1.5)

# graph 2
cols = "cadetblue4"
boxplot(time ~ medium,
  col = c("goldenrod","firebrick"),
  ylab = "Time",  xlab = "Medium",
  varwidth = T,
  main = "Performance times by medium",
  col.main = cols,
  col.axis = cols,
  las = 1, col.lab = cols,
  names = c("","","",""))
mtext(text = c("Brass band", Concert band",
  "Organ", "Orchestra"),
  side = 1, cex = .6,
  at = c(1,2,3,4), line = 1)

# graph 3
pro = subset(Nimrod, level == "p")
am = subset(Nimrod, level == "a")
plot(density(pro$time), ylim = c(0,.028),
  main = "Professional vs. amateur groups",
  xlab = "Time in seconds",
  col = "navy", lwd = 2,
  bty = "n", xlim = c(100,350),
  family = "HersheyScript",
  cex.main = 1.4, cex.lab = 1.3)
lines(density(am$time), lty = "dotted",
  col = "lightblue4", lwd = 2)
legend("topright", c("Amateur","Professional"),
```

```
  cex = .8, text.col = c("lightblue4","navy"),
  bty = "n")

# graph 4
data2 = Nimrod[order(Nimrod$time),]
dotchart(data2$time,
  labels = data2$performer, cex = .34,
  main = "Performance Time by Performer",
  xlab = "Performance time", pch = 19,
  col = c("violetred1", "violetred4"),
  lcolor = "gray90",
  cex.main = 1.9, col.main = "violetred4",
  cex.lab = 1.4,
  family = "HersheySerif")
detach(Nimrod)
```

Troubleshooting: Why Doesn't My Code Work?

Beginners at almost anything will make mistakes. Fortunately, beginners with R receive error messages when they make mistakes, indicating what needs to be changed. Unfortunately, those messages are often cryptic and seem to be written in a language that only vaguely resembles English. A little experience with R will smooth the difficulties in a short time. The following pages include some examples of easily made errors and messages that accompany them. You should know that I have made each of the following errors myself, some of them many times!

Misspelling

One of the most common mistakes is simple misspelling. R, however, apparently does not have the word "misspelling" in its vocabulary and therefore labels this problem in sundry other ways:

```
> attach(trees)
> plt(Girth, Height)
Error: could not find function "plt"
```

In this example, R suggested that we wanted to use a function that does not exist, or is hiding, but it was a simple spelling error! Retype the command with the correct spelling:

```
> plot(Girth, Height)
```

Actually, you do not need to retype the whole command. In the preceding example it is not a big deal, but sometimes you will have a long line that it would be quite tedious to repeat. In that case, there are two shortcuts:

- Copy and paste the incorrect line to the most recent prompt (>) and fix the error before pressing Return (or Enter).
- Press the up-arrow key; the previous line will be copied, and you can edit it. If you press the up-arrow key twice, the command two lines above will be copied, and so on.

Here's another example:

```
> plot(Girth, Height, color = "red")
Warning messages:
1: In plot.window(...) : "color" is not a graphical parameter
2: In plot.xy(xy, type, ...) : "color" is not a graphical
   parameter
3: In axis(side = side, at = at, labels = labels, ...) :
   "color" is not a graphical parameter
4: In axis(side = side, at = at, labels = labels, ...) :
   "color" is not a graphical parameter
5: In box(...) : "color" is not a graphical parameter
6: In title(...) : "color" is not a graphical parameter
```

This set of messages looks terrifying, but when you read each line, you can see that R simply cannot get over our using the word "color." To find the correct abbreviation, type **?plot**, and all is forgiven. Simply change color to col, as shown here, and this now works just fine:

```
> plot(Girth, Height, col = "red")
```

Take a look at this next example:

```
> library(poltrix)
Error in library(poltrix) : there is no package called 'poltrix'
```

Indeed, there is no package named poltrix. Check the spelling!

```
> library(plotrix)
```

No problem now! Notice that each of the three examples in this section were, interpreted loosely, spelling errors. Nonetheless, R gave three entirely different responses. This shows that error messages are not always to be interpreted literally. You just need to have a little experience to understand what the messages could mean.

Confusing Uppercase/Lowercase

Remember that R treats uppercase and lowercase versions of the same letter as if they were completely different letters. In this example, R cannot find the object height because there is no such object:

```
> attach(trees)
> plot(Girth, height)
Error in xy.coords(x, y, xlabel, ylabel, log) : object 'height'
not found
```

Change height to Height and the command will work. If you cannot remember the right variable name, you can use the str(trees) command or head(trees) to find the precise name.

Too Few (or Too Many) Parenthesis Signs

In the following example, R does not execute the command and prints + instead of >:

```
> plot(density(Girth)
+
```

This means that R was expecting something more. In this particular case, typing one more right (close) parenthesis sign, after the +, would make everything work.

In the next example, there are too many parentheses. The error message points to the culprit:

```
> plot(density(Girth)))
Error: unexpected ')' in "plot(density(Girth)))"
>
```

When using parenthetical expressions, the number of left parenthesis signs must be equal to the number of right parenthesis signs. If you have long commands, it is a good idea to count "lefts" and "rights" before you press the Return key.

Forgetting to Load a Package

Remember that any extra packages that you have installed—not in base R—must be loaded for each session in which you intend to use them. Suppose that you want to do some analysis of the Nightin gale dataset from the HistData package, and you receive this message:

```
> attach(Nightingale)
Error in attach(Nightingale) : object 'Nightingale' not found
>
```

This is similar to the error message that a misspelling generates, but it's produced for a very different reason. The solution here is to load HistData first:

```
> library(HistData)
> attach(Nightingale)
```

You can then use any commands or datasets in HistData without having to load it again until you quit R. If you want to use anything in HistData the next time you start R, you will need to load it again.

Forgetting to Install a Package

Many examples in the book load a package by using the library() command. Remember that to load a package, you first must have installed it by using the install.packages() function, or you'll see a message such as this:

```
> library(abctools)
Error in library(abctools) :
    there is no package called 'abctools'
```

You only need to install a package once. It will reside on your computer forever. However, you must load it for every session in which you need it.

When I typed the command in the preceding example, I did not have the abctools package installed on my computer. I could install it by using this command:

```
> install.packages("abctools")
```

It would be even better if I used the command:

```
> install.packages("abctools", dependencies = TRUE)
```

This command not only installs abctools, it also installs any other packages that abctools might depend on; that is, packages that abctools itself uses. On Windows-based computers, you can also install packages by going to the Packages menu and selecting Install Package(s). A "CRAN mirror" window opens; either select a mirror site or use the one that is already highlighted and press OK. Then, select the package you want. Mac users can go to the Packages & Data menu, select Package Installer, click the Get List button, and then select a package.

After the first few chapters, this book does not remind you to install a package every time library() appears. I assume that you already know you need to do this, having done it several times. If you are not sure whether you have previously installed a package, you can see what packages you have by using this command:

```
> installed.packages()  # "installed" not "install"
```

This command might give you more information than you want, but it works on all R systems. A more convenient way to see what you have on Windows-based machines is to go to the Packages menu and select Load Packages. For Macintosh computers, go to the Packages & Data menu and select Package Manager.

A Dataset in a Loaded Package Is Not Found

When you load a package, the datasets included in that package should be available to use:

```
> library(reshape2)    # load a package
> head(tips)           # use a dataset in that package

  total_bill  tip    sex smoker day    time size
1      16.99 1.01 Female     No Sun Dinner    2
2      10.34 1.66   Male     No Sun Dinner    3
3      21.01 3.50   Male     No Sun Dinner    3
4      23.68 3.31   Male     No Sun Dinner    2
5      24.59 3.61 Female     No Sun Dinner    4
6      25.29 4.71   Male     No Sun Dinner    4
```

This one worked just as it should have. Sometimes, though, something goes wrong and R cannot find the data:

```
> library(epiDisplay)
Loading required package: foreign
Loading required package: survival
Loading required package: splines
Loading required package: MASS
Loading required package: nnet
Warning message:
'.find.package' is deprecated.
Use 'find.package' instead.
See help("Deprecated")

> head(Ectopic)
Error in head(Ectopic) : object 'Ectopic' not found
```

`Ectopic` is a dataset in the package `epiDisplay`, but even though the package has just been loaded, R says it cannot find the dataset. When that happens, you can add one more step, calling the `data()` function, to load the particular dataset that you want:

```
> data(Ectopic)
> head(Ectopic)
  id outc     hia gravi
1  1 Deli   ever IA  1-2
2  2 Deli   ever IA  3-4
3  3 Deli  never IA  1-2
4  4 Deli  never IA  1-2
5  5 Deli  never IA  1-2
6  6   IA   ever IA  1-2
```

Now, all is right with the world!

Leaving Out a Comma

Commas show R where one argument ends and another begins. What happens if you leave one out?

```
> plot(Girth, Height col = "red")
Error: unexpected symbol in "plot(Girth,Height col"
```

The unexpected symbol was anything other than a comma. Arguments must be separated by commas:

```
> plot(Girth, Height, col = "red")
```

Copy-and-Paste Error

The command that follows was copied from a successful execution of that same command earlier in the session. The error message might leave you scratching your head:

```
> > head(Nightingale)
Error: unexpected '>' in ">"
```

The problem here is that the copy included the prompt symbol, >, so that the command line, when pasted, had two of them. The way around this problem is do one of the following:

- Copy only the part of the line after the >.

- After you have pasted, delete the second > before pressing the Return key.

Directory Problems—Cannot Load a Saved File

You might have trouble retrieving a file that you know you have previously saved. Even if you spell everything correctly, R might not find the file. Possible error messages are:

```
cannot open the connection
```

and/or:

```
no such file or directory
```

The most likely reason for such an error is that you are not searching the right directory—in other words, the file is not in your working directory.

First, read the section "The Working Directory" on page 10. If that does not answer all your questions, open the working directory to see if the file in question is really there. On Windows-based computers, go to the File menu and select "Display file(s)." On a Mac, go to the File menu and select Open Document.

On either platform, if the file is not in the working directory you will need to search for it and do one of the following:

- Move it to the working directory.
- Change the working directory to be the directory where the file is located by using the setwd() command.
- In the load() command, give the entire path to the file. For example, if the file you wanted was *cands.rda* in the directory */Users/yourname/Desktop/R Things/*, you would use the command:

```
load("/Users/yourname/Desktop/R Things/cands.rda")
# note quotes!
```

Ensure that you spell everything correctly and include all the slashes, quotes, and so on.

Missing File Extension

This not an R problem, *per se*, but something that could easily cause a problem for R users. Consider the dataset created in the section "Reading from an External File" on page 16. It was entered into a spreadsheet and exported as a CSV file. On either Windows-based or Macintosh computers, depending on what options you have selected—or neglected to select—the filename may appear to be *Nimrod.Tempo.*

This is because your computer is set up not to show file extensions. If we believe the filename and issue an R command with that name, R indicates that no such file exists:

```
> Nimrod <- read.csv("Nimrod.Tempo", header = TRUE)
Error in file(file, "rt") : cannot open the connection
In addition: Warning message:
In file(file, "rt") :
  cannot open file 'Nimrod.Tempo': No such file or directory
```

If we simply add the extension to the filename, there is no problem:

```
> Nimrod <- read.csv("Nimrod.Tempo.csv", header = TRUE)
```

A similar problem can arise with scripts that you try to source if you leave off the file extension, *.R*:

```
> source("NimTotals")
Error in file(filename, "r", encoding = encoding) :
  cannot open the connection
In addition: Warning message:
In file(filename, "r", encoding = encoding) :
  cannot open file 'NimTotals': No such file or directory
```

On the other hand:

```
> source("NimTotals.R")  # works fine!
```

Do Not Assume That All Packages Use the Same Argument Abbreviations

Although many packages are quite consistent with base R in their use of arguments and abbreviations, not all of them are, as the error message in this next example demonstrates:

```
> scatterplot3d(Solar.R, Ozone, Wind, col = "blue")
Error in scatterplot3d(Solar.R, Ozone, Wind, col = "blue") :
  argument 4 matches multiple formal arguments
```

The col argument is almost a universal standard among R packages, but consulting the help file for scatterplot3d reveals that it is not the right option for that package. Instead, you need to use the following argument:

```
> scatterplot3d(Solar.R, Ozone, Wind, color = "blue")
```

Now, this works just fine.

Outdated Packages/Package Incompatibility

Many packages depend on certain other packages being available. If a package does not load, it might be because some other required package is absent. If an error message indicates this, for instance by naming a package or command that could not be found, it might only be necessary to install the required package. Sometimes, the particular versions of installed packages can be the problem. To check this, use the following command:

```
> library(help = packagename)
```

For example, if you have trouble loading Rcmdr, type the following:

```
> library(help = Rcmdr)
```

You will see a basic information file about the package, which includes the required/suggested packages and the necessary versions. Here is a small excerpt from this file, after the naming of the authors:

```
Depends:        R (>= 3.0.0), grDevices, utils, splines,
                    RcmdrMisc (>= 1.0-2), car (>= 2.0-21)
Imports:        tcltk, tcltk2 (>= 1.2-6), markdown, knitr,
                    abind
Suggests:       aplpack, colorspace, effects (>= 3.0-1),
                    e1071, foreign, grid, Hmisc, lattice,
                    leaps,lmtest, MASS, mgcv,
                    multcomp (>= 0.991-2), nlme, nnet,
                    relimp, rgl, rJava, RODBC, sem
                    (>= 2.1-1)
```

This excerpt indicates that the version of Rcmdr installed on this computer requires R version 3.0 or later. It also depends on several other packages, such as grDevices, utils, and so, having been installed. Further, some packages must be of a certain version; for example, car must be version 2.0-21 or later. If you do not have the proper matches, Rcmdr will either not load or not work properly. The easiest way to fix this problem is simply to reinstall Rcmdr, with its dependencies:

```
> install.packages("Rcmdr", dependencies = TRUE)
```

This will install/reinstall the latest version of Rcmdr and the latest versions of its dependencies. If this does not work, you might need to reinstall R.

The help file for the package also references imports, such as tcltk, which is crucial to the GUI of Rcmdr. If you do not have this package, which normally comes as part of R, you should reinstall R. Be sure that you install the *binary* version. If your computer is a Mac running OS X 10.9 or higher, you will also need to install XQuartz.

Finally, there are some suggested packages. Without these, parts of Rcmdr might work, but not all of it.

R Functions Introduced in This Book

Here is a list of functions used in this book, for quick reference. It is far from a complete list of R functions. For further information about a given function, *x*, see the index, or type **help(*x*)** or **?*x*.**

Data Input/Output

load( )
    Reload an R dataset previously created by using save( ).

open.ncdf( )
    Open an *.ncdf* file (ncdf package).

Quandl( )
    Read a Quandl dataset (Quandl package).

read.csv( )
    Read a file in *.csv* format and create a data frame.

read.fwf( )
    Read a fixed-width file.

read.spss( )
    Read an SPSS dataset (foreign package).

read.table( )
    Read a file in table format and create a data frame.

read.txt()
: Read a file in *.txt* format and create a data frame.

read.xport()
: Read an SAS XPORT file (foreign package).

readWorksheetFromFile()
: Read an Excel spreadsheet (XLConnect package).

save()
: Write an R object to the working directory or a specified file.

xmlToDataFrame()
: Read an XML file (XML package).

Datasets

attach()
: Select a particular dataset for the following analysis.

data()
: Determine what datasets are available (with no argument) or load a dataset.

data.frame()
: Combine two or more vectors to make a new data frame.

detach()
: Deselect a dataset; that is, following commands no longer analyze that dataset.

edit()
: Edit a dataset.

fix()
: Edit a dataset.

head()
: View selected lines of a dataset, from the top.

str()
: Determine the structure of an object.

subset()
: Create a subset of a specified data frame.

```
tail()
```
View selected lines of a dataset, from the bottom.

Graphical Functions 1—Creates Graph

```
barplot()
```
Produce a bar plot.

```
bland.altman.ade()
```
Produce a Bland-Altman plot (epade package).

```
boxplot()
```
Produce a box plot.

```
coplot()
```
Produce a coplot (conditioning plot).

```
cor.plot()
```
Produce a corrgram (psych package).

```
corrplot()
```
Produce a corrgram (corrplot package).

```
dotchart()
```
Produce a dot chart.

```
dotplot.mtb()
```
Produce a dot chart as in Minitab (plotrix package).

```
ehplot()
```
Produce an Engelmann-Hecker-Plot (plotrix package).

```
fan.plot()
```
Produce a fan plot (plotrix package).

```
ggpairs()
```
Produce a generalized pairs plot (GGally package).

```
ggplot()
```
Produce many types of plots (ggplot2 package).

```
ggscatmat()
```
Produce a scatter plot matrix with corr coefficients on top (GGally package).

```
gpairs()
```
Produce a generalized pairs plot (gpairs package).

`grid()`
  Draw a grid on the current plot.

`heatmap()`
  Produce a heat map.

`heatmap.2()`
  Produce an enhanced heat map (`gplots` package).

`hexbin()`
  Produce a hexbin plot (`hexbin` package).

`hist()`
  Produce a histogram.

`Hist()`
  Produce a histogram for multiple groups (`RcmdrMisc` package).

`histbackback()`
  Produce back-to-back histograms (`Hmisc` package).

`histogram()`
  Produce histograms for multiple groups (`lattice` package).

`histStack()`
  Produce a stacked histogram (`plotrix` package).

`image()`
  Create a heat map.

`levelplot()`
  Produce a false-color plot (`lattice` package).

`missiogram()`
  Produce a plot of missing values (`epade` package).

`missmap()`
  Produce a plot of missing values (`Amelia` package).

`mosaic()`
  Produce a mosaic plot (`vcd` package).

`mosaicplot()`
  Produce a mosaic plot.

`pairs()`
  Create a scatter plot matrix.

`pie()`
>   Produce a pie chart.

`pie3D()`
>   Produce a three-dimensional pie chart (`plotrix` package).

`plot()`
>   Produce a scatter plot or other plots.

`PlotBubble()`
>   Produce a bubble plot (`DescTools` package).

`pyramid()`
>   Produce a pyramid plot (`epiDisplay` package).

`qq()`
>   Produce a quantile-quantile (QQ) plot (`lattice` package).

`qqnorm()`
>   Produce a QQ plot with theoretical quantiles.

`qqplot()`
>   Produce a QQ plot.

`scatter3d()`
>   Produce a three-dimensional scatter plot with a regression surface (`car` package).

`scatterplot()`
>   Produce a scatter plot with advanced features (`car` package).

`scatterplot3d()`
>   Produce a three-dimensional scatter plot (`scatterplot3d` package).

`scatterplotMatrix()`
>   Produce a scatter plot matrix with advanced features (`car` package); also ++spm()++.

`scatter.ade()`
>   Produce a scatter plot with advanced features (`epade` package).

`smoothScatter()`
>   Produce a smooth scatter plot.

`spineplot()`
>   Produce a spine plot (spinogram).

`stem()`
> Produce a stem-and-leaf plot.

`stem.leaf()`
> Produce an advanced stem-and-leaf plot (`aplpack` package).

`stripchart()`
> Produce a strip chart.

`sunflowerplot()`
> Produce a sunflower plot.

`xyplot()`
> Produce a scatter plot (`lattice` package).

Graphical Functions 2—Adds Features to Existing Graph

`abline()`
> Draw a straight line on an existing graph.

`axis()`
> Add an axis to the current plot.

`legend()`
> Add a legend on the current plot.

`lines()`
> Put curved lines on the current plot.

`mtext()`
> Put text in the margins of the current plot.

`par()`
> Set graphical parameters, or query about same.

`plotmath`
> See ?`plotmath` to include math expressions on graphs.

`points()`
> Draw points on the current plot.

`polygon()`
> Draw/fill a polygon.

`qqline()`
  Add a line to a QQ plot.

`rug()`
  Draw a rug plot on the current plot.

`text()`
  Put text in the plotting area of the current plot.

Miscellaneous

`asTheEconomist()`
  Style imitator for lattice graphs (`latticeExtra` package).

`c()`
  Combine the arguments, forming a vector.

`cat()`
  For printing output from functions.

`colors()`
  Give R color names.

`demo()`
  Run a demonstration of selected R capabilities.

`dev.off()`
  Complete writing to a graphical device and save a file.

`jpeg()`
  Open a file to be saved in *.jpeg* format; must conclude with
  `dev.off()`.

`order()`
  Reorder the rows of a data frame by the values of a selected variable.

`par()`
  Set graphical parameters, or query about same.

`png()`
  Open a file to be saved in *.png* format; must conclude with
  `dev.off()`.

`print()`
  Print output.

```
rgl.snapshot()
```
Save a screenshot as a *.png* file (`rgl` package).

Packages

```
available.packages()
```
Check what packages are available for download.

```
install.packages()
```
Download and install one or more R packages.

```
installed.packages()
```
Check what packages are installed on a computer.

```
library()
```
Load a previously installed package into the current R session.

Statistics

R has *many* statistics functions not covered in this book. The ones we looked at include:

```
aggregate()
```
Divide data into subsets, computing summary statistics for each subset.

```
cor()
```
Calculate the Pearson correlation coefficient.

```
CrossTable()
```
Produce a contingency table in SPSS or SAS format (`gmodels` package).

```
density()
```
Compute kernel density estimates.

```
dist()
```
Compute the distance between rows of a matrix.

```
ecdf()
```
Compute an empirical cumulative distribution function.

```
Ecdf()
```
Compute an empirical cumulative distribution function (`Hmisc` package).

`hclust()`
>   Perform a hierarchical cluster analysis.

`lm()`
>   Compute a linear model (e.g., a regression).

`max()`
>   Compute the maximum value of a vector.

`mean()`
>   Compute the mean of a vector.

`median()`
>   Compute the median of a vector.

`min()`
>   Compute the minimum value of a vector.

`quantile()`
>   Find quantiles of a vector.

`scale()`
>   Center and/or scale columns of a matrix.

`sd()`
>   Compute the standard deviation of a vector.

`summary()`
>   Compute several summary statistics of a vector.

`table()`
>   Compute one-way or two-way frequencies.

`var()`
>   Compute the variance of a vector.

User-Defined Functions and Scripts

`function() {}`
>   Create a user-defined function.

`source()`
>   Execute a script.

Workspace and Directories

`ls()`
> Determine what objects are in the current workspace.

`getwd()`
> Find the current working directory.

`setwd()`
> Change the working directory .

Index

Symbols

lwd agument, plot() and lines() functions, 139

M

Macintosh systems
  GUI capabilities, 6
  Numbers spreadsheet, 16
  sourcing a script, 25
  starting R, 2
  using the data editor, 16
  XQuartz, 296
main = argument, hist() function, 86
marginal values (marginals), 24
math achievement scores
  box plot analysis of SES data and,
    exercises, 78
  box plot of, 69
  breaking down by sex and minority status, 71
  strip chart of, 67
mathematical functions, commonly
  used, 3
matrices, 183
  (see also scatterplot matrix)
  creating, 218
  transposing, 227
mean, 5
  getting for Nimrod dataset, 21
  operation finding (FUN = mean),
    112
mean difference, 165
mean() function, 21, 225
median, 25
  in box-and-whiskers plot of math
    achievement scores, 69
mfrow argument, par() function, 67
miscellaneous functions, 303
missing values
  Amelia and epade packages, 233
  handling in R, 10
mosaic plots, 235-245
  plot of clinic, death, and anc, 240
    with anc highlighted, 241
    with anc highlighted and color
      added, 242
  plot of death by anc (treatment),
    236
  residual analysis, 243

  residual shading of results, 244
  table of frequencies data, 237
mosaic() function, 236
  argument as formula, 236
  making certain relationships
    stand out, 240
mtcars dataset, 33, 221
mtext() function, 55
multcomp package, sbp dataset, 81
musical tempo data, reading into R
  (example), 17

N

ncdf package, 273
netCDF files, 273
Nimrod dataset, 17
  analyzing using R commands, 21
  box plots of time broken down by
    level and medium, 73
    improved graph, 75
  codebook, 18
  graphs based on, 26
  using subset in generalized pairs
    matrix, 196
nlme package, 67
nominal variables, 19
normal distribution, 101, 172
  comparing tip variables to, 173
normalizing variables, 174, 225

O

objects, 4
  listing all in your workspace, 5
observations, 15
octothorpe character (#), introducing
  comments, 8
oned (diagonal strip chart), 186
openintro package, 251
operators (arithmetic) in R, 2
overfitting, 98

P

packages
  available, retrieving list of, 7
  forgetting to load, problems
    caused by, 289
  functions for, 304

About the Author

John Jay Hilfiger is a statistician, with an MS in biostatistics. He has worked as a statistical/computer analyst in three major universities (Rochester, Iowa, Cornell). He has also made heavy use of his data background in positions as associate dean and as director of institutional research. In addition, Hilfiger is a composer/arranger (over 100 publications) and has been a music professor (masters and PhD in music). A big part of his experience has been helping other people analyze their data with numbers, graphs and insight; writing this book is an extension of that pursuit.

Colophon

The animal on the cover of *Graphing Data with R* is a *Red-and-yellow barbet (Trachyphonus erythrocephalus)*. It is part of the Lybiidae family, which contains 42 species of birds. The red-and-yellow barbet can be found in uneven terrain such as riverbeds, cliffs, and termite nests or mounds of Eastern African countries, such as Kenya and South Sudan.

This bird has a distinct, colorful look. Plummage is made up of black, red, and yellow coloring, with white spots on much of the black parts (mostly the wings and back). Males also have black foreheads and a slight crest, while both sexes have a lot of red coloring to their heads. The neck and breast include a reddish-orange that changes into yellow in the remainder of the lower body. The tail is colored with black and yellow bars. Females and juveniles are duller in coloring than males, and have more yellow and white than orange and red. Adults can grow up to nine inches in length with a wingspan of four inches, and weigh about 72 grams.

The red-and-yellow barbet is omnivorous and their diet consists of various fruits, seeds, and insects. They are known to eat smaller birds as well. Because of the minimal changes of season in their environment, red-and-yellow barbets only move around for the purpose of attaining food.

Breeding prep and raising of the young extends beyond the breeding pair, as there is always one or more assistants to help. Nesting sites are usually termite mounds in which the birds will dig a tunnel. A nesting chamber made up of feathers and grass can be found at the end of this tunnel. They lay between two and six eggs per brood. Once eggs hatch, parents and helpers mostly feed the chicks insects, as the chicks are in need of protein. Once the hatchlings are ready to leave the nest... they don't. Instead, they will stick around to become helpers for the next brood, until it's time for them to start a family of their own.

Many of the animals on O'Reilly covers are endangered; all of them are important to the world. To learn more about how you can help, go to animals.oreilly.com.

The cover image has been colorized by Karen Montgomery, based on a black and white engraving from *Cassell's Natural History*. The cover fonts are URW Typewriter and Guardian Sans. The text font is Adobe Minion Pro; the heading font is Adobe Myriad Condensed; and the code font is Dalton Maag's Ubuntu Mono.

Have it your way.

O'Reilly eBooks

- Lifetime access to the book when you buy through oreilly.com
- Provided in up to four, DRM-free file formats, for use on the devices of your choice: PDF, .epub, Kindle-compatible .mobi, and Android .apk
- Fully searchable, with copy-and-paste, and print functionality
- We also alert you when we've updated the files with corrections and additions.

oreilly.com/ebooks/

Safari Books Online

- Access the contents and quickly search over 7000 books on technology, business, and certification guides
- Learn from expert video tutorials, and explore thousands of hours of video on technology and design topics
- Download whole books or chapters in PDF format, at no extra cost, to print or read on the go
- Early access to books as they're being written
- Interact directly with authors of upcoming books
- Save up to 35% on O'Reilly print books

See the complete Safari Library at safaribooksonline.com

©2014 O'Reilly Media, Inc. O'Reilly logo is a registered trademark of O'Reilly Media, Inc. 14373

Get even more for your money.

Join the O'Reilly Community, and register the O'Reilly books you own. It's free, and you'll get:

- $4.99 ebook upgrade offer
- 40% upgrade offer on O'Reilly print books
- Membership discounts on books and events
- Free lifetime updates to ebooks and videos
- Multiple ebook formats, DRM FREE
- Participation in the O'Reilly community
- Newsletters
- Account management
- 100% Satisfaction Guarantee

Signing up is easy:

1. Go to: oreilly.com/go/register
2. Create an O'Reilly login.
3. Provide your address.
4. Register your books.

Note: English-language books only

To order books online:
oreilly.com/store

For questions about products or an order:
orders@oreilly.com

To sign up to get topic-specific email announcements and/or news about upcoming books, conferences, special offers, and new technologies:
elists@oreilly.com

For technical questions about book content:
booktech@oreilly.com

To submit new book proposals to our editors:
proposals@oreilly.com

O'Reilly books are available in multiple DRM-free ebook formats. For more information:
oreilly.com/ebooks

©2014 O'Reilly Media, Inc. O'Reilly logo is a registered trademark of O'Reilly Media, Inc. 14373

Milton Keynes UK
Ingram Content Group UK Ltd.
UKHW021814231023
431202UK00009B/58